CBT Fundamentals

CBT Fundamentals: Theory and Cases

Vanessa Skinner and Nick Wrycraft

Open University Press

Open University Press
McGraw-Hill Education
McGraw-Hill House
Shoppenhangers Road
Maidenhead
Berkshire
England
SL6 2QL

email: enquiries@openup.co.uk
world wide web: www.openup.co.uk

and Two Penn Plaza, New York, NY 10121-2289, USA

First published 2014

Copyright © Vanessa Skinner & Nick Wrycraft, 2014

All rights reserved. Except for the quotation of short passages for the purpose of criticism and review, no part of this publication may be reproduced, stored in a retrieval system, or transmitted, in any form or by any means, electronic, mechanical, photocopying, recording or otherwise, without the prior written permission of the publisher or a licence from the Copyright Licensing Agency Limited. Details of such licences (for reprographic reproduction) may be obtained from the Copyright Licensing Agency Ltd of Saffron House, 6–10 Kirby Street, London EC1N 8TS.

A catalogue record of this book is available from the British Library

ISBN-13: 978-0-33-524773-8 (pb)
ISBN-10: 0-33-524773-3 (pb)
eISBN: 978-0-33-524784-4

Library of Congress Cataloging-in-Publication Data
CIP data applied for

Typesetting and e-book compilations by
RefineCatch Limited, Bungay, Suffolk

Fictitious names of companies, products, people, characters and/or data that may be used herein (in case studies or in examples) are not intended to represent any real individual, company, product or event.

Praise for this book

"This is a useful addition to any CBT reading list. A range of reflective components, together with exercises and a range of case studies, encourages the reader to contribute to their learning experience in a participatory way. It will make a welcome addition to students wanting to explore the area of psychosocial interventions."

Bruce Wallace, Visiting Lecturer in Mental Health at University of Bedfordshire, UK

"This new book provides a good, authoritative introduction to CBT and how it might be applied to a range of different settings. Taking as its starting point the underpinning theory of CBT, the book examines the core knowledge and skills required of the practitioner. The case study format and style make it easy to read and follow whilst keeping the content fresh. I will be encouraging my students to make use of the book as part of their studies in mental health nursing."

Paul Linsley, Principle Lecturer in Health and Social Science at Lincoln University, UK

Contents

About the authors ix
Preface x
Acknowledgements xii

1. **Introduction** 1
2. **Theoretical background, including the core concepts of CBT** 6
3. **The practice of CBT** 36
4. **Mild to moderate depression** 52
5. **Low self-esteem, anxiety and depression** 68
6. **Panic disorder with agoraphobia** 87
7. **Social anxiety disorder** 104
8. **Obsessive compulsive disorder** 121
9. **Obsessive compulsive disorder – mental compulsions** 140
10. **Generalised anxiety disorder** 158
11. **Post-traumatic stress disorder – single episode trauma** 174
12. **Perfectionism** 191
13. **Assertiveness** 213
14. **Clinical supervision in supporting practice** 230

Conclusion – developing yourself as a therapist 244

Glossary 246
References 250
Index 258

About the authors

Vanessa Skinner is a cognitive behavioural psychotherapist who has worked in the field of mental health for over 16 years. She qualified as a registered mental health nurse in 2001, later training and specialising in therapeutic group work. She gained both a BSc (Hons) and a postgraduate diploma in cognitive behavioural therapy and is working towards her MSc in CBT. She is accredited by the British Association for Behavioural and Cognitive Psychotherapies as a psychotherapist, trainer and supervisor. She also holds a postgraduate certificate in learning and teaching in higher education and is a member of the Higher Education Authority.

Vanessa currently works as a cognitive behavioural psychotherapist for the University of Cambridge Counselling Service; prior to this she was employed as a lecturer and supervisor in cognitive behavioural therapy at Anglia Ruskin University, where collaboration with Nick Wrycraft on *CBT Fundamentals: Theory and Cases* began. Their current work brings together a wealth of theoretical and practical experience for anyone wanting to develop their understanding of how the principles of CBT can be applied in real-world settings.

Nick Wrycraft is a qualified mental health nurse, and worked in a variety of mental health nursing settings and research in primary care before joining Anglia Ruskin University. Over the last 10 years he has taught on a variety of different mental health courses, although most extensively in pre-registration mental health nursing. Nick's doctoral research was on clinical supervision groups in primary care settings. He has previously edited *An Introduction to Mental Health Nursing* in 2009 and *Case Studies in Mental Health Nursing* in 2012 and is currently involved in further writing projects.

Preface

In this book there are a number of case studies focused on people experiencing a range of different aspects of anxiety and depression. Although the cases mainly pertain to adults, they include clients at different stages of life, various genders and ethnicities and social and economic circumstances. They demonstrate how anxiety and depression can be experienced in everyday life settings and workplaces and homes, as well as within relationships and everyday life situations that we all might recognise.

The case study format and style in which the chapters are written encourage the reader to engage with the text by actively using the components of CBT, and fulfils several purposes. Firstly, the features are intended to socialise readers to the CBT model, and introduce the specific components of a session. Through engaging with these features, it is hoped that readers will be able to form a personal understanding of the meaning and role of these components of CBT. However, these features also permit the reader to set personal learning goals, reflect on what they have gained from their reading, and identify other actions that might be taken to address any remaining learning needs. Furthermore, the varied range of cases in the book reflects the need for CBT to be adaptable and flexible to the different features of each particular case and client.

In the introduction in Chapter 1, we familiarise the reader with the structure of the book and discuss Kolb's (1984) reflective cycle. Chapters 2 and 3 then progress to consider the principles and practice of CBT. In Chapter 2 we outline the background of the development of CBT, before going on to explain the core concepts of CBT theory and models of treatment, and some fundamental concepts of CBT that are applied to the case studies that follow. In Chapter 3 we discuss the practice of CBT, focusing on the components of a CBT session, outlining the items on the Revised Cognitive Therapy Scale (CTS-R: James *et al.* 2001) and then identifying how the CTS-R is applied to the components of CBT and used to measure the competence of the therapist.

In Chapters 4–13 there are 10 case studies. In Chapter 4 we consider mild to moderate depression and its cognitive and behavioural attributes, and the theory of behavioural activation focused on activity scheduling is applied to the case of a 49-year-old male called Will. In Chapter 5 the focus is on low self-esteem, anxiety and depression, applying Fennell's (1997) model of low self-esteem and encouraging the application of a self-compassionate thinking style and working with assumptions in relation to the case of Sophie, a 32-year-old care assistant. Chapter 6 is concerned with panic disorder with agoraphobia and identifying the features of this problem, and how it impacts on friends and family and their responses in turn impact on the problem, and considering how treatment might still progress in spite of obstacles in the case of a 62-year-old recently bereaved woman called Mary.

In Chapter 7 the focus is on social anxiety and the most important features of this disorder to target in treatment, and a CBT model is then applied to the case of a 45-year-old woman called Ailsa. Chapters 8 and 9 discuss obsessive compulsive disorder (OCD), with Chapter 8 focusing on developing an understanding of OCD and understanding the nature of this problem, how to assess the person and engage with them, developing a formulation, and understanding how therapeutic interactions might be applied in the case of Gail, a 36-year-old single mother. Chapter 9, on mental compulsions, applies Wells's (1997) cognitive OCD model, provides an understanding of the concept of metacognitive thinking and how to work with this in treatment, before providing an explanation of thought–action–fusion, its connection with magical thinking and how to work with avoidant and neutralising safety behaviours in therapy in the case of Lang-Hoo, a 27-year-old Chinese male student. Chapter 10 considers the features of generalised anxiety disorder (GAD) and its relation to other disorders, while outlining a model for GAD and discussing the application of relevant treatment strategies for GAD in the case of Eddie, a 62-year-old male builder. In Chapter 11 we then discuss post-traumatic stress disorder (PTSD), considering the main features of this problem, explaining the application of Ehlers and Clark's (2000) model to a single case episode of PTSD and then relating the theoretical principles of treatment for PTSD to practice in the case of Juliet, a 27-year-old female healthcare professional. In Chapter 12 we consider perfectionism, offering a definition of this problem and its relationship to other problems, developing a formulation using an appropriate model and considering working with ambivalence to change, before discussing how a range of CBT strategies are used to effect change in the case of Sigurd a 27-year-old male student. Chapter 13 discusses how to work trans-diagnostically to develop an idiosyncratic formulation working with interpersonal difficulties, considering some of the difficulties that may be experienced in treatment and then working with assumptions driving both assertive and non-assertive behaviour with regard to Adita, a 23-year-old Asian woman. Finally, Chapter 14 defines clinical supervision and discusses the benefits and advantages to practice, and then outlines the models of Proctor (1986) and Hawkins and Shohet (2012), before discussing the competencies in CBT based clinical supervision.

Acknowledgements

We would like to thank family and friends for their encouragement and support throughout the writing process, as well as Noel Sawyer for teaching Vanessa CBT, and Alex, Emily and Hamish for their perseverance and patience.

1   Introduction

 Reader's agenda

Take a few moments to consider your own agenda or reasons for reading this chapter and make a note of them here:

-

-

The aim of this chapter is to:

- Familiarise you with the contents of the book
- Socialise you to the CBT format/structure of the book
- Introduce you to the reflective learning cycle.

Managing your time

Take a moment to consider how long you plan to spend reading this chapter, and make a note here:

There will be a reminder later in the chapter to check whether you have kept track with this.

The contents of this book

Over recent decades cognitive behavioural therapy (CBT) has gained prominence as the recommended treatment of choice for the majority of mental health issues. This is especially the case for depression and anxiety, which are also overwhelmingly the most frequently occurring mental health problems nationally and internationally. Within the UK healthcare sector this has in turn led to the recognition of the need to make CBT more widely available and easily accessible and the development of a wider range of mental healthcare workers and specialist roles and training. It is also a common expectation in numerous areas that mental healthcare workers possess skills in CBT as a basic requirement of their role.

The case studies in this book are intended to provide an understanding of the application of CBT for a range of common mental health problems, from depression to different anxiety-based problems. It is likely that these mental health issues will be frequently encountered by people in their everyday life in different ways as well by healthcare professionals in the course of their work.

However, a common misconception is that as depression and anxiety-based problems occur so frequently and guidance suggests that they can be effectively addressed within a brief number of CBT sessions, they are more amenable to intervention than other mental health issues. Although CBT offers a well-resourced and evidence-based framework, the effectiveness of therapy ultimately depends on the skills, competence and capacity of the healthcare worker implementing the approach to engage in working with people with depression and anxiety.

Implementing an effective CBT-led approach requires empathy, perception, self-awareness, compassion, honesty, flexibility and a wide range of therapeutic skills and competencies to be effective. The case studies in this book reflect the realities and challenges of practice, whereby depression and anxiety-related problems are often acutely disabling for the person. For the healthcare worker understanding the problem is often elusive, progress is frequently slower than would be hoped for and the practitioner often feels their capabilities to be in question.

In order to develop an in-depth understanding of the CBT approach it will help for readers to actively apply the therapeutic models to their own learning experience. Throughout the book there are a range of exercises and activities which readers are invited to engage with and which will enhance their learning.

In Chapter 2 the core concepts of CBT are explained. The development of CBT is briefly considered, and then the chapter broadens out to consider the models which inform the CBT approach adopted in this book. Central terms are highlighted, explained and also defined in the glossary. In Chapter 3 the practice of CBT is discussed, referring to the terms used and the common progression of CBT sessions in relation to the most commonly used method of rating sessions, the Revised Cognitive Therapy Scale (CTS-R) of James *et al.* (2001).

Socialisation to the structure of the book

One aim of CBT is to encourage independent learning. To this end, we have planned each chapter using the standard format of a CBT session, modelling the basic cognitive behavioural approach to a therapy session (James *et al.* 2001).

This logical structure promotes personal engagement with the material; for example, to help you focus, you will be encouraged to identify and write down your own agenda for reading at the outset of each chapter, including any gaps in your knowledge and understanding of the subject that you wish to fill.

To maximise efficiency, you are encouraged to set a timeframe for how long you wish to spend reading each chapter, as well as completing 'check-ins' during the reading to ensure you keep on track with this.

Throughout the chapters you will also be asked to contribute to a series of mini-summaries, as well as to a concluding summary, referring back to your original agenda items and summarising what you have learned, how this fits with what you already know and how you plan to carry your learning forward in practical terms for 'homework'. The book takes a broad, pragmatic approach, and additional reading is suggested at the end of each subject.

Although we will not be able to respond individually, you will also be encouraged to note down and send us feedback and impressions of what was helpful. This will be valuable in helping us plan for the future. Feedback is a vital tool for learning and is a central two-way feature of CBT practice.

We have tried to write in a style that is straightforward and jargon-free. However, as with any profession, CBT has its own specialised language, so this could not be avoided entirely, and we have included a glossary at the end of the book for clarification and learning. Words included in the glossary are printed in **bold**.

> To sum up: To encourage independent learning, each chapter is set out in the format of a CBT session. This requires involvement and participation in setting your own agenda items for reading each chapter and for making sure that you have covered these by the end. You will also be encouraged to complete homework tasks between chapters, and suggestions for additional reading will be provided.

Reflection and the learning cycle

One clear aim of any healthcare teaching is to produce responsible professionals, capable of managing their own continuing professional development needs. Professional bodies all stress the importance of reflective practice as part of this ongoing process (Nursing and Midwifery Council 2008; British Association for Behavioural and Cognitive Psychotherapies 2010).

By setting a personal agenda for reading this chapter you have already begun to actively and deliberately engage in the process of reflection. Kolb and Fry (1975) suggest that there are four stages to this process:

(i) Having an experience
(ii) Reflecting on the experience
(iii) Analysing your experience in light of what you already know
(iv) Planning for a different experience.

Each stage is necessary to avoid getting stuck in the rut of perpetually repeating unhelpful patterns of thinking and behaviour.

It is important to recognise that most mental health difficulties involve problems with completing the cycle at one stage or another. This makes a thorough working knowledge of the cycle important as it is a valuable therapeutic tool for initiating change.

Although the cycle of reflection is traditionally set out in the same order, in reality the cycle is flexible and has no distinct 'beginning' or 'end', but involves a cyclical

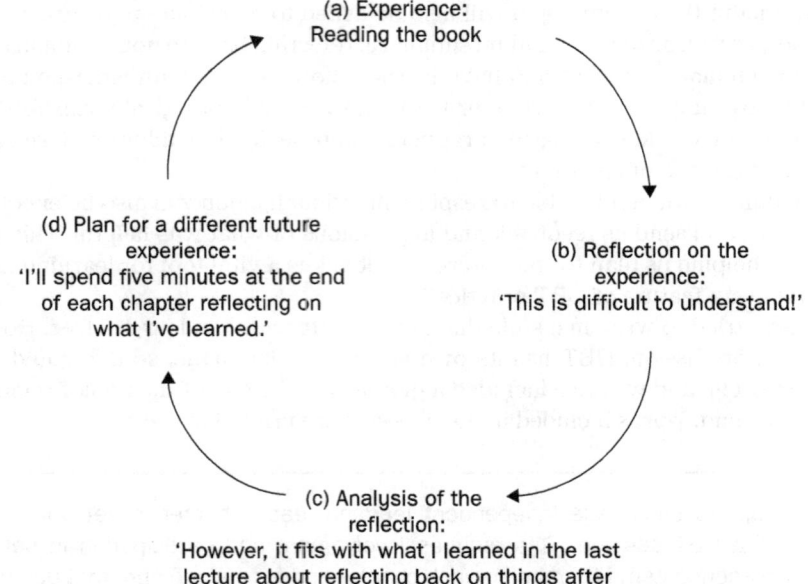

Figure 1.1 The learning cycle

process with learners entering the cycle at different points to complete the reflective process (Figure 1.1).

By way of practical application of the cycle, this book encourages engagement with the reflective process at point (a) by engaging you with the experience of reading the chapter. You are then likely to move to point (b) when reflecting on what you are reading, before (c) analysing any new information in the light of what you already know and integrating new information with what you already know. Finally, it is hoped that you will (d) specifically plan to use your new understanding the next time you (a) have a new experience that you can apply the information to. In this way you carry on round the cycle, continually learning as you go.

This reflective cycle is one of a many **models** that you will be introduced to during the course of learning CBT. Models are particularly helpful as they provide practical fameworks for understanding and applying abstract concepts.

 In summary, reflection is a skill that involves:

(i) Having an experience
(ii) Pondering on the experience
(iii) **Analysing** the experience by taking a close examination of its constituent parts
(iv) **Synthesising** new learning from the experience with pre-existing knowledge to gain new understanding.

Time invested applying the reflective cycle to your own learning will be well rewarded as reflective skills are essential to your becoming an effective practitioner.

Check-in

Now take time to reflect back on the agenda items set at the outset. Review and summarise what you have read so far, making key notes of any learning here:

Did you manage to keep to your original timeframe? If you did not, what have you learned from this? Make a brief note here:

How can you take any learning from this forward to the next chapter?

Homework

We suggest you now use the reflective cycle to consider, analyse and integrate any new understanding you have gained so far about the subject into your old understanding of it.

To complete the reflective cycle it would be helpful to plan how to apply this in your next practical experience and then carry your plan forward so that you maximise your learning. It might be helpful to start this now while you are thinking about it and to make a note of any plan you make here.

Completing this exercise will be an important part of your development as an independent and reflexive practitioner.

2 Theoretical background, including the core concepts of CBT

 Reader's agenda

Take a few moments to consider your current understanding and experience, if any, of the theory, principles and core concepts that underpin CBT. It will be helpful to identify gaps in your knowledge that you hope to fill by the end of the chapter. Use the space below or a separate notebook to make notes to reflect back on later.

•

•

The aim of this chapter is to help you:

- Understand how cognitive behavioural therapy developed
- Grasp the core concepts underpinning CBT theory and treatment
- Explain the basic models which inform the CBT approach
- Relate the theoretical fundamentals of CBT to the case studies that follow.

Managing your time

Take a moment to consider how long you plan to spend reading this chapter, and make a note here:

This chapter introduces the theory and fundamentals that underpin CBT and is designed to help you think about the individual case studies that follow in an analytic and systematic manner. The case studies themselves address a range of common mental health problems and will help you to consolidate your learning from this chapter by demonstrating how the fundamentals can be flexibly applied within real-world settings.

Before introducing the theory and fundamentals of cognitive behavioural therapy we will briefly set the scene for the emergence of CBT in the 1960s.

Behaviour therapy, the precursor to CBT, was developed out of early work on behavioural psychology undertaken in the late nineteenth and early twentieth centuries. Initially behaviourism was very unpopular because it endeavoured to study human behaviour in the same scientific way that behaviour in animals was studied, thus putting people 'on a par' with animals. Darwin's *Origin of the Species* had recently been published, all of which was seen as contributing to a perceived threat to the established order of things at that time (Watson 1970).

Up until this point, psychology had been largely dominated by self-analysis, which behaviourists now regarded as rooted in magic and superstition because it could not be measured scientifically. Thus the backdrop of this emerging creation–evolution divide makes it easy to understand how some ideas about therapy came to be unhelpfully polarised at that time.

Work undertaken by early behaviourists such as Thorndike and Skinner was based on two principles of learning, *classical conditioning* and *operant conditioning*. Classical conditioning applies to involuntary behaviour and is the process by which reflex or automatic responses occur, for example, salivation in response to the smell of food. On the other hand, operant conditioning is shaped by the consequences of behaviour; by manipulating the consequences, behaviour can be either **positively** or **negatively reinforced** to encourage or discourage desired behaviour; for example, obedience can be encouraged by reward and disobedience by being ignored or punished.

Bandura recognised the significance of **cognitions** in the learning process and later expanded on classical and operant conditioning to include **social learning theory**, or learning gained by modelling and imitation. This requires the observer to attend, retain and reproduce the behaviour observed, as well as have the motivation to do so.

Over the last forty years, cognitive psychologists have criticised behaviourism as being simplistic and have focused on human thought and the process of knowing as motivation for human action (Zimbardo *et al.* 1995). It was during the 1960s that Aaron Beck laid down the original model for cognitive therapy, which was devised to offer a short-term structured way of solving present problems for clients suffering from depression. It made the connection between cognitions and emotion, demonstrating that the meaning the client gave to any given situation could influence thoughts, particularly in a dysfunctional negative automatic way (Wills and Sanders 1997). Eventually an amalgam of cognitive and behavioural therapies evolved, which incorporates relationships between thinking, feeling *and* behaviour, and recognises the impact the environment can have on all of these.

CBT is concerned with 'here and now' problems and is aimed at providing opportunities to develop new adaptive learning experiences. In order to do this it is necessary to focus on specific rather than global issues (Kirk, in Hawton *et al.* 1989). CBT is time-limited and seeks to teach clients an awareness of the thoughts that are causing them distress and how this is being maintained, using the CBT model. The eventual aim is to teach clients to become their own therapist, with emphasis on relapse prevention (Beck 1995).

Core concepts and theoretical background

The role of positive and negative reinforcement

> Consider your current understanding, if any, of the role of positive and negative reinforcement in mental health difficulties and jot this down:
>
> •
>
> •
>
> Now consider any deficits in your understanding and make a note of anything you hope to understand better.

Behaviour is often interpreted as purposeful, that is, directed toward some end. However, during the mid-twentieth century a number of **empirical** studies on animals by Skinner interpreted behaviour as being selected on the basis of *past* consequences.

One limitation of Skinner's studies is that they only focused on observable effects on the environment and did not take into account unobservable internal processes, such as cognitions. By manipulating conditions within a highly controlled environment Skinner demonstrated a relationship between behavioural response and environmental change that is contingent on the behaviour. These contingent environmental changes are called behavioural **reinforcers** (Fuller 1995; Hawton *et al.* 1989).

To illustrate:

According to Skinner's theory, the fact that you are continuing to read this chapter suggests that your efforts are either being:

(a) reinforced by positive consequences or rewards (for example, as you continue to read you are learning something useful) or
(b) reinforced negatively by avoidance of something aversive (for example, if you stop reading you will start to feel anxious about an impending assignment that you do not know enough about).

These examples illustrate the principle of reinforcement: that short-term benefits that are contingent on the behaviour promote the behaviour.

Dysfunctional behaviours such as addictions are positively reinforced by the immediate reward of the 'hit', whereas anxiety disorders are negatively reinforced by escape and avoidance behaviour which immediately reduces the anxiety. In either case, the immediate benefit, either positive or negative, usually overrides the potential for longer-term outcomes, either positive or negative.

It is the lack of short-term incentive that is problematic when trying to bring about change. However, a word of caution: reinforcers are not always easy to identify or by any means obvious. For example, I may try to reinforce some good behaviour in you by offering you chocolate as a reward; however, I may not know that you are on a diet and chocolate is something negative which will make you feel worse. Likewise, it is important to recognise that while the behaviour of the above mentioned addict is positively reinforced by the pleasurable 'hit', it is also negatively reinforced by the avoidance of other more difficult emotions.

Fear and avoidance

In line with Skinner's observations, anxiety disorders in particular are usually negatively reinforced and thus maintained by avoidance of a fear stimulus. This principle can be illustrated using the 'fear and avoidance' model (Figure 2.1). Where fear, for example of dogs, is negatively reinforced by avoidant behaviour (i.e. the fear reduces if you cross the road and avoid the dog), the avoidance results in a lack of familiarity with dog behaviour. This unfamiliarity leads to less confidence in one's ability to deal with dogs, which in turn reinforces the fear of them.

To anyone afraid of dogs (or you might substitute anything that you are personally afraid of), it is understandable that you would avoid the fear stimulus because you perceive it as threatening. Perceived threat produces a physiological reaction (release of the hormone adrenaline), which itself can feel aversive. Interestingly, the adrenaline rush itself often becomes part of what the person fears and tries to avoid.

The aim of therapy is therefore to encourage approach rather than avoidance behaviour. To the individual in question this seems counter-intuitive, and skill is needed to provide conditions under which it will feel safe enough to undertake this work; the individual needs to feel in control at all times, as the case studies that follow will demonstrate. Of course, helpful approach behaviour can be encouraged by **positive reinforcement**, such as immediate praise or reward from the therapist.

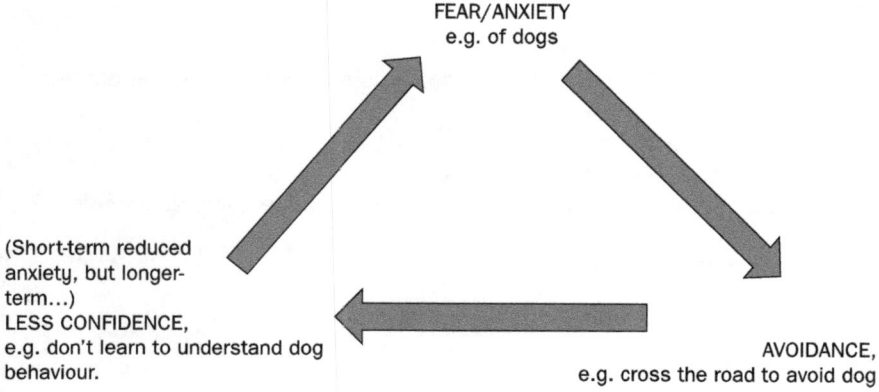

Figure 2.1 The fear and avoidance model

(Rachman and Hodgson 1974)

Homework

It is important to consolidate your understanding of how both positive and negative reinforcement work in the establishment and maintenance of emotional disorders.

Briefly summarise, *in your own words,* your understanding of how this applies in the personal experiences you mentioned at the outset. Be specific and explain how the role of reinforcement worked out in your examples:

Practice immediately and consistently rewarding desired behaviour (your own or someone else's) over a period of time and note the effects of this on the behaviour.

Further reading: Hawton *et al.* (1989: Chapter 1).

Summary

If any behaviour has consistently rewarding consequences, whether the positive addition of something pleasurable or the negative removal of something aversive, the action is likely to be repeated. In CBT anything that reinforces unhelpful behaviour needs clear identification and forms a key target for treatment.

 Check-in

Check back on the original time scale you scheduled for at the outset.

- Are you on schedule?
- How much time do you have left?
- Do you want to make adjustments or prioritise some subheadings?

Writing it down will serve as a reminder:

Levels of cognition

 Before reading on, list here all the different nouns for the word 'cognition' that you can think of:

So far in this chapter cognitions have been referred to in general terms to include automatic thoughts, assumptions, beliefs, memories and images. To target specific problems appropriately and effectively, it is important to identify and understand the different levels or 'layers' involved within a person's belief system. According to Beck *et al.* (1979), these levels include:

1   Automatic thoughts
2   Assumptions
3   Beliefs (or schemas).

All three levels can include memories and images.

It is important to distinguish between the three cognitive levels as not all levels are suitable or effective to work with initially. It may help to picture the three cognitive levels like a boat at sea that is connected by a rope to its anchor. The boat that bobs about on the surface represents automatic thoughts; the rope, which is heavy but flexible, represents assumptions and at the deepest level; the anchor, difficult and heavy to move, represents beliefs. Although all three are connected, it is much easier to work with automatic thoughts; therefore this is nearly always the first choice, only working with assumptions and beliefs if and when it becomes necessary to do so. We will now discuss each level in more detail.

Automatic thoughts

Automatic thoughts can be defined as the unplanned, transient flow of words and images that pass through our minds moment by moment in specific situations. They are often fleeting but emotionally active and may have repetitive themes. Like familiar furniture, they may go unnoticed by the individual much of the time, which can make them difficult to identify.

It is often the emotional reaction to the thought that gets noticed, so it can be helpful to work backward from the feeling by asking what was going through the person's mind at that time. Although many thoughts might be identified, it is important to work with the one that carries the 'emotional charge', that is, the thought that bothers the person most in that situation. This is sometimes referred to as the 'hot thought', and is closely connected to related assumptions and beliefs (Padesky and Greenberger 1995).

The following are examples of situation-specific automatic negative thoughts:

'This is impossible, I can't do it.'
'People at the party won't like me.'
'This work is rubbish!'

> **Micro-summary**
>
> Negative automatic thoughts are transient, situation-specific and carry an emotional charge. It is important to work with the thought carrying the strongest emotional charge.

Assumptions

Assumptions can alternatively be referred to as 'conditional beliefs' or 'rules for living'. They appear as either 'if . . . then . . .' statements, or as imperatives such as 'I must . . ./I should . . ./I ought . . .'.

Assumptions are generally helpful as they help make the world predictable and save time with decision making, for example, 'if I turn on the tap, then water will come out'. This can be taken for granted, and you do not have to think what will happen each time you turn on the tap.

Assumptions are more stable and enduring than automatic negative thoughts. They guide responses and behaviour across a wide range of situations, making them highly influential within the belief system. However, because they are *assumed* they are not always obvious and may need to be inferred from actions.

When a person holds their assumptions rigidly and inflexibly, their behavioural responses are restricted, even when this is clearly causing them problems. For example, if our assumption 'if I turn the tap then water will come out' is held too rigidly and water fails to come out because the washer is stuck, we will continue turning the tap pointlessly as the old assumption fails to adapt to the new circumstance.

Rigid assumptions limit options and frequently result in a narrow, frustrating and unsatisfying way of life, fostering resentment, anxiety and depression, as can be construed from the following examples:

'I must always put others ahead of myself.'
'I must always do my best or I won't be good enough.'
'I must never let others know the real me or they won't like me.'

Assumptions tend to be learned from past experience, and are sometimes deliberately passed on as 'wise' family sayings, such as 'if a job's worth doing then it's worth doing properly'.

Make a list of any personal rules or assumptions that you can identify. Think about any family sayings that have been passed on to you and include them.

-

-

-

Note the impact these have had on your life so far.
Remember: assumptions themselves can be helpful, but the rigidity with which they are held may not be!

Core beliefs

There are a number of differences between the terms 'core beliefs' and 'schemas', although these are frequently employed interchangeably within CBT literature. It is not our purpose to discuss these differences here, and for convenience this text employs the less technical term 'core beliefs'.

Core beliefs are the 'deepest' level of cognition and act as filters that process and code stimuli (Beck *et al.* 1979). When activated they tend to be regarded as 'the truth', rather than as personal beliefs or opinions. They are normally expressed in just one or two words and are held as absolute and dichotomous; for example, 'I'm lovable', 'I'm unlovable'. The cognitive model suggests that early experiences shape the development of core beliefs and that being long-standing means they are usually difficult to influence.

Beliefs are held across three domains – the self, others, and the world (Beck *et al.* 1979). It is important to identify all three, as there is interplay between them. For example, the combination of beliefs

'I'm vulnerable'
'The world is dangerous'
'Others are malicious'

is likely to result in anxiety and depression; whereas the combination

'I'm vulnerable'
'The world is dangerous'
'Others are kind'

is more likely to result in anxiety and dependency.

All three levels of cognition are interconnected. For example, the absolute negative core belief 'I'm unlovable' might give rise to the conditional assumption 'if I always do what others want they might like me', and will determine the type of automatic thoughts that will occur, 'he won't like me'. Figure 2.2 demonstrates the three cognitive levels.

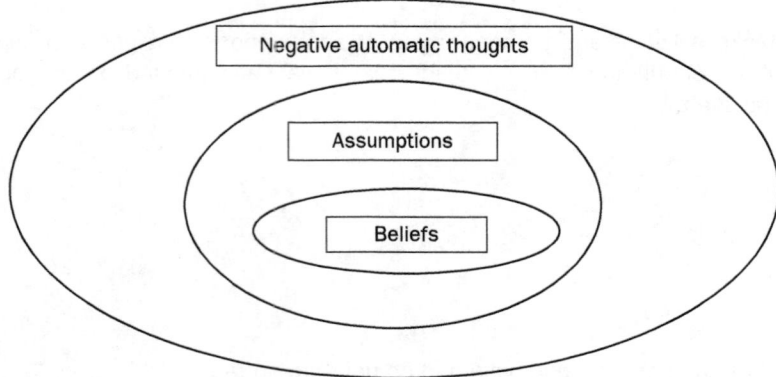

Figure 2.2 The three cognitive levels

Working systematically with negative automatic thoughts and assumptions over time naturally calls core beliefs into question, loosening their absolute hold and eventually making them easier to work with.

As beliefs involve a fundamental sense of self, others and the world, it would be unethical to expose and question these unless there is a sound therapeutic rationale for doing so. Working with core beliefs is not generally employed when working with Axis I difficulties, although it is central to treatment when working with Axis II, lifelong, personality-driven difficulties (James 2001; Padesky and Greenberger 1995).

Summary

Core beliefs give rise to assumptions and determine the content of automatic thoughts. They are the deepest level of cognition and are usually learned early in life.

Core beliefs are held as 'truths' rather than opinions, and trying to change them directly can produce strong resistance which is likely to be unhelpful.

Think of something that you hold to be true (e.g. that your eyes are the colour they are), and imagine someone trying to persuade you that they are not!

Further reading: Westbrook et al. (2007: 125–127).

Check-in

Is the chapter covering the points you hoped to cover?

Make a note of any points that are still outstanding; if they have only been partly covered, or not covered at all, you may consider some extended reading on that topic.

Are there any clues from the text about where you might look to extend your research?

Core Concepts of CBT:

The interacting cognitive subsystems model

There are many different ways in which we acquire knowledge; think for a moment about how you know what you know, and write your thoughts about this here:

Now consider how these various ways of knowing things influence the strength of your belief in what you know. (For example, is your belief in things you have been *told* as strong as your belief in things that you have learned from personal *experience*?)

Make some notes on your observations:

The subject of how we learn has greatly interested researchers and there are a number of theories about how we process information. The interacting cognitive subsystems model (Teasdale and Barnard 1993) has been perhaps the most influential within the world of CBT. It suggests that there are two information processing subsystems, **propositional** and **implicational**, that interact at a cognitive level.

The theory is complex; however, put simply, information which is coded within the *propositional* system appears to be rational, specific, represented in words and based on the individual's own logic. In contrast, information which is coded in the *implicational* system appears to be based on experience and often involves images or memories from experience. Reasoning from this system is less logic-based and more emotional, often involving a 'felt sense' of things, and seems to apply in a more general or global way. In lay terms, the propositional subsystem is involved with 'head' knowledge, while the implicational subsystem is involved with 'heart' knowledge.

> The following dictionary definition of 'cognition' captures the sense of both propositional and implicational learning involved in the acquisition of knowledge: 'The mental action or process of acquiring knowledge and understanding through thought, experience, and the senses' (*Oxford Dictionary of English*, 2003).

 Exercise

Close your eyes for a moment and think about some of your most powerful learning in life, noting the context in which the learning occurred:

Did your thinking involve verbal memories or images? Did you have an emotional reaction to this? If so, it is likely that your implicational coding system was activated. Significant learning often occurs within the context of strong emotions.

The propositional and implicational subsystems interact well together when the information coded in each of them forms a consistent account of things. However, when the two subsystems are hindered from interacting consistently, it often results in distorted, biased and extreme beliefs, leading to emotional and behavioural disorders. The aim of treatment is therefore to develop consistency between the two subsystems (Teasdale 1996; Bennett-Levy 2003; Bennett-Levy *et al.* 2004).

Commonly, some elements of CBT are considered to specifically target one subsystem or the other, but this is likely to be a simplified understanding of the processes involved. In reality, the most powerful and effective strategies are those that impact on both the implicational and propositional subsystems together (Bennett-Levy *et al.* 2004). This is one reason why the reflective cycle is considered to be a key means of professional skill development and learning, as it promotes consistency between both subsystems, synthesising theoretical knowledge (propositional learning) with practical experience (implicational learning) (Kolb 1984).

Summary

In your own language summarise your understanding of the ICS model and its relevance to CBT.

Further reading: Bennett-Levy (2003).

CBT assessment

CBT assessment differs markedly from general mental health assessment. Outline any differences that you are already aware of, as well as anything that you would like to understand about CBT assessment.

-
-
-

CBT assessment is an ongoing process which is more formally structured than generic mental health assessment; its primary aims are to build rapport, to identify current problems, to set treatment goals, and to obtain sufficient information on which to build a **formulation** and to plan treatment (see below). Because CBT is concerned with here-and-now problems, history taking is less prominent than in generic mental health assessment, although careful attention should always be given to assessing risk.

Information about the main problem is gathered by asking the '4WFINDS' questions, '*w*hat?', '*w*hen?', '*w*here?', '*w*ith whom?', and finding the *f*requency, *n*umber, *i*ntensity and *d*uration of its occurrence, as well as the **synthesising** question, what *s*ense does the person make of their difficulty? Two specific CBT models are outlined here that will help with gathering relevant information, and provide structure to questioning.

The four-systems model

The 'four systems' is a simple, generic CBT model that assists with gathering assessment information in a way that helps make sense of things. The four systems comprise:

- Thoughts, including images and memories, which are often predictive; these tend to be exaggerated, negative and extreme
- Physiology, which is activated by the autonomic nervous system
- Moods
- Behaviour, including excesses and deficits.

As these systems are interlinked, change in one domain affects each of the others and the system tends to self-perpetuate. An example of the model is presented in Figure 2.3. Both *internal* events (for example, loosing concentration momentarily) and *external* situations (for example, reading the book) can trigger the system.

Understanding this model broadens the scope for questioning to include what the person was thinking just prior to the shift in their mood, how this impacted on them physiologically, how they behaved as a result of these cognitive and affective changes and whether this behaviour was helpful or otherwise, as well as what, if anything, might have been more helpful.

Although the four-systems model is an effective tool for gathering information and demonstrating the elements of CBT, it does not explain *how* a problem is maintained and is not therefore suitable as a tool for **formulating** (see below) problems, as the maintenance element of any formulation is fundamental to understanding how treatment will proceed. This is quite a complex matter and for this reason we will return to it later.

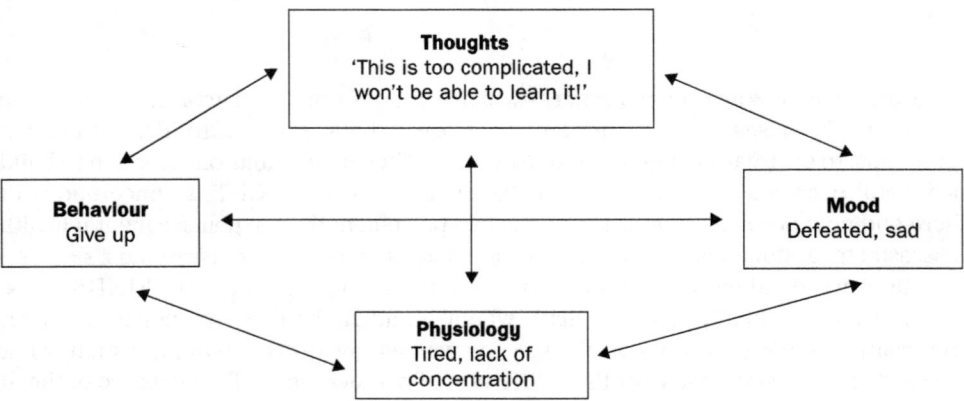

Figure 2.3 The four-systems model

Adapted from Greenberger and Padesky (1995)

> **Homework**
>
> CBT encourages scientific experimentation. Curiosity and open mindedness are vital ingredients of all good experimenters. Practice using the four-systems model on yourself and start noticing how your mind, body, mood and behaviour are linked and how the environment impacts on the system. Again, it is important to take notes about your findings. Try to encourage others to become curious about how their four systems link too.
>
> **Further reading:** Padesky and Mooney (1990).

The ABC model

Another tool to analyse presenting problems is the ABC model. To grasp this, imagine you are undertaking a CBT course; there is an exam and many in the group feel anxious because of this, while others are much less bothered. If it is the *exam* that is making people anxious, why isn't everyone equally anxious about the same exam? Clearly other factors, or **variables**, must be involved.

Although initially it looked as if A, the activating event (in this case the exam), leads to C, the consequence, (in this case the emotional response of anxiety), thus,

A_____leads to_____C
(The exam)   (Anxiety)

it becomes evident that more is involved in the generation of anxiety than the exam alone, and that other factors must be influencing things between A and C.

To find the **variable** we need to explore what the exam *means*. Answers are likely to depend on things like past exam experience, workshop attendance, revision and preparation. It is therefore the meaning or beliefs, B, that individuals hold about taking exams that accounts for the difference in their anxiety levels. It is the identification of B, the idiosyncratic intermediary belief, that is the vital ingredient in CBT. It is this B that can be influenced in treatment to impact more favourably on C:

A_____B_____C
(The exam)   (meaning = 'I might fail!')   (Anxiety)

If the individual is anxious because they have not prepared for the exam, this requires a change in behaviour (i.e. doing the revision) in order to influence beliefs, B, about the consequence, C, but it is still the *meaning* or *belief* about not having prepared ('I haven't revised, therefore I might fail') that brings about the consequence (in this case anxiety). Hence, the main ingredients of CBT are beliefs and behaviours; both need clear identification as they form the focus of therapy.

> **Homework**
>
> Next time you experience a negative consequence (C) to an activating event (A) use the ABC model to identify your cognition or belief (B). Note down your belief and how it influenced the consequence or outcome. Repeat the exercise a few times and think about your belief system. Do the same beliefs crop up often?
>
> Become familiar with the ABC model; it can be used flexibly and forms the basis for gathering important information on which many CBT interventions are based.
>
> **Further reading:** Hawton et al. (1989: 25).

Summary: How we use CBT models

In summary, models help to organise and clarify thinking by using frameworks to make sense of problems. You may have noticed that the ABC model includes many elements of the four-systems model; for instance, both models include cognitions and behaviours, but arranged differently to illustrate and elicit different aspects of the problem.

It is important to familiarise yourself with these two models and consolidate your learning by completing the homework assignments before moving on.

Formulation

Once relevant cognitive and behavioural details have been gathered during CBT assessment, it becomes possible to make sense of the difficulty by collaboratively devising a CBT formulation. This involves mapping out the problem, including its development, together with an analysis of the factors that are maintaining it, thus providing a rationale for treatment and making it clear what to target in treatment.

The formulation is an adaptable working hypothesis for testing reality. For the individual to 'own' and view it as meaningful, it is important to use their own **idiosyncratic** details and language and to compose it collaboratively in session.

This process engenders hope and reduces anxiety and depression by bringing order to the chaos and by introducing fresh ideas about how to improve the situation. The formulation is the interface between abstract, general CBT theories, and practice.

There are a number of 'disorder-specific' CBT formulation models that include the important central feature for that particular disorder. These will be demonstrated in the case studies that follow. However, while it is good to base treatment on a strong and scientifically sound footing, people are individuals and it can be potentially **invalidating** to use any model as a standard prescription that must be followed to the letter. It is more helpful to view models as flexible tools that can be adapted to individual problems.

Focus on maintenance: Safety behaviours

Often difficulties are rooted in the past as well as in a person's genetic predisposition, neither of which are directly treatable. The legacy of these influences, that is, (i) how the person still perceives things and (ii) how they subsequently behave as a result of these perceptions, often fails to get updated. These form maintenance patterns that hinder progress with effective living; therefore updating these in line with current reality becomes the focus of therapy.

These maintenance patterns can be understood in terms of feedback loops or cycles. The cycle starts with a stimulus – either internal or external – which triggers a round of negative thoughts, feelings, physiological reactions and behavioural responses (the four systems).

However, the four-systems model does not demonstrate how the problem is *maintained* as it does not include the perceived short-term advantage of the behaviour that **reinforces** the problem, feeding back into the loop or cycle and maintaining, or sometimes worsening, the problem. These problematic behaviours are **conceptualised** in CBT terms as **safety behaviours**. This term indicates the hoped-for function of the behaviour, which is to keep the individual safe in a situation where potentially they might feel unsafe.

Safety behaviours may be overt (e.g. avoiding dogs), or covert (e.g. counting to 10 to prevent the dog from biting). Either way, the paradoxical effect of safety behaviours is that they maintain the problem by preventing disconfirmation of the negative belief that the person holds about the event. The person is left with the idea that the feared consequence (being bitten) did not happen only because they engaged in the safety behaviour (avoiding or counting).

Superstitions

To illustrate how beliefs and the behaviours they prompt can form maintain patterns, consider how superstitions work.

If a person believes that walking under a ladder will result in something unlucky happening, they will avoid the ladder. Then, when nothing bad happens, they ascribe this to avoiding walking under the ladder (rather than to the fact that nothing bad happens most days).

Thus, when they come across another ladder they are more likely to do the same thing again, because the belief has been negatively reinforced; thus the superstitious belief is maintained and promoted.

Thus prevention of disconfirmation of the belief locks people into loops of thinking and behaviour that feel 'safe' but which prevent the necessary learning that would undermine or contradict the erroneous belief. The formulation therefore needs to include any idiosyncratic safety behaviours if it is to provide an effective guide for treatment.

Therefore at assessment it is important to identify what the person does to reduce their short-term discomfort when afraid or depressed. Although safety behaviours are idiosyncratic, each mental health disorder has a typical style or set of associated safety behaviours. Table 2.1 gives some examples: this list is not exhaustive, but illustrates

Table 2.1 Some examples of disorder-specific safety behaviours, adapted from James et al. (2001)

Disorder	Safety behaviour
Panic	Monitoring and regulating breathing/pulse Sitting down or holding on to something to prevent collapse Only going out with another person present
Social anxiety	Self-monitoring and self-absorption, including excessive self-reflection on personal 'performance' following social contact Avoidance of attracting attention (wearing dark clothes, sitting in the corner, avoiding eye contact, etc.) Holding objects tightly (e.g. pen, cup) to avoid tremor being noticed
Obsessive compulsive disorder	Preventative or neutralising behaviours (mental and physical), such as checking, washing, or engaging in rituals like counting or saying a prayer, etc. to prevent bad things from happening Taking responsibility to excessive degree
Generalised anxiety disorder	Worrying and ruminating to anticipate threat, mental control, trying to suppress thoughts, scanning for danger, distraction
Health anxiety	Self-monitoring and checking for signs and symptoms of illness Reassurance seeking including GP and specialist tests Avoidance of others with health problems Selective attention to, or avoidance of, health-related issues (TV, journals, etc.)
Post-traumatic stress disorder	Dissociation or 'spacing out' Thought suppression Avoidance of trigger situations including places reminiscent of the trauma
Depression	Avoidance of other people/isolation Inactivity Self-criticism

how knowledge of the type of safety behaviours involved with a specific disorder can help to inform assessment questions.

Each case study that follows will include a formulation of the problem, including unhelpful thoughts and behaviours that are maintaining it. (Note that in this book the words 'formulation' and 'conceptualisation' are used interchangeably to refer to this map or 'framework' of the problem.)

In your own words

To help understand how safety behaviours work, think about a problem that you are currently struggling with and briefly sum up how safety behaviours are involved in maintaining it. A useful question to help identify safety behaviours is: 'If there was a fly on the wall watching when X is happening, what would it observe happening?'

Further reading: Sanders and Wills (2005: 33–36).

Summary

During assessment the problem is analysed, or broken down into its constituent parts; these parts are then synthesised into a coherent map or formulation that demonstrates how the various elements link and maintain the problem. This formulation is viewed as a working 'hypothesis' which is subject to change and which is used to guide treatment.

Check-in

Look back at your original decision about how much time you were prepared to spend on this chapter. Consider here if it is feasible to complete the chapter in the amount of time remaining. Remember, you need to leave time to complete the exercises. You may decide to prioritise some subheadings.

If you are running over time you may decide either to extend your time frame, or to delay reading further for another time.

Make a note here of any changes you decide on, including when you plan to complete the chapter and how much time you think you will need. This will be useful to refer to, and will help you manage your time more effectively.

Time I planned to spend:

Time spent so far:

Planned change:

Treatment strategies: The fundamentals

Exposure and response prevention
Avoidance and escape are primary, adaptive behavioural responses to anxiety (Marks 1987). However, routinely adopting avoidance and escape behaviour can prove maladaptive, as less exposure to the feared stimulus and its accompanying adrenaline 'rush' prevents both **habituation** and learning.

This resulting unfamiliarity increases anxiety and reduces confidence, resulting in a fear and avoidance cycle. The principle of exposure and response prevention (ERP), that is, exposure to the perceived threat and prevention of the desired response to avoid or escape, has a sound evidence base for treating anxiety disorders (NICE 2005). As a treatment strategy ERP can prove difficult, as the person may fear becoming overwhelmed by their raised anxiety level during the process. One fundamental element of successful treatment is the development of a trusting therapeutic relationship. Without this, treatment dropout poses a considerable risk. The individual needs to feel in control when facing their fears, and be allowed to dictate the speed at which they feel safe enough to proceed.

Treatment progresses with the individual being encouraged to design a **graded hierarchy** of situations that they would find distressing. This is so that the exposure work can proceed in a controlled manner, working from their own list at their own pace, gradually from their least to their most distressing situations.

Imagine your own fears, such as heights, public speaking or spiders. If you had to have treatment for this, how would you want this to proceed?

(a) With a therapist encouraging you to just face the fear straight out, 'all-or-nothing' style?
(b) Using self-help?
(c) With a therapist supporting and encouraging you to gradually build up to facing your worst fear in a controlled manner?

Measuring the person's distress levels at the outset of any exposure exercise and at regular intervals throughout is encouraging for both client and therapist as this indicates whether treatment is working and works to positively reinforce treatment (see Figure 2.4).

Occasionally a person may appear to be progressing well through their hierarchy with little distress, but they are actually 'blocking' their emotional responses. Without exposure to emotion, no habituation can take place and treatment will be ineffective. If this is the case, treatment starts again on the hierarchy, making sure the person focuses on their emotional responses, describing and rating them throughout.

ERP targets the powerful implicational subsystem, allowing the individual to relearn, through the experience of habituation, that both the stimulus and the physiological response it provokes are largely benign. However, by including a cognitive

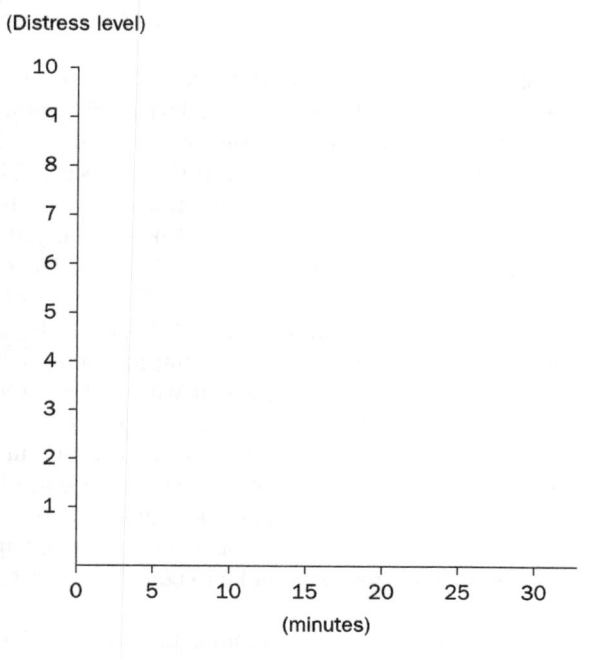

Figure 2.4 Chart to measure subjective levels of distress

element to ERP it is possible to target both propositional and implications subsystems, thus improving treatment outcomes (Bennett-Levy *et al.* 2004). This will be discussed further in the section on behavioural experiments below.

> ✏️ Briefly summarise your understanding of the principles of ERP and outline the various considerations that must be taken into account at the outset of treatment.

Behavioural activation

> ✏️ Write a couple of sentences that describe your current understanding and experience of behavioural activation, including any problems that you have encountered and any gaps in your knowledge.

Behavioural activation is a well-researched intervention for treating depression. It targets passive, avoidant behaviour that results in a narrowed lifestyle that offers little in the way of positive reinforcement (Lewinsohn *et al.* 1976; Jacobson *et al.* 1996; Cuijpers *et al.* 2007). Avoidances may be behavioural (such as watching endless TV to avoid getting on with life), cognitive (involving ruminating on the depression) or emotional (such as overeating or use of alcohol or drugs to eliminate uncomfortable emotions), all of which negatively reinforce the depression. Clearly, to alleviate depression, changes are necessary.

For any change to be meaningful and sustained, Veale (2008) recommends first exploring the person's value system to ensure that any planned goals are in line with their values. Values differ from goals and represent what a person wants their life to stand for in the long run; they require long-term commitment to a way of life. On the other hand, goals are shorter-term aims and may or may not be in line with values, although as Veale advocates, goals that are in line with values are more likely to be meaningful and motivating. For example, you might want to become a competent cognitive behavioural therapist, this is what you value and want your life to stand for, whereas a goal in line with this value might be to complete your first assignment by the end of the year.

With values in mind, the depressed individual is taught to analyse the unintended consequences of the avoidant behavioural 'solutions' they currently adopt, noting the effects of these on their depressed mood and on the achievement (or otherwise) of their values.

Their identified values can then form the basis for scheduling activity which will help them move forward; this generally includes targeting avoidant behaviours that currently prevent progress. The aim is to make small, carefully planned changes that positively reinforce the new behaviour. The intervention is powerful as behavioural change impacts on the implicational subsystem, providing new learning from experience.

Although called behavioural activation, treatment also targets self-attacking cognitive styles and ruminative thinking. Employment of the ABC model to analyse the function of these cognitive behaviours often demonstrates that they provide escape from thoughts and feelings associated with interpersonal difficulties. The therapist can encourage a more active approach to resolving relationship problems.

> **Summary**
>
> Behavioural activation takes a practical approach to treating depression, identifying various reinforcing behaviours the individual employs as their solution to the depression. Identification of an alternative, valued direction in which the individual would prefer to move provides a basis for scheduling activity toward that end. The depressed individual is helped to see that they do in fact have choices, and that their choices can influence their mood.
>
> What have you learned?
>
>
>
> **Further reading:** Veale (2008).

Thought records

> The four-system model raises awareness that thoughts impact on physiology, emotion and behaviour. Make a note of anything you want to know or are not sure about thinking or thought records.

Thought records are initially targeted toward propositional learning, later using this work as a basis to design strategies that impact on implicational learning. However, no

28 CBT Fundamentals

strategy is exclusive and both propositional and implicational learning are likely to be involved to some extent.

Before undertaking cognitive work it is important to explain the rationale for this and to discuss potential benefits to the individual. Cognitive work can be painful, and starting at automatic negative thought level can help to mitigate this.

The aim of thought records is to help the individual stand back from their currently upsetting appraisals of events and to analyse and re-evaluate them, thus broadening their cognitive perspective within the moment.

Because thought records are technical, it is important to practise them in session until the individual is confident to use them independently. Encouraging the person to write down their thoughts word for word engages them in the process and promotes ownership of their work. Initially these are written within a five-column format (a completed five-column thought record for someone with social anxiety is shown in Figure 2.5).

Date	Emotions	Situation	Automatic thoughts	Behaviour
13.06.12	Anxious 75%	Thinking about hanging the washing out.	'The neighbour will be looking; she'll think I'm odd.'	Don't hang the washing out.
13.06.12	Anxious 50% Guilty 75%	Partner coming home.	'I should have got the washing dry. He'll think I'm lazy.'	Hide the wet washing and distract partner by asking him questions.
14.06.12	Angry at self 80%	Looking at pile of wet washing.	'I'm so stupid, why don't I just hang it out?'	Wait until the neighbour goes out before hanging the washing out.
14.06.12	Stupid 100% Angry at self 100% Anxious 100%	Wanting to get the washing in as it must be dry.	'I should have been watching to see if the neighbour got back. If she's back she'll see me and might come out to talk.'	Wait for partner to come in, pretend to be really busy and ask him to get the washing in.

Figure 2.5 Five-column thought record

Firstly, the individual has to recognise their negative automatic thoughts. Typically an incident that has caused distress during the week is discussed in therapy, a note is made of the date, the emotions provoked and the situation. If the person is unable to identify their negative automatic thoughts immediately, it can be useful to enquire what was going through their mind just before they noticed the emotion, or what it was they were saying to themselves at that moment.

Using the five columns raises awareness of negative thinking while at the same time familiarising the person with the four-systems model. It is important to write thoughts and feelings as they occur or at least to jot them down in the moment, to be completed later.

From the range of thoughts identified the person then highlights the most upsetting thought; this is usually the one with most potential for bringing about change as it carries the emotional 'charge'.

Once the person is familiar with recording their thoughts using five columns they can be introduced to the next step, which is to evaluate their 'strongest' thought using a seven-column thought record (see Figure 2.6). This process needs to be introduced slowly and consistently so that the person thoroughly understands what is being asked of them and feels relatively confident that they can complete these independently outside of the session.

The seven-column record uses only columns 1–4 from before. This time the fifth column is used to collect evidence the person is using as a basis for their thoughts. This stage is important as it exhausts the person's 'yes but . . .' arguments before starting on the next column. However, if the person is depressed it may be better to miss this column out because focusing on reasons for their negative thoughts could lower their mood still further.

Once all of this evidence has been recorded, the sixth column can be introduced to gather evidence which suggests the original thought might *not* be true. The person may find this difficult because cognitive biases (see below) are narrowing their perspective. Gentle, non-persuasive questioning is often needed to open this up:

'What could be another way of seeing this?'
'How would your (non-depressed) friend see this?'
'What else suggests it might not be completely true?'

Finally, taking evidence from both of these columns into account, the person is encouraged to produce a more accurate and balanced way of thinking about the situation, writing this in the final column.

The re-evaluated thought often represents a **paradigm shift** and is not likely to be as believable as the original negative thought, even though it may be acknowledged as more realistic. It is important to measure the person's strength of belief in this new thought, as this can be used to measure future change against. The new thought can then provide a basis for planning further strategies to test it for accuracy and 'fit'.

Thought records provide a useful resource for identifying cognitive biases which generally favour pre-existing core beliefs and assumptions. Cognitive biases are

Date	Emotion %	Situation	Automatic thoughts	Evidence for the thought	Evidence that suggests it's not 100% true	More balanced thought (including % strength of belief)
21.06.12	Anxious 60%	Thinking about going shopping	'What if I see someone I know?' 'If they come over and talk I'll stumble over my words and they'll think I'm odd.'	Last time Mrs. G. spoke to me I felt so anxious my mind went blank. I felt stupid and she must have thought I was stupid. (emotional reasoning and mind reading)	On Monday Mr. B. said hello and we had a chat about his dog. Because we focused on the dog it was OK and the conversation felt natural.	If someone talks to me I will probably feel anxious, but if I focus on the other person and what they are saying it might be OK. Strength of belief 40%

Figure 2.6 Seven-column thought record

exaggerations of erroneous thinking that are common when emotions are aroused and include:

- Mentally filtering out and dwelling on a single negative event
- **Dichotomous, all-or-nothing** thinking
- Catastrophic thinking
- Over-generalising many conclusions from one negative event
- Magnifying the importance of negative events while minimising the importance of positive ones
- Jumping to conclusions
- Mind reading
- Name-calling – 'I'm such an idiot!'
- Reasoning from one's emotions, 'I feel anxious; therefore there must be something to be anxious about!'

From regular practice with thought records, the individual learns both how to reflect on action (after the event), and in action (during the event), and to recognise and counter their negative thinking biases.

> **A word of warning**
>
> Thought records can prove counter-therapeutic in some cases. Dwelling on and analysing thoughts can be counter-therapeutic for people with ruminative and OCD thinking, where a mindfulness approach is more appropriate (see any reputable text on mindfulness for information as it is beyond the scope of this book).
>
> Also of note is that using thought records with angry thoughts may produce defensiveness and resistance which may increase the person's anger, and should therefore be undertaken very cautiously, if at all.

> **Homework**
>
> Practice catching your own negative automatic thoughts in emotionally provocative situations. Record these as they happen, using a five-column thought record (reflecting in action), then expanding this into a seven-column thought record after the event (reflecting on action). Try to identify your own thinking biases and notice if there are patterns or themes that emerge; remember to remain curious!
>
> **Further reading:** Greenberger and Padesky (1995).

Behavioural experiments

Behavioural experiments include many features of exposure and response prevention; however, their strength is in the fusion of both behavioural and cognitive elements, thus engaging both the implicational and propositional subsystems in the learning process. Whereas ERP is a behavioural strategy, behavioural experiments are ultimately a means toward cognitive change; learning is made explicit by analysing and drawing conclusions from the outcomes of pre-planned behavioural experiments.

Behavioural experiments draw on the same principles employed in scientific testing, only using belief systems as the foundation for experimentation. The process usually involves the following stages:

1. Constructing a theory to be tested
2. Designing a method for testing the theory
3. Carrying out the tests/experiments
4. Gathering the data from these
5. Analysing the data and drawing conclusions.

> **Measurement**
>
> Drawing conclusions from data depends on accurately measuring the outcomes; there are a number of symptom specific, **valid** and **reliable** CBT tools for this, including the PHQ–9 (Kroenke et al. 2001) and GAD7 (Spitzer et al. 2006), as well as more global measures such as CORE-OM (Barkham et al. 2001).
>
> However, idiosyncratic data can necessitate personalised data collection tools. While these may have only **face validity,** they are often more personally relevant, as the case studies that follow will illustrate.

The most productive approach to behavioural experiments is to strengthen alternative, more adaptive belief systems, rather than to spend time dismantling old ones (Padesky 1994). Accomplishing this involves experimenting with balanced thoughts generated from thought records, working with modified, more flexible assumptions and testing beliefs about the value of safety behaviours. Experiments may involve discovery, hypothesis testing, deliberate manipulation of **variables,** or may be simply observational. Experimental techniques may include role play, modelling or use of surveys to gather data.

Much thought needs to be given to setting up behavioural experiments as individuals are unlikely to engage in the process unless they feel safe enough to do so. This requires a pre-existing collaborative, open and respectful therapeutic relationship. Because experiments are perceived to have an element of risk, it is important to set them up as win–win ventures, no matter what the outcome. Toward this end, Sawyer (2007) gives ten top tips for setting up behavioural experiments:

1 Explore the feared consequence.
2 Explore how the individual would know if it was happening.
3 Ask what they would think, feel and do if it did happen.
4 Enquire about the likelihood of it happening.
5 Enquire about how awful this would be.
6 List all the safety behaviours employed to manage the situation.
7 Evaluate how likely these really are to prevent the feared outcome from happening.
8 Enquire whether it's *true* that the fear consequence *will* happen, or whether they *worry* it will happen?
9 If they believe it *will* happen, enquire whether other people are just as worried about this.
10 If the person acknowledges they are *worried*, enquire whether this could explain their anxiety symptoms and how they might feel if they could view it differently.

When planning behavioural experiments it is helpful to start with low-cost ventures, chosen by the individual concerned. The experiment should clearly target the relevant cognition, remembering it is more helpful to build on new cognitions than to demolish old ones. Any experiment should take into account emotional and physiological reactions that may be triggered by the experiment and medical clearance from the person's GP may be needed in cases where there may be underlying physical heart problems such as epilepsy or heart disease.

> **Summary**
>
> Behavioural experiments are a powerful method for working with cognitions at an implicational level. They may feel risky for the individual undertaking them and for this reason collaboration and careful planning are keys to success.

> **Homework**
>
> Working with the thought records from your last homework exercise and using Sawyer's ten top tips, devise a behavioural experiment to test out your new thought. You may need to undertake several experiments before your strength of belief in the new thought becomes meaningful.

Conclusion

> **Conclusion and consolidation of your learning**
>
> This chapter has introduced a number of core CBT concepts, including:
>
> - The principles that underpin and provide a rationale for treatment
> - Models for gathering assessment information
> - Basic treatment principles and strategies.
>
> To help you recall and explain any learning about these concepts, answer the following:
>
> 1. Classical conditioning applies to involuntary behaviour and is the process by which reflex responses occur. True or false?
>
> 2. How does operant conditioning differ from classical conditioning?

3   Behaviour is positively reinforced by the addition of a reward. Explain how behaviour can be negatively reinforced.

4   Explain the relationship between core beliefs, assumptions and negative automatic thoughts.

5   Information coded within the propositional system is rational, represented in words and based on personal logic, whereas information coded within the implicational system is based on experience and often involves a 'felt sense' of things. True or false?

6   What is the purpose of CBT assessment?

7   Can you name each of the elements involved in the four systems?

8   What does the B in the ABC model stand for, and when might you use the model?

9   What is one important feature of any formulation and why?

10 What is the benefit of collaboratively devising a graded hierarchy when working with ERP?

11 What is the benefit of identifying a person's valued directions in life when working with behavioural activation?

12 Why is it important to work towards strengthening a new, more balanced thought rather than undermining a negative thought?

13 What are five stages involved in setting up a behavioural experiment?

If there were any questions that you found difficult to answer you may wish to revisit parts of the chapter to consolidate your learning before moving on to apply these principles to the case studies that follow.

Feedback

Think about your experience of reading this chapter and note any feedback for the authors here:

At the end of the book you may wish to collate the feedback together to forward to the following address: nick.wrycraft@anglia.ac.uk

3 The practice of CBT

Reader's agenda

Take a few moments to consider your current understanding and experience of practising CBT. Next identify gaps in your knowledge that you hope to fill by the end of the chapter. Use the space below or a separate notebook to make notes to reflect back on later.

-
-

The aim of this chapter is to help you:

- Understand the components of a CBT session
- Become familiar with the items on the Revised Cognitive Therapy Scale (CTS-R: James *et al.* 2001)
- Understand how the CTS-R is applied to the different components of CBT and is used in measuring therapist competence.

Managing your time

Take a moment to consider how long you plan to spend reading this chapter, and make a note here:

There will be a reminder later in the chapter to check whether you have kept track with this.

Introduction

CBT is a problem-focused and time-limited therapeutic approach that emphasises collaborative working between the therapist and client and aims to teach the client practical skills that they will continue to use at the end of therapy.

CBT proceeds upon a number of principles and is characterised by an emphasis upon:

- The development of the therapeutic alliance with the client
- Working in an actively collaborative partnership
- Developing an individualised and specific formulation and conceptualisation of the client's problem(s)
- Using a problem focused and goal orientated approach
- Being time limited
- Using a structured approach
- Teaching the client to identify, understand and respond to unhelpful thoughts and beliefs
- Using a variety of techniques to help the client bring about change in their thinking, mood and behaviour
- Teaching the client to become their own therapist

(Beck 2011)

In this chapter we will consider how the elements of CBT sessions are rated using the Revised Cognitive Therapy Scale (CTS-R) devised by James *et al.* (2001). However, first we will consider the common features that are characteristic to CBT sessions.

Almost all CBT sessions will include the components listed in Table 3.1. The first component, *orientation*, involves:

- Explaining the theory supporting CBT
- Discussing how the presenting problems of the client can be conceptualised and addressed using the CBT approach
- Educating the client regarding the structure of CBT sessions and the mutual expectations, roles and responsibilities of the client and the therapist.

Orientation ought to occur in the initial session, yet also be frequently reiterated in further sessions as often as possible, in order to effectively socialise the client to CBT. Framing explanations of the model in relation to the client's own experience and examples will also help provide a sense of personal relevance to application of the CBT model (Culley and Teten 2008).

Table 3.1 Components of CBT

Component	Phase
Orientation Checking in Agenda setting	Introduction phase (phases 1–3)
Periodic summaries Setting homework	Content phase (phases 4–5)
Summarising the session and client feedback	Concluding phase (phase 6)

Checking in has the potential for digression, so it helps to limit this part of the session to a maximum of 5–10 minutes. Among the features of checking in are:

- An informal update and renewal of the acquaintance that helps build the therapeutic alliance
- To update on any significant and relevant events that have happened to the client since the last session
- Gauging the client's mood and identifying any changes
- Considering any discrepancy between the therapist's perception of the client's mood and their subjective view.

Agenda setting ought to occur early on in the session, and is the process through which the client and therapist decide how to allocate the time in the session. Emphasis needs to be put on collaboration and negotiation between the therapist and client, and agreeing the order and time allocated to items that each feels ought to be considered in the session. For some clients at an early stage in treatment and still developing familiarity with the model, the therapist may need to take a more active role. However, to socialise the client with the model there needs to be an emphasis on facilitating the client's active and equal participation at every opportunity (Cully and Teten 2008). When setting the agenda part-way through a number of sessions, it is necessary to review items from the previous session and the homework assignment, to engender a sense of continuity and integration to the therapy.

The next component is *periodic summaries*. A summary ought to be provided after the agenda identifying what the session will cover. The sessions ought to then be punctuated at regular intervals with at least two summaries, clarifying what has been discussed, identifying new learning and the emergence of new perspectives and action points. The therapist offering regular summaries during sessions provides a coherent thread and logical sense of continuity and progression to the issues being discussed. Summaries are also an opportunity to ensure that there is a shared understanding between the therapist and client, and is an opportunity for any differences to be resolved.

The process of *setting homework* tasks ought to:

- Be collaboratively discussed and agreed within the session
- Identify a clear and specific task
- Be a task that the client can realistically achieve
- Be a task that the client feels motivated to complete
- Be linked to work that has occurred within the session
- Have a clear rationale linked to CBT that the client understands and is aware of the contribution that this makes to their therapy
- Be innovative in the way that information is captured for example the use of recording forms.

The final component is *summarising the session and client feedback*. Consistent with the offering of periodic summaries, the therapist ought to deliver an overview at the end of the session. This may take the form of a chronological account of the issues that were discussed. However, it is also important to ask for the client's feedback in terms of what was helpful or unhelpful.

Look at the above components and place them in order, with the one that you are best at first and the most challenging last. What has led you to choose this order? Write down your strengths and learning needs in relation to each component.

Having discussed the components of CBT sessions, we will next consider the Revised Cognitive Therapy Scale of James *et al.* (2001) and identify how therapists can be rated with regards to their level of competence in delivering CBT.

The Revised Cognitive Therapy Scale

The CTS-R of James *et al.* (2001) is the most commonly used rating scale for assessing therapist competence and is based on the cognitive cycle of thoughts, feelings, physiology and behaviour/planning (Figure 3.1). It proceeds on the basis that in therapy the client is facilitated by the therapist to move from a dysfunctional formulation or conceptualisation to a more helpful way of thinking.

The CTS-R scale comprises of 12 items in two groups: general items and cognitive therapy specific items. The general items (1–5) relate to aspects of the practice of CBT that assist in helping the client to adopt more helpful ways of thinking and responding to the triggers that produce and maintain problems. In contrast, items 1 and 6–12 are cognitive therapy specific and assess the therapist's competence and skills in supporting the client to move through the cognitive cycle. Note that item 1 belongs to both the general and cognitive groups.

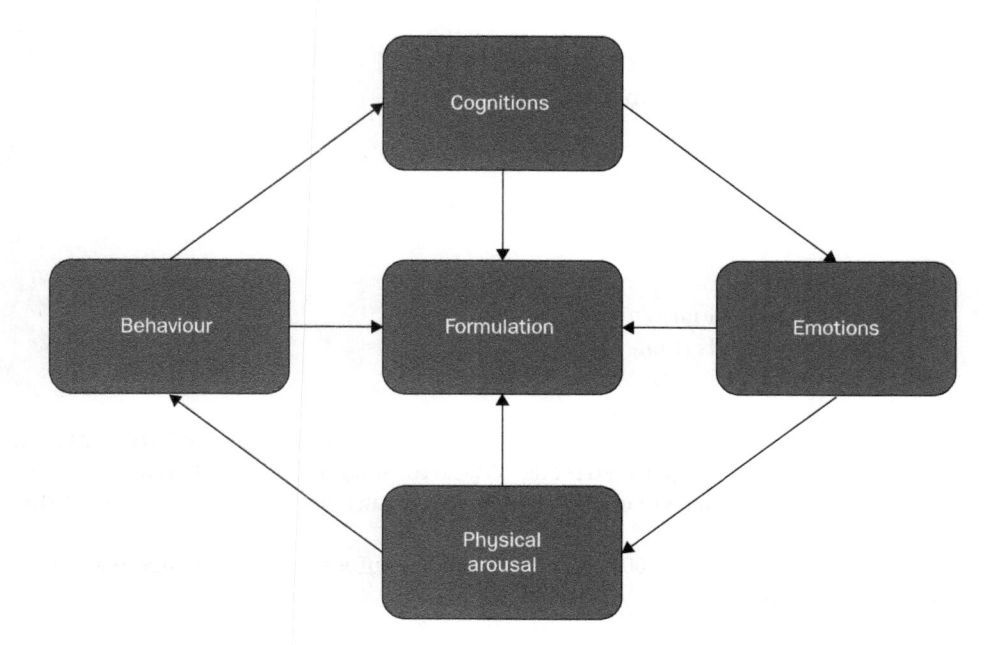

Figure 3.1 The cognitive cycle
(adapted from James *et al.* 2001)

General items

1. Agenda setting and adherence
2. Feedback
3. Collaboration
4. Pacing and efficient use of time
5. Interpersonal effectiveness

Cognitive therapy specific items

1. Agenda setting and adherence
6. Eliciting appropriate emotional expression
7. Eliciting key cognitions
8. Eliciting behaviours
9. Guided discovery
10. Conceptual integration
11. Application of change methods
12. Homework setting

The cognitive aspects can be grouped within the cognitive cycle of Figure 3.1:

Cognitions/thoughts

- Eliciting key cognitions (item 7)
- Change methods (item 11)

Feelings/emotions

- Eliciting emotional expression (item 6)

Arousal/physiology

- Eliciting emotional expression (item 6)

Behaviour/planning

- Eliciting behaviours (item 8)
- Change methods (item 11)
- Homework (item 12)

In the process of CBT the stages of the cycle overlap, interrelate and are mutually influential. The cognitive cycle also feeds into the formulation (conceptualisation), and as therapy progresses this will change which then in turn impacts upon the rest of the cognitive cycle.

The CTS-R (James *et al.* 2001) is scored using Dreyfus's model of competence. The stages of competence are:

Incompetent. There are errors and behaviour falling below that expected of a competent practitioner and that lead to unhelpful therapeutic outcomes.

Novice. Rigid observance of taught rules and a lack of capacity to adapt to situation specific factors or use initiative and discretion.

Advanced beginner. All aspects of the task are given equal and individual attention. There is evidence of the ability to adapt to differing situations and to exercise discretionary judgement.

Competent. Tasks are connected within an overarching conceptual view within which further plans are made and standard evidence based interventions are applied.

Proficient. There is a grasp of the client's issues in terms of complexity and scope, and the ability to prioritise tasks, arrive at decisions rapidly and clear proficiency and skill.

Expert. Rules are not used; however, the therapist has a deep insight into the client's issues and is able to apply situation-specific problem-solving methods. High-level skills are demonstrated even in very challenging situations.

In applying the Dreyfus model, therapists are scored in terms of competence from 0 to 6 in relation to each of the 12 items. The scoring system operates as shown in Table 3.2. Consistent with these scores the classifications in Table 3.3 are suggested.

Table 3.2 Scoring system

Classifications	Score
The item is not apparent, or there is inept performance	0
Inappropriate performance and significant problems	1
Competence is apparent but there are problems	2
Competence but some problems or a lack of consistency	3
Good performance of the item but with minor problem or inconsistency	4
Performance of a higher level with very limited problems or inconsistencies	5
High-level performance, even in the presence of difficulties or challenges	6

Table 3.3 Classifications

Classifications	Score
0–1 incompetent	0–1
1–2 novice	1–2
2–3 advanced beginner	2–3
3–4 competent	3–4
4–5 proficient	4–5
5–6 expert	5–6

The maximum score that can be achieved is 72, although it is suggested that the highest scores are awarded only for outstanding practice, or for working in highly adverse situations (James *et al.* 2001). The minimum competence standard is advised as being 36, or a minimum of a score of 3 in each of the 12 categories (James *et al.* 2001).

> **Check-in**
>
> Using the 0–6 rating scale, how would you rate yourself in relation to the 12 items of the CTS-R?
>
> | Item | Score 0–6 |
> |---|---|
> | 1. Agenda setting and adherence | |
> | 2. Feedback | |
> | 3. Collaboration | |
> | 4. Pacing and efficient use of time | |
> | 5. Interpersonal effectiveness | |
> | 6. Eliciting appropriate emotional expression | |
> | 7. Eliciting key cognitions | |
> | 8. Eliciting behaviours | |
> | 9. Guided discovery | |
> | 10. Conceptual integration | |
> | 11. Application of change methods | |
> | 12. Homework setting | |
>
> What were your scores and why did you award yourself these marks? Overall what are your strengths and areas for development?
>
> Refer back to your plan for how much time you will spend and on which parts of the chapter. Are you on target?

To summarise so far, we have discussed the conceptual framework of the CTS-R, the two groups of general items and cognitive therapy specific items and how these are scored. Next we will discuss the requirements of each of the 12 items in the CTS-R.

Agenda setting

In assessing competence with regard to this item, the agenda ought to include:

- At least two items that are clearly and specifically stated
- Items that have been agreed and prioritised in a collaborative process between therapist and client
- The items on the agenda can be related to cognitive therapy and the client's formulation
- The agenda contains items appropriate to the client's current level of progress in therapy, consistent with previous sessions
- The agenda reflects the client's current concerns
- The items are sufficient and there are not too many to address within the time-frame of the session
- Homework is included as a standing item
- Although this item is entitled 'agenda setting', the assessment of this item includes whether the agreed agenda was actually followed in the session.

While working in partnership is a central objective to forming an effective therapeutic alliance and contributes to positive outcomes for other items on the CTS-R as well, collaboration is only scored in the agenda setting and collaboration items.

Feedback

Feedback occurs in two forms: the therapist offering periodic summaries at frequent intervals during the session; yet also regularly seeking feedback regarding the client's perspective.

Periodic summaries have a number of purposes. They:

- allow information to be 'chunked' together to permit common themes to emerge
- provide points in the session for issues to be highlighted
- provide opportunities for the client to gain insight into issues and appreciate new learning
- help to keep the discussion focused and consistent with the agenda
- provide a sense of structure, flow and sequence to the session.

Seeking feedback from the client also provides a number of benefits. These include:

- helping the client to make therapeutic progress
- actively demonstrating collaborative working and an effective therapeutic alliance

- providing the therapist with the client's view
- establishing what the client finds to be positive and negative about therapy and the therapist's approach
- allowing for the identification of discrepancy or differences in understanding between the therapist and client
- establishing whether the client understands the therapeutic approach that is being used.

When scoring this item James *et al.* (2001) identify the following criteria:

- Feedback occurs regularly throughout the session.
- The feedback is appropriate, has therapeutic content, is useful for the client and has relevance.
- The manner of delivery of the therapist's feedback is sensitive and responsive to the reactions and cues of the client.
- Suggestions are sought from the client in terms of what to do next.
- The client's input is elicited and wherever possible they are encouraged to make choices.
- There are major summaries at the beginning and end of the session.

Collaboration

Collaboration requires commitment on the part of the therapist to working in partnership with the client. Although at times there may be a need for the therapist to adopt a more didactic approach, for example early in therapy, when the client has yet to gain familiarisation with the model, the therapist ought to actively involve the client and create opportunities for their participation and capacity to make choices wherever possible.

In scoring this item, the areas that are considered include the following:

- The use of verbal skills in interpersonal communication and discretion in encouraging the client and deciding when to speak and when to listen, when to challenge and when to withdraw, when to offer suggestions and when to let the client generate their own solutions
- The use of non-verbal skills, for example active listening and the demonstration of positive, yet professional body language and interaction with the client
- Sharing written summaries, formulations and conceptualisations with the client, and joint working on problems in terms of actions and interventions.

Pacing and efficient use of time

The therapist ought to ensure that the time in the session is managed effectively. Among the considerations are that there is a beginning, middle and end, the items on the agenda are addressed and the therapy is delivered at a pace that is relevant to the client's rate of learning. It is also important to avoid digressions, or, where these happen, to act to quickly refocus the session. However, in some cases it may be necessary that the pacing of the session is flexible, and the agenda may be altered to reflect changes in priority that emerge during the session. The therapist ought to ensure that the session does not exceed the allotted time and suitable time is permitted for the homework task to be discussed.

In scoring this item, the areas that are considered are as follows:

- The session flows and has clear phases.
- The session has a suitable pace.
- The pace of the session matches the rate of learning of the client.

Interpersonal effectiveness

Forming a positive relationship with the client is central to an effective therapeutic alliance, yet as in all effective relationships this is built upon mutual trust and confidence in the other person. The therapist needs to demonstrate Rogers's (1980) core components of empathy, genuineness and positive regard, so that the client will feel able to engage, trust the therapist, and have confidence in the relationship. *Empathy* validates the client's responses through demonstrating an interest and identification with their perspective and experience. *Genuineness* refers to credibility, honesty and professional identity, yet also a sense of constancy and authenticity. *Unconditional positive regard* pertains to treating the client with respect, and without the biasing influences or expectations of preconceptions or stigma.

In scoring this item, it is these same three areas that are considered:

- Empathy – the therapist demonstrating an understanding of the clients' feelings and the capacity to promote change based on this insight
- Genuineness – a mutually trusting relationship is established between the therapist and client
- Unconditional positive regard – the client feels accepted and valued as a person by the therapist.

Eliciting appropriate emotional expression

In this item the focus is upon the therapist's ability to use their verbal and non-verbal communication skills to support the client in expressing enough emotion to promote positive change. In both cases too much or too little emotion will impede the process. If the client is apathetic they will not feel motivated to change, whereas if they are experiencing very high levels of anger or anxiety in the session these emotions may impede their ability to change **cognitions**. Therefore the therapist is required to amplify the client's level of expressed emotion consistent with a level that will support change. This skill is referred to as *emotional shift*, where in some cases it is necessary to contain emotions, yet at other times encourage the client to express emotion.

In scoring this item, the three areas are:

- Skills in facilitating the client to access a range of emotions
- The capacity to support the client in using emotion therapeutically, or containing it where appropriate
- Facilitating appropriate emotional expression and the access of different emotions.

Eliciting key cognitions

In cognitive therapy there is a focus upon the connection between cognitions and emotions and how these act together to maintain problems. Cognitions include thoughts, assumptions and beliefs, and this item concerns the therapist helping the client to identify important cognitions or hot thoughts that contribute to problems. The therapist identifies the cognitions that contribute to the client's distress which are often in the form of negative **automatic thoughts** (NATs), or beliefs about the world that feed into negative emotions, although these are not always obvious. Often NATs or beliefs continue to exist in spite of a wealth of contradictory evidence. For example:

- Minimising or reducing the importance of positive factors within situations
- Catastrophising by exaggerating the impact of minor events
- Extreme thinking, or perceiving situations in terms of radical opposites.

In scoring this item, the three areas are as follows:

- Identifying cognitions that link to distressing emotions
- The skill and range of techniques that are used and relevance to the client's specific needs, for example Socratic questioning, monitoring, downward arrowing, imagery and role playing
- Identifying the appropriate level at which to work relevant to the client's progress and stage in therapy.

Eliciting behaviours

Behavioural problems occur in the form of withdrawal, avoidance, compulsions and safety-seeking behaviours. Often these reinforce negative thoughts and feelings, for example social phobia leads to the person avoiding the feared situation(s), and therefore not acquiring the skills to be able to engage effectively in social settings. Clients also engage in safety-seeking behaviours to ameliorate their distress, yet again in the long term these maintain the problem and perpetuate the dysfunctional cycle.

In scoring this item, the areas are as follows:

- The therapist identifies behaviours linked to distressing feelings, such as safety-seeking behaviours.
- The therapist demonstrates skills, and a range of techniques appropriate to the client's particular case. These include Socratic questioning, appropriate monitoring, imagery and role play.

Guided discovery

This item refers to the style of questioning adopted by the therapist to help the client develop hypotheses to explain their current problem and in developing possible solutions. Guided discovery involves the therapist adopting a continually enquiring approach. Often this involves Socractic dialogue and frequently asking the client questions to encourage them to scrutinise the connections between aspects of the cognitive cycle. The purpose of guided discovery is to support the client in gaining insight into issues for themselves, through integrating concepts, making connections and forming hypotheses about the problem that they wish to resolve.

The techniques that are used allow the client to make links *laterally*, between the day-to-day phenomena which produce and maintain problems, for example recognising NATs, dysfunctional behaviours and physical sensations; but also *vertically*, through uncovering historical patterns and influences that contribute to current problems, such as parenting issues and experiences in childhood.

Through questioning the therapist assists the client in making connections. The questions can be specifically linked to certain situations, such as 'Do you always feel hurt when your friend criticises what you have chosen to wear?', or more general, such as 'Do you often feel hurt when people comment on what you are wearing?'

In framing questions the therapist needs to gauge the client's current level of understanding of the problem, their stage of therapy and grasp of the model of CBT. The intention is that the questions permit the client to make connections themselves and provide helpful cues and triggers.

In scoring this item, two aspects are considered:

- The extent to which the therapist adopts an open and inquisitive questioning style
- The use of effective techniques and Socratic questioning to encourage the client to discover information, in better understanding their problem(s), and identifying possible solutions.

Conceptual integration

In the conceptual integration (see Figure 3.2) the client is made aware of the cognitive rationale for their problem(s) and the underlying and maintaining features and triggers. After the initial assessment an understanding of the client's problem(s) or formulation is developed. In the formulation the cognitive cycle is applied to and used to explain the client's problem(s), linking with and involving the lateral and vertical aspects that were identified in item 9 (guided discovery).

At the next session the therapist and client develop the formulation collaboratively. This performs the dual function of offering an explanation of the problem(s), yet also acting to socialise the client to the model and developing an understanding of how thoughts influence feelings that then have an impact upon physical sensations and behaviours and how these aspects overlap. In this way the therapist and client have a shared understanding of the theoretical understanding of the client's problem(s)

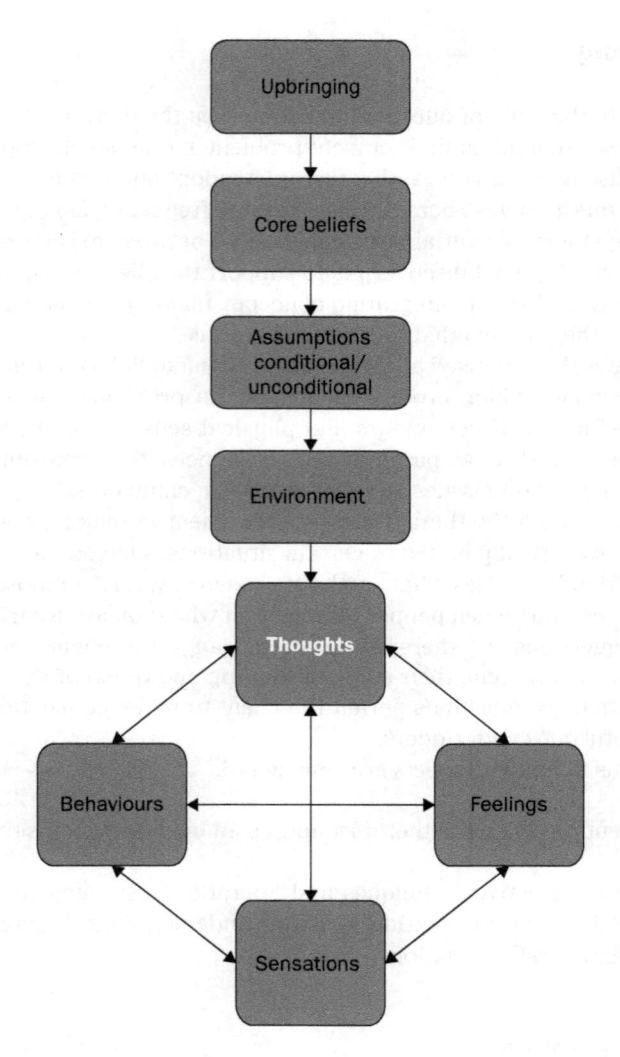

Figure 3.2 The conceptual integration
(adapted from James et al. 2001: 22)

and the client can begin to become their own therapist through understanding the model and being able to apply it to problems. The conceptualisation also provides structure and focus for therapeutic work and offers the client insight into the problem(s) and a basis for possible solutions.

Two aspects are considered in scoring this item:

- An appropriate conceptualisation that is consistent with therapeutic goals
- The conceptualisation offers a basis for interventions or positively focused actions.

Application of change methods

In this item the focus is upon the therapist's use of cognitive and behavioural techniques that are consistent with the formulation and appropriate to the client's stage of therapy. The therapist's abilities in selecting and applying methods that create emotional shifts and assist the client in gaining perspective are considered.

Although a wide knowledge of various techniques is required, several other competencies also contribute. These include the rationale for the selection of the techniques that are used, and the therapist's manner, skill and ability to apply these to the particular needs of the client, with sensitivity to their stage of therapy. For instance, a diary may be used as a method of assessment but later again as a method of reviewing cognitive processes. While if a client's core beliefs are challenged early in therapy before a trusting rapport has developed, the therapeutic alliance may be undermined. Within therapy sessions it is important that there is an emphasis upon practising and rehearsing interventions and changes that the client will carry out between sessions in building the client's skills and confidence in achieving the homework task.

In scoring this item, the aspects that are considered include:

- The suitability and range of cognitive and behavioural methods. The cognitive methods include: cognitive change diaries; continua; distancing; responsibility charts; evaluating alternatives; considering advantages and disadvantages; and imagery restructuring. Among the behavioural methods are: behavioural diaries; behavioural tests; role play; graded task assignments; response prevention; reinforcement of the client's work; modelling; applied relaxation; and controlled breathing.
- The skills of the therapist in applying the methods.
- The appropriateness of the methods to the client's understanding of the model and stage of therapy.

Homework setting

The focus of this item is the therapist's capability in setting homework tasks. As a brief, time-limited therapy, the long-term focus is for the client to be able to apply the skills learned in therapy sessions in their lives. Therefore homework acts as a bridge between therapy sessions and real life. Homework serves three main purposes for clients:

- Testing hypotheses
- Incorporating new learning
- Encouraging the client to experiment with using new behaviours.

In scoring this item the aspects that are considered are as follows:

- Time is allocated within the session for the homework to be discussed.
- The task is developed from the content of the session.
- The homework task is negotiated between the therapist and client.

- The homework task has clear and specific agreed goals or expectations.
- The client understands the relevance of the homework to their therapy and the formulation.

Conclusion

In this chapter we have considered the competencies that are involved in delivering CBT sessions, and the CTS-R as a means of rating therapist competence. The CTS-R is intended to provide a method of identifying skills and areas for development in delivering CBT sessions.

Check-in

Look again at the 12 items of the CTS-R listed below. Using the 0–6 rating scale (Table 3.4), how would you now rate yourself in relation to each of the 12 items?

Item	Score 0–6
1. Agenda setting and adherence	
2. Feedback	
3. Collaboration	
4. Pacing and efficient use of time	
5. Interpersonal effectiveness	
6. Eliciting appropriate emotional expression	
7. Eliciting key cognitions	
8. Eliciting behaviours	
9. Guided discovery	
10. Conceptual integration	
11. Application of change methods	
12. Homework setting	

Table 3.4 Dreyfus's competence scoring criteria

Criteria	Score
the item is not apparent, or there is inept performance	0–1
inappropriate performance and significant problems	1–2
competence is apparent but there are problems	2–3
competent but some problems or a lack of consistency	3–4
good performance of the item but with minor problem or inconsistency	4–5
performance of a higher level with very limited problems or inconsistencies	5–6
high level performance, even in the presence of difficulties or challenges	6

Adapted from James et al. (2001)

> Refer back to the items that you identified on your agenda at the beginning of the chapter. Have these been met? If there are any learning needs that remain, what further actions do you need to take?
>
> List the three main learning points for you in reading this chapter:
>
> 1
>
> 2
>
> 3

Feedback on this chapter

Think about your experience of reading this chapter and note any feedback for the authors here:

At the end of the book you may wish to collate the feedback together to forward to the following address: nick.wrycraft@anglia.ac.uk

4 Mild to moderate depression

Reader's agenda

Most people have some understanding of what it is like to feel low for a few days or even weeks. Consider any experience that you or others around you may have had. What would you say typifies these experiences?

Take a few moments to consider your own agenda or reasons for reading the chapter and make a note of them here:

-

-

The aim of this case study is to:

- Identify the main cognitive and behavioural attributes of mild to moderate depression
- Explain the theory of behavioural activation
- Apply the theory of behavioural activation to a case study, focusing on activity scheduling.

Managing your time

Take a moment to consider how long you plan to spend reading this chapter, and make a note here:

There will be a reminder later to help you keep on track with this.

Background and introduction

Will is a 49-year-old married man who eventually visited his GP after months of persistent tiredness. He was sleeping for 2 or 3 hours during the day as well as 7 or 8 hours at night, and had put on nearly a stone in weight over the past 6 months. Around that time he had been made redundant from his employment as a telecommunications engineer and the problem had become steadily worse since then.

Will was not surprised when his GP advised that he might be suffering from depression and when his score on the Patient Healthcare Questionnaire (PHQ-9: Kroenke *et al.* 2001) suggested the depression was in the mild to moderate range (see Box 4.1).

Box 4.1 Symptoms indicative of depression

The following symptoms may be indicative of depression if they persist for longer than a fortnight:

1. Depressed mood
2. Decreased interest or pleasure in doing things
3. Significant weight loss or decrease in appetite, or weight gain or increase in appetite
4. Inability to sleep, or sleeping much more than usual
5. Agitation or slowing down
6. Tiredness or lack of energy
7. Feeling worthless or excessively or inappropriately guilty a lot of the time
8. Finding it hard to think or concentrate or make decisions
9. Repeated thoughts about death and suicide.

Adapted from American Psychiatric Association (2000).

What might help Will to make an informed decision about treatment for his depression?

Will was offered the choice between antidepressant medication, which the GP explained could take 3–4 weeks to take effect and may have some side effects, or eight sessions of cognitive behavioural therapy with a psychological wellbeing practitioner (PWP) attached to his GP surgery.

Having recently read a favourable article about CBT in the weekend paper, Will was curious and agreed to CBT, considering it preferable to taking medication. Will's access to information about depression via the news media was timely as it allowed him to consider information about CBT in more detail and in his own time before consenting to treatment. As concentration is often a problem with depression, written information tends to be more helpful than verbal information alone, as it can be read through more than once (Saver *et al.* 2007).

Assessment and formulation

As recommended by the NICE guidelines (National Institute for Health and Clinical Excellence 2010), the PWP was able to see Will for assessment within 2 weeks of his referral. He was seen in a treatment room at his GP surgery, which he found a reassuringly familiar environment.

Why is it important to socialise the individual to the format of CBT sessions?

Will had little personal experience of mental health problems and felt nervous about seeing a mental health practitioner. He was pleased to find the PWP was 'a bloke', and was further put at ease when the practitioner explained what to expect in CBT sessions. This included explaining how at the start of each session an agenda would be set, that they would stop half-way through to make sure Will felt OK about the session and to make sure that they were keeping to the agenda items. It was explained how Will would be asked to summarise what he got from each session at the end; he had read about CBT homework and was prepared for this aspect of therapy. Initially they contracted for eight sessions, spaced weekly, then fortnightly, with the final session as a three-month follow-up. Will felt safer and more prepared to engage in therapy knowing what to expect and where he stood.

What types of risk is it important to assess for in mild to moderately depressed individuals?

It is particularly important when assessing for depression to explore present and past risks relating to self-harm or suicide, including thoughts, plans and intentions, and whether or not the person has the means to carry these through. To an inexperienced practitioner this may seem like a difficult topic to introduce, and in practice it may be more helpful to discuss the subject a little later in the assessment, once the individual is speaking more openly about things.

The PWP talked about confidentiality at the outset and it was agreed that if at any point during treatment anyone's safety was seen to be compromised the PWP would need to share this information with the GP. In this regard the PWP assured Will that if this became necessary he would discuss it with Will first. Will expressed appreciation for this openness and reassured the PWP that he had no thoughts of harming himself or anyone else and had never considered suicide. He remembered only once before feeling particularly low for any extended period; this had been in his late teens when he had failed his driving test on three consecutive occasions. In spite of there being no history of self-harm, the PWP asked Will if he would let him know if and when things changed at any point and provided him with emergency contact details as a matter of course.

Another aspect of risk considered was self-neglect. While Will lived a fairly settled and predictable life with his wife, still his lifestyle and diet had changed since being made redundant. He was snacking frequently throughout the day now and getting little exercise; as a result he had put on almost a stone in weight over the past 6 months. This had the potential to affect his health and psychological wellbeing over time. In view of this the PWP arranged an appointment for Will with the practice nurse to check his weight, blood pressure and general health.

Will also noticed he was starting to shower less frequently. He clearly felt awkward talking about this, which he said made things seem 'more real, more of a problem' to him. He realised that, had he lived alone, self-neglect could have become more of an issue, but his wife's persistent encouragement, though unwelcome at times, had helped minimise this issue.

The tendency to isolate himself socially was also having an impact. Will missed work and the friendships he had had there. In the past when he experienced problems in his marriage he had talked to his mates about this. Now, on his own, he tended to brood, making problems feel worse. His ability to problem-solve also appeared to be diminishing as a result of the depression, making matters worse. These areas of risk became a priority in therapy.

How might a collaborative approach to behavioural activation be introduced from the outset?

The PWP encouraged a collaborative approach to note-taking, by asking Will to write his own notes, offering him the pen and pad and suggesting 'How about you jot that down in case we forget it?' whenever something important or relevant was said or planned. At the end of each session both Will's and the PWP's notes were photocopied for Will to take home with him. This had the effect of activating Will in the session and helping him to take ownership of the work undertaken in the session, making it more likely that he would engage with and act on it.

When checking if Will was OK with this system of note-taking, he said he found this openness refreshing; having a copy of the notes was helpful for him to review the session at home and share with his wife.

List four benefits that having a shared formulation of the problem accomplishes.

1

2

3

4

Please see suggested answers in italics below

During assessment the PWP encouraged Will to sketch out the formulation of the problem as they went along. They *worked collaboratively* together on several versions of this until finally coming up with a 'map' that captured the main elements and which formed *a shared understanding of the problem* (see Figure 4.1).

Emphasis was put on capturing the aspects currently maintaining the problem, helping to *demonstrate how Will's thoughts, emotions and behaviours were linked in unhelpful ways*. Developing the formulation *familiarised Will with the CBT process*. It was explained how the formulation would be used to *plan treatment goals and strategies*, providing *a theoretical overview and rationale* for their work.

The formulation was based on Veale's (2008) model for behavioural activation and was chosen for two main reasons:

1. The model provided a clear fit with Will's passive and avoidant patterns of behaviour.
2. The PWP was familiar and confident working with this model for depression.

How might the PWP begin teaching Will to become his own therapist, demonstrating equality and collaboration from the outset?

The PWP taught Will how to use the ABC model to obtain information relevant for the formulation. Will was encouraged to map out the effects that the:

(A)ctivating event
(his overall experience of being depressed)
was having on

↓

his (B)eliefs and (B)ehaviours
(which involved short-term avoidance and escape
from depressive thoughts and feelings)
and how these, in turn, resulted in longer-term

↓

(C)onsequences, both personally and socially,
which in turn fed back into his experience of the

↓

(A)ctivating event, his depression (and so on).

Will established five main relevant behaviours and their consequences using this ABC model. The PWP encouraged him to map these all together, demonstrating how the behaviours unintentionally served to maintain Will's depression, thus they collaboratively formulated the difficulty into a shared understanding of the problem (see Figure 4.1). From this formulation it became clear that Will was experiencing little in the way of satisfying activity that might provide positive reinforcement and a way out of the depression.

In the centre of the formulation (1) Will put the (A)ctivating event, his overall

Mild to moderate depression

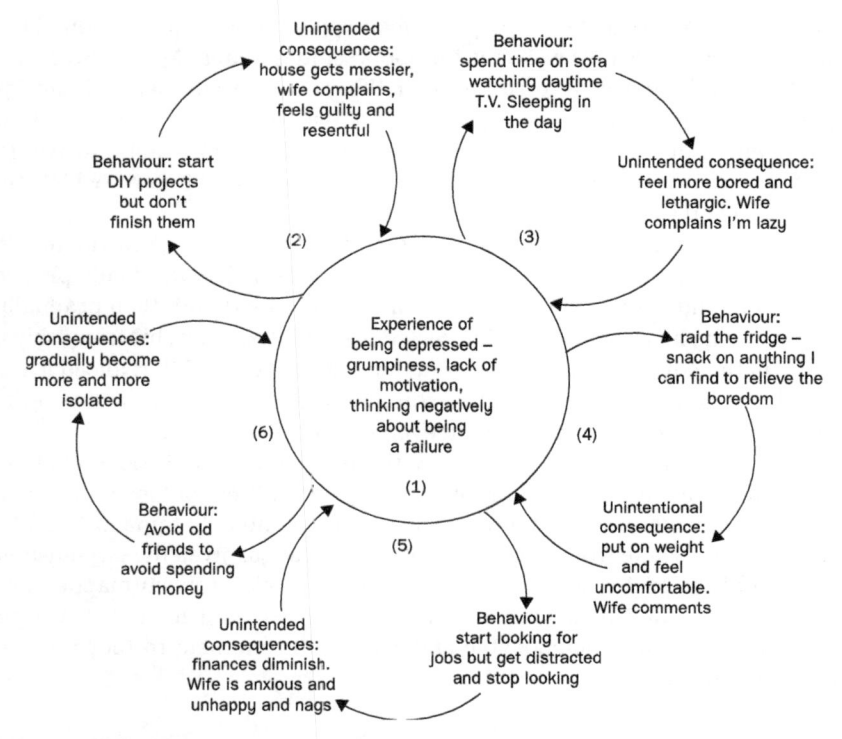

Figure 4.1 Will's formulation for behavioural activation based on Veale (2008)

Diagram (centre): Experience of being depressed – grumpiness, lack of motivation, thinking negatively about being a failure (1)

(2) Behaviour: start DIY projects but don't finish them → Unintended consequences: house gets messier, wife complains, feels guilty and resentful

(3) Behaviour: spend time on sofa watching daytime T.V. Sleeping in the day → Unintended consequence: feel more bored and lethargic. Wife complains I'm lazy

(4) Behaviour: raid the fridge – snack on anything I can find to relieve the boredom → Unintentional consequence: put on weight and feel uncomfortable. Wife comments

(5) Behaviour: start looking for jobs but get distracted and stop looking → Unintended consequences: finances diminish. Wife is anxious and unhappy and nags

(6) Behaviour: Avoid old friends to avoid spending money → Unintended consequences: gradually become more and more isolated

experience of being depressed, including how the depression made him feel grumpy, unmotivated and 'a failure'. This experience fed into the five identified different avoidant (B)ehaviour spirals and their resulting unintended social (C)onsequences. Each 'petal' or 'spiral' of the formulation focused on one aspect of avoidance or escape from Will's uncomfortable thoughts or feelings as follows:

(2) Initially being made redundant had given Will time to do the things that needed doing around the house and he had started a number of DIY projects but had not completed them. As an unintended consequence, the house had become messier and his wife was disappointed and annoyed, nagging him to finish the jobs, which he no longer felt he had the energy to do. This made him even grumpier, increasing his thoughts about being a failure and his depressed mood (2 back to 1).

(1 to 3) As a result of the tiredness, Will was spending longer and longer on the sofa watching TV, often falling asleep in the daytime for up to 2 hours. This avoidance of activity had the unintended effect of making him feel even more bored and lethargic, and again his wife would complain and call him 'lazy', which led back to him thinking he was a 'failure' and further depressed his mood (3 back to 1).

(1 to 4) While watching TV, Will would often snack on anything he could find to distract himself and relieve the boredom. As an unintended consequence, he had gradually put on weight, just under a stone in 6 months, which made him feel uncomfortable. His wife commented on this from time to time, which made him even grumpier. Again, this increased his thoughts about failure and his depressed mood further (4 back to 1).

(1 to 5) Will had intended to find a job right away after being made redundant, and had started searching various websites for opportunities available. However, after his initial enthusiasm he got distracted by other things on the internet and had by and large given up on the job search, although he had to attend the Job Centre fortnightly, which he found 'grim'. As a consequence, finances had become tight and Will felt he had lost his role as 'provider', leading back into thoughts of failure, which further depressed his mood (5 back to 1).

(1 to 6) At first Will had continued going out for a drink once a fortnight with his old mates from work but because of the lack of finances he had gradually phased this out, avoiding telling his mates the real reason for not going until they gradually lost contact, presuming he was no longer interested. As a consequence, his friendship circle had shrunk until he had virtually stopped going out. Although Will realised it was *his* withdrawal that had led to this situation, still it contributed to his thoughts of having failed as a 'mate' and depressed his mood even further (6 back to 1).

While the formulation highlighted how these avoidance and escape behaviours were unhelpfully maintaining the problem, the PWP still empathised and validated Will's experience, acknowledging how it was understandable that up until now he had tried to avoid and escape from these thoughts and feelings, given the circumstances.

Will found it helpful to see the various aspects of his problem mapped out into 'loops' of behaviour and their unintended consequences, as it made the prospect of tackling things look more manageable and it allowed treatment to focus on each of these aspects in turn.

Check-in

Are you on track with your time-keeping as planned at the outset of the chapter?

Make a note here of any adjustments you need to make.

Have any questions arisen that you want to add to your original agenda for reading the chapter?

It is often difficult for depressed individuals to set meaningful goals because of a sense of helplessness and hopelessness. How might this problem be addressed?

Will had originally visited his GP to get over his tiredness. Beyond this, he had difficulty thinking about treatment goals, seeing things as 'a bit pointless'.

To help with this impasse the PWP suggested that Will visualise how, if things went well, he would like them to be in a year's time. He encouraged Will to close his eyes for a moment and imagine this. Imagining goals can be helpful as it can bring about a positive emotional change in relation to the images generated; this appears to strengthen the probability of their future outcome (Holmes and Mathews 2005, 2010).

Although Will agreed to do this, he found it difficult to visualise anything being much different, so the PWP prompted him with some ideas: 'can you imagine having finished decorating the bedroom, or perhaps even having a job?'

With encouragement, Will was able to see these things. He also pictured going shopping with his wife at the weekends again, as well as taking the dog for walks along the beach on holiday, as they had done regularly in the past.

However, once Will opened his eyes again he ridiculed the exercise as 'a silly pipe dream'. Nevertheless, the exercise provided an opportunity to explore with Will the things that he valued about going shopping with his wife and walking the dog on holiday. This in turn helped with setting some short- and longer-term goals which involved more normal social functioning.

Behavioural activation involves activity scheduling. What kind of activity is it important to schedule and why?

When working with behavioural activation it is important to establish 'valued directions', that is, directions in which the person would value their life moving, so that any activity planned is meaningful to the individual, rather than being activity for activity's sake. While these values can inform goals, they are not goals in themselves, but have been described as 'a compass', giving direction to a person's life (Veale 2008).

It is important that any values identified by the individual are not the values the person *thinks* they should have because *others* will approve, but are their own (for example, not valuing completing the DIY tasks because *his wife* wanted them completed, but because of what it would mean about him – that he was a competent husband, which he valued being).

During initial sessions the PWP explored Will's values across a number of areas, including how he valued being as a husband, what was important to him about his health and physical wellbeing, and, more broadly, what he wanted his life to stand for. These values formed a basis for thinking about medium- and shorter-term goals.

Socially, Will valued having something to contribute and to talk about. In the short term he could see how getting out of the house each day would give him something apart from TV to talk about to his wife. He also valued feeling fit and in the short to medium term wanted to exercise, cut down snacking, and lose weight.

In line with his identified values Will specified the following goals:

- To stay awake during the day, limiting sleep to 7–8 hours at night
- To increase physical activity to include daily exercise (walking/jogging each day and going swimming twice a week)
- To reduce weight to $12\frac{1}{2}$ stone within 12 weeks and to 12 stone within 18–20 weeks by eating regular healthy meals and limiting snacks to healthy options (to discuss with the practice nurse)
- To complete the unfinished DIY projects: (1) fixing and painting the front gate; (2) papering and painting the small bedroom; (3) clearing out the gutters; and (4) tidying the garden
- To recommence his job search in a more proactive manner – buying local and national papers on relevant days and 'putting out feelers'.

As well as measuring Will's progress against these goals, they agreed to use the PHQ-9 to measure progress each session, starting from a score of 17 at assessment.

CBT homework is often used as a method of gathering data about problems. How might exploration of potential homework difficulties be helpful when homework is being planned?

In session Will drew up a chart to record his week's activity on for homework. The plan was to fill in his activities throughout the day as he went along, keeping this as simple as possible (see Table 4.1).

Being familiar with using behavioural activation for depressed individuals, the practitioner was aware that, while this exercise appeared simple, there were a number of common pitfalls that could occur. He therefore asked Will if *he* could foresee any difficulties that might arise, and used this as an opportunity to highlight the problems that others had experienced. Thus he aimed to pre-empt and normalise any difficulties that Will might encounter.

While Will could not foresee any difficulties, the practitioner explained how it was common for people to return the next session without the activity schedule, saying they had 'forgotten' or 'lost' it, not because they had *actually* forgotten or lost it, but often for a variety of other reasons.

Table 4.1 Activity schedule

	Morning	Afternoon	Evening
Thursday			
Friday			
Saturday			
Sunday			
Monday			
Tuesday			
Wednesday			

He then asked Will how he might feel about bringing the schedule back to share if it mainly featured 'watched TV', 'snacked on crisps' or 'argued with wife'. Will could see that this would be difficult and appreciated that this had been discussed ahead of time, so that any problems that might crop up were out in the open to begin with.

Another pitfall the PWP highlighted was how negative thoughts could make the activity schedule difficult to complete (for example, 'How on earth is this going to help?'), and therefore not to be surprised if this happened. Despite these potential problems, he still asked Will to complete the schedule as accurately as possible as he went along, because that would be most helpful. Will agreed to try.

How might discussing the completed activity record be used therapeutically within the session?

Will returned the following week having completed his activity schedule for homework as agreed (see Table 4.2). The agenda for the session was agreed and prioritised as follows:

1. Homework – the activity diary (standing item), 20 minutes.
2. Planning activities in line with valued directions/goals for the next week's homework, 20 minutes.
3. Summing up, 10 minutes.

Will acknowledged that knowing he would have to bring the schedule back had influenced his activity levels, although this had not been deliberate. He had added the word (different) to activities where writing them down had made a difference.

Talking the PWP through each day's activity, Will explained how on the Thursday afternoon after their last appointment, he had decided to walk the dog further than he

Table 4.2 Activity schedule, week 1

	Morning	Afternoon	Evening
Thursday	PWP appointment	Walked the dog, further than usual (different)	Watched TV with wife
Friday	Watched TV	Shopping with wife	Watched TV
Saturday	Watched TV	Walked the dog with wife (different)	Watched TV
Sunday	Lie in, read papers online	Visited garden centre with wife (different)	Watched TV
Monday	Watched TV	Watched TV	Walked dog briefly
Tuesday	Appointment with practice nurse	Watched TV	Watched TV
Wednesday	Watched TV	Planned more healthy snacks with wife	Watched TV

usually did, along the canal towpath about half a mile from his home. The sun had shone and the dog had really enjoyed being let off the lead, running up and down 'like a mad thing'. There had been a family of ducklings that Will had not expected to see, and it was nice having something to talk about to his wife when he got back. His wife had even offered to wash the dog off afterwards, which he had been dreading, so it had gone well overall.

Will smiled as he talked about the dog running about as just seeing it in his mind's eye lifted his mood again for a moment. The PWP pointed this out to Will, who agreed, 'Yes, maybe'.

Will had been surprised when on Saturday afternoon his wife had suggested they walk the dog together. Again this had been quite enjoyable as he had taken her to see the ducklings. They had met a neighbour whom Will had not seen for ages and chatted about the dog, the ducklings and the start of the cricket season, which Will had found 'quite nice'. Again, he smiled when telling the PWP about this, which the PWP again pointed out.

On the Sunday, Will's wife had suggested a trip to the garden centre. Will had not wanted to go because they did not have any money to spend, but it crossed his mind that he would have to bring the activity schedule back with nothing on it for that day otherwise, so he reluctantly agreed. The garden centre had been busy, so they spent most of the time outside walking round the displays, which had been colourful. Will's wife bought a small plant and had seemed happy with that. Will had not liked the crowds, but again, they talked together about the displays later when they got home, which had been quite nice.

On the Tuesday, Will's appointment with the practice nurse revealed that he had developed raised blood pressure. Will had felt angry at himself for becoming so unfit; his wife had been upset about the news, which had made him feel guilty and his mood had dipped considerably at this point in the week.

The next day his wife had tried to engage him in planning some healthy snacks for the week, but Will only found this depressing and they had bickered. Thinking about this in session lowered Will's mood, but being experienced at working with depressed individuals, the PWP did not let Will's shift in mood affect his own mood negatively, but remained hopeful.

Will said that after that point he had given up somewhat, and just stayed watching TV again. He had started think that therapy 'was all just a desperate attempt' and that 'I might as well just give up; I'll fail at it anyway'.

How might you work with negative thoughts when using behavioural activation?
Make a note of any ideas here:

As they were focusing on behavioural activation the practitioner refrained from getting caught up in the content of Will's negative thinking about failure, instead highlighting the context (activating event) and outcome (consequence) of his cognitive responses, asking Will 'What did you do next when you thought about failing and giving up?'

Focusing on behaviour helps to discourage both **ruminating** on thoughts of failure, and fusing the content of one's thoughts with one's identity (for example, 'Because I failed it means I'm a failure.') It can also help to reduce verbal self-attacking (for example, 'I'm so stupid letting this happen') and so has many advantages as a treatment for depressed individuals.

The PWP reminded Will about how they had used the ABC model before to analyse situations for the formulation, and suggested that they use the same strategy again to look more carefully at what had happened to bring his mood down so markedly at this point.

Again, the practitioner activated Will by asking him to find his list of valued directions and goals in the file. Once Will had found these the PWP asked him if he noticed any relationship between his activities, his valued directions and his moods, over the whole week. Will looked from the activity schedule to the valued directions list.

He observed how when the (A)ctivating event led to (B)ehaviour in line with his valued directions, the (C)onsequence had been that his mood had lifted, at least to some extent. On the other hand, when the (A)ctivating event had led to (B)eliefs and (B)ehaviour working against his valued directions ('I'm a failure so I might as well give up'), the (C)onsequence had been that his mood had dropped and he had returned to feeling grumpy and depressed again.

Will stated that, although it seemed somewhat obvious looking at it written down, he had not thought about the (B) in between things like this, assuming it was the raised blood pressure that directly caused the low mood rather than his response to it.

The practitioner asked Will how his mood might have been affected if, despite finding he had high blood pressure, he had kept to his valued directions anyway, even if he had not felt like it, perhaps going for a walk rather than going back to watching TV. Will could see that it would have been more helpful.

The rest of the session was spent planning activity for the coming week, in particular moving Will toward his valued direction of becoming fitter. This session had been something of a 'breakthrough' for Will in seeing how much moving towards his valued directions could influence his mood for the better, even when he did not immediately feel like taking that course of action in the moment.

Sessions 3–8

The next six sessions were spent positively reinforcing Will's new approach behaviours and building in specific activities to move him in the direction he valued, using the ABC model to analyse and adjust things as necessary. The sessions were now spaced fortnightly, which allowed more time for Will to achieve what he set out to do.

Initially Will concentrated on his goal of increasing his physical activity, which led him to tackle some of the unfinished DIY projects. In session 6 he reported how, on his travels with the dog, he had found some good bits of wood in a skip, and he had not only fixed the broken garden gate, but also built a rose arch over it, inspired by a display on his original trip to the garden centre.

This project helped him regain a sense of competence as a husband which he valued, and his wife's pleasure about the arch positively reinforced his active behaviour. An added benefit had been that neighbours had stopped and spoken to him while he was working in the garden, providing positive social interaction.

Will's score on the PHQ-9 improved steadily until by session 7 it indicated that he was no longer depressed (see Table 4.4). A 'continued improvement plan' was drawn up for Will to take things forward (see Table 4.3). By the three-month follow-up session Will had not only maintained his PHQ-9 score but was actively looking for employment. It was mutually agreed to end treatment at this point, as planned.

Table 4.3 Continued improvement plan

What have you learned from these sessions?	I have learned how to become less grumpy by working out what it is I really value in life – about myself, my way of relating to others (especially my wife), about how I want to be. I then need to behave in ways that move me in these 'valued directions', even if I don't immediately feel like moving at all.
What strategies have you found most helpful?	The (A)–(B)–(C) way of analysing what's going on, so I can decide how I want to respond to the (A)ctivating event, in line with my values. Scheduling in activity to do and then doing it, but not overdoing things either.
What do you need to do to maintain/extend change?	Keep on scheduling in things to do in line with what I value in life. Take the initiative a bit more still. Make sure I keep on meeting with other people and don't isolate myself. *Find a job!*
What might lead to a set back?	An (A)ctivating event that floors me for some reason or another (probably because of what I'm thinking about it), and makes me want to avoid activity again.
How would you recognise this?	I'd stop doing things and cut myself off from others. I'd become grumpier, people would complain about this even if I didn't notice it.
Can you identify skills you have learned, resources, people and agencies that could help manage this set back?	Imagine how I'd like things to be and move toward that. The (A)–(B)–(C). Talk to my wife about things before they get bad. Read through this plan and implement it. See the GP before it gets bad.

Client Name .... Therapist Name .... Date ....

Treatment outcomes

Will had met a number of his treatment goals by the final follow-up session, but, more importantly, he had identified the direction in which he wanted his life to move. He was on course and was confident, with a strategy to adopt if and when things went off course. His remaining goals were to get down to his original weight of $12\frac{1}{2}$ stone (he was hovering around 12 stone 12 pounds), and to find paid employment. In the interim he was considering some voluntary work to avoid having big gaps in his CV.

Will's score on the PQH9 had steadily improved over the eight treatment sessions until he no longer registered as depressed (see Table 4.4). These gains were maintained at the three-month follow-up.

Table 4.4 PHQ-9 scores

	Session 1	Session 2	Session 3	Session 4	Session 6	Session 7	Session 8
PHQ-9 score	17	16	12	10	8	4	4

Reflections

The PWP was very happy with the way in which treatment had progressed. He was experienced at working with mild to moderately depressed individuals and was familiar with many of the pitfalls of working with behavioural activation in particular. Having confidence in the strategy had helped him to remain hopeful and optimistic about treatment, even when Will was expressing negative thoughts that a less experienced practitioner might have found 'catching'.

The PWP had considered using a more complex activity schedule to include recording activity hourly throughout the day. While doing this has the advantage of including more detail, filling it in can be demanding, particularly at the outset of treatment when the depressed individual is finding any activity difficult. There is also a risk that if the schedule is too complicated it is less likely to be completed.

The practitioner had found it helpful to activate Will in the sessions as this enabled him to grasp treatment principles quickly and to own the treatment, thus empowering him. By staying with one main intervention (activity scheduling), and one model (the ABC model), the PWP had worked simply and effectively, specifically targeting problematic behaviours detailed on the formulation.

Working behaviourally provided Will with **implicational learning** from the outset. In particular, finishing the DIY tasks had produced a sense of competence, reducing his negative thoughts about failure without having to work **propositionally** with them. The activities undertaken (e.g. walking the dog and fixing the gate) had provided opportunities for social inclusion which had increased Will's sense of wellbeing.

One factor in treatment outcomes had been that Will had no significant history of depression, whereas chronically depressed individuals often take longer to treat and the course of therapy is more likely to fluctuate. Another factor had been that Will's wife was supportive once she saw him making an effort, and had encouraged and empowered him to get up and about. Thus behavioural activation provided a relatively simple and very effective way to work with Will on his depression.

> **Conclusion and consolidation of your learning**
>
> Reflecting on the case study aims outlined at the outset of the chapter, summarise:
>
> 1 The main cognitive attributes of mild to moderate depression
>
> 2 The main behavioural attributes of mild to moderate depression
>
> According to the ABC model, what does:
>
> 1 A stand for?
>
> 2 B stand for?
>
> 3 C stand for?
>
> What is the significance of (B)?
>
> Can you explain the principle behind behavioural activation in no more than three sentences?

Reflecting on the original gaps in your knowledge that you hoped the chapter would address, what questions about treating mild to moderate depression still remain?

What might you do next to find out about these remaining questions?

Homework

While activity scheduling initially looks quite straightforward, people often find it surprisingly difficult to do in real life. In order to understand what it feels like to keep an activity schedule and the difficulties that can arise, try keeping one yourself for a week, recording your activity every hour. This will provide insight into the nature of activity scheduling and may provide ideas about how to introduce the strategy so as to successfully engage depressed individuals in the process.

Further reading: Veale and Willson (2007).

Feedback

Think about your experience of reading this chapter and note any feedback for the authors here:

At the end of the book you may wish to collate the feedback together to forward to the following address: nick.wrycraft@anglia.ac.uk

5 Low self-esteem, anxiety and depression

Reader's agenda

'Low self-esteem' is a **trans-diagnostic** problem. Research into the concept suggests that a healthy self-stance is strongly linked to the ability to show self-compassion and this case study draws on these research findings (Gilbert 2007).

Take a few minutes to think about someone you may know with low self-esteem. What typifies their thinking style and behaviour?

How do you feel being around this person?

Take a few moments to consider your own agenda or reasons for reading the chapter and make a note of them here:

•

•

•

The aim of this case study is to:

- Help you make sense of and apply Fennell's (1997) model of low self-esteem
- Encourage a self-compassionate thinking style
- Introduce you to working with assumptions.

Low self-esteem, anxiety and depression   69

Managing your time

Take a moment to consider how long you plan to spend reading this chapter, and make a note here:

There will be a reminder later in the chapter to check whether you have kept track with this.

Exercise

'Low self-esteem' is a commonly used expression, before reading the case study it would be helpful to define the term in relation to it. Take a few moments to think about your understanding of the term and jot down a few ideas here:

-
-
-
-

Now compare your ideas with the definition in Box 5.1. What do you notice about any similarities and differences?

General practitioner assessment

Sophie is a 32-year-old healthcare assistant, a job which she finds rewarding but exhausting. Initially she approached her GP asking for 'a pick-me-up' because of feeling tired and generally unhappy. Her score on the Patient Healthcare Questionnaire (PHQ-9: Kroenke *et al.* 2001) indicated that she was moderately to severely depressed and her GP found that she was also anxious about her relationship with her husband, Paul, who was a tree surgeon for a large corporation. She described Paul as 'much better than me', and feared that he would eventually get bored with her and leave. The GP referred her for CBT for anxiety and depression as a result of low self-esteem.

> **Box 5.1 Definition of self-esteem**
>
> Definitions for self-esteem range widely:
>
> > 'Pride in one-self, self-respect.' (*American Heritage Dictionary of the English Language*, 4th edn, 2000)
> >
> > 'Respect or a favourable opinion of yourself.' (*Collins English Dictionary*, 2003)
> >
> > 'The recognition of one's strengths and acceptance of one's weaknesses, without self-reproach.' (Quoted by a client in 2013, of unknown origin)
>
> It is the sense of this latter definition that is used in this case study. The definition embraces the spirit of self-compassion, which means that one's sense of self-worth is not contingent just on one's achievements but can be sustained even in the face of mistakes or when things have not gone so well.

CBT assessment and formulation

> List three typical signs of low self-esteem that might become evident during assessment.
>
> 1
>
> 2
>
> 3
>
> (Suggested answers follow in italics.)

At CBT assessment Sophie was apologetic about taking up the therapist's time. She described feeling tired and unhappy despite 'having nothing to be unhappy about', as she had a good job and 'a lovely husband'. She described feeling unworthy of Paul and anxious that he would leave her for someone more attractive, although he had given her no reason to think this and often reassured her that he loved her.

From this it was clear that Sophie *didn't feel good about herself* and found it *difficult to accept Paul's love and attention*. She also found it *difficult to accept herself as she was*, judgementally describing herself as, 'ungrateful' and 'undeserving' of the good things that she had. She had been married for only 18 months but had *a strong sense that she would not be up to the challenges that marriage posed and that the marriage would fail because of her* (Fennell and Brosan 2011). Sophie did not experience thoughts of harming herself or anyone else.

What other information is relevant for developing an initial working formulation of the problem?

When asked why she thought Paul had not left her up until now, Sophie could not say, but behaviours she adopted to prevent this happening included constantly trying to please him, for example by always cooking his favourite meals (rather than ones she preferred), agreeing with him and going along with his preferences rather than voicing her own. She constantly sought reassurance that Paul loved her and would not leave her.

When asked about the effects of these safety behaviours, Sophie acknowledged that Paul no longer asked her opinion since she always deferred to him anyway, and how she had started to feel resentful about this. She also realised that her need for constant reassurance was upsetting for Paul, but she found it difficult to stop doing.

> From this limited information, draw up a simple formulation of Sophie's problem, including any maintaining elements.
>
> How does your formulation compare with the **conceptualisation** in Figure 5.1?

From this information and with the lower part of Fennell's (1997) model of low self-esteem in mind, the therapist encouraged Sophie to 'map out' what was happening (see Figure 5.1), starting with her anxious predictions about Paul leaving (1), which

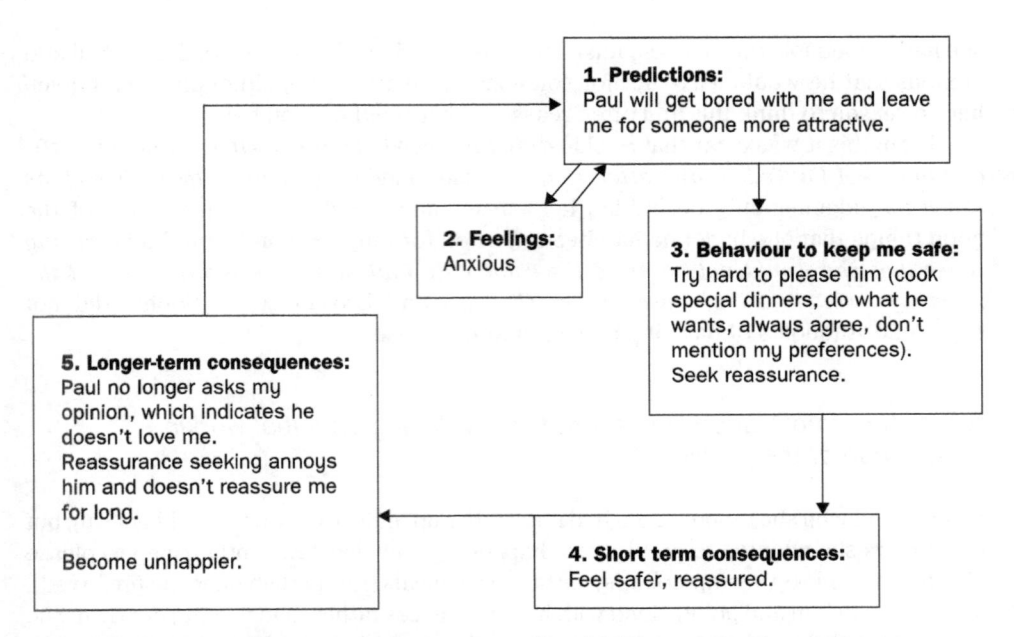

```
                    ┌─────────────────────────────────┐
                    │ 1. Predictions:                 │
           ┌───────▶│ Paul will get bored with me and │
           │        │ leave me for someone more       │
           │        │ attractive.                     │
           │        └─────────────────────────────────┘
           │                    ▲  │
           │                    │  ▼
           │        ┌──────────────┐   ┌─────────────────────────────────┐
           │        │ 2. Feelings: │   │ 3. Behaviour to keep me safe:   │
           │        │ Anxious      │   │ Try hard to please him (cook    │
           │        └──────────────┘   │ special dinners, do what he     │
           │                           │ wants, always agree, don't      │
┌──────────────────────────┐           │ mention my preferences).        │
│ 5. Longer-term           │           │ Seek reassurance.               │
│ consequences:            │           └─────────────────────────────────┘
│ Paul no longer asks my   │                           │
│ opinion, which indicates │                           ▼
│ he doesn't love me.      │           ┌─────────────────────────────────┐
│ Reassurance seeking      │◀──────────│ 4. Short term consequences:     │
│ annoys him and doesn't   │           │ Feel safer, reassured.          │
│ reassure me for long.    │           └─────────────────────────────────┘
│                          │
│ Become unhappier.        │
└──────────────────────────┘
```

Figure 5.1 First formulation based on Fennell's (1997) model of low self-esteem

looped into her feeling anxious (1–2) and back again (2–1), as feeling anxious reinforced her belief that the predictions must be true **(emotional reasoning)**. This loop resulted in Sophie adopting a number of behaviours to reduce the risk of Paul leaving (1–3). These behaviours were designed to reduce her anxiety in the short term (3–4), but in the longer term (4–5) paradoxically resulted in more evidence to support her anxious predictions, leaving her even more anxious and unhappy as the cycle perpetuated itself (5–1).

This 'loop system', as Sophie called it, made sense and demonstrated how the behaviours she adopted had become part of the problem. This formulation provided a sufficient basis to work from initially.

What other information is relevant if longer-term work on the problem is needed and why would this be helpful to know now?

Good therapists start treatment at the level of **automatic thoughts**, as this strengthens and underpins the individual's functional cognitions (James 2001). However, it is often helpful to be aware of the broader picture, including core beliefs and assumptions that underpin the problem so that these can be targeted more accurately from the outset, establishing a solid basis for sustained longer-term work (Beck 1995).

The therapist therefore took other details, including a family history. Sophie was the middle child of three. She described her older brother as a 'high flyer', getting top marks at school and gaining a highly paid professional career. Her younger brother was autistic, which meant much attention had centred on him while she was growing

Low self-esteem, anxiety and depression   **73**

up. Sophie herself had felt rather overlooked in the family, doing moderately well at school and spending much of her time attending to her younger brother's needs, which always seemed more important than her own.

This family background had shaped Sophie's belief system, and together they identified the key cognitions that were causing Sophie difficulty, beginning with her negative automatic thoughts: 'My opinion doesn't matter', 'Why would he [Paul] bother?' and 'Why is he [Paul] still with me?'

To access Sophie's beliefs and assumptions the therapist asked her: 'If it was true that your opinion didn't matter, what would it say about you?' Sophie responded in resigned manner: 'It means *I'm not important.*'

Identifying this belief lowered Sophie's mood; in response, the therapist slowed right down, paying attention by acknowledging the belief and showing empathy for the feeling it generated.

The therapist enquired about some of Sophie's other negative automatic thoughts, which revealed the beliefs (in italics) that 'If Paul didn't bother with me it would mean *I'm worthless*' and 'If Paul doesn't stay with me it would mean *I'm unlovable*'. Again, the therapist attended to Sophie's emotional responses, gently enquiring how she managed in day-to-day life given that she held these beliefs about herself. After a pause, Sophie responded with her rule that 'I work really hard and try all the time to make people happy'.

After a thoughtful pause, the therapist commented on how difficult this must make life for Sophie, to which she nodded sadly in agreement. At this point the therapist suggested they might move away from these beliefs and assumptions for the time being and maybe come back to them later in another therapy session. Sophie said she thought this would be important to do as it felt relevant.

For Sophie's key beliefs and assumptions to guide longer-term therapy, they needed to form part of an overall **conceptualisation** of the problem, and the therapist drew another formulation based on the full version of Fennell's (1997) model of self-esteem (see Figure 5.2).

Why might the therapist refrain from sharing the complete formulation (including beliefs and assumptions) with Sophie straight away, and when might it be appropriate to do so?

As core beliefs and assumptions generally involve long-term constructs of a person's personality, it is advisable to take a stepped-care approach towards working with them (James and Barton 2004). Knowing this, the therapist decided a good place to start treatment would be with the collaboratively designed initial formulation which included Sophie's anxious predictions (see Figure 5.1).

However, having a more complete formulation (see Figure 5.2) would be helpful in targeting treatment accurately as it included Sophie's early experiences (1), her resulting 'bottom line' beliefs (2) and the assumptions she adopted to cope with these beliefs (3). It also included how, despite her assumptions working quite well over long periods of time, a critical incident (4) had been getting married, as she constantly felt her efforts were not enough when either (5) her standards were not met because Paul

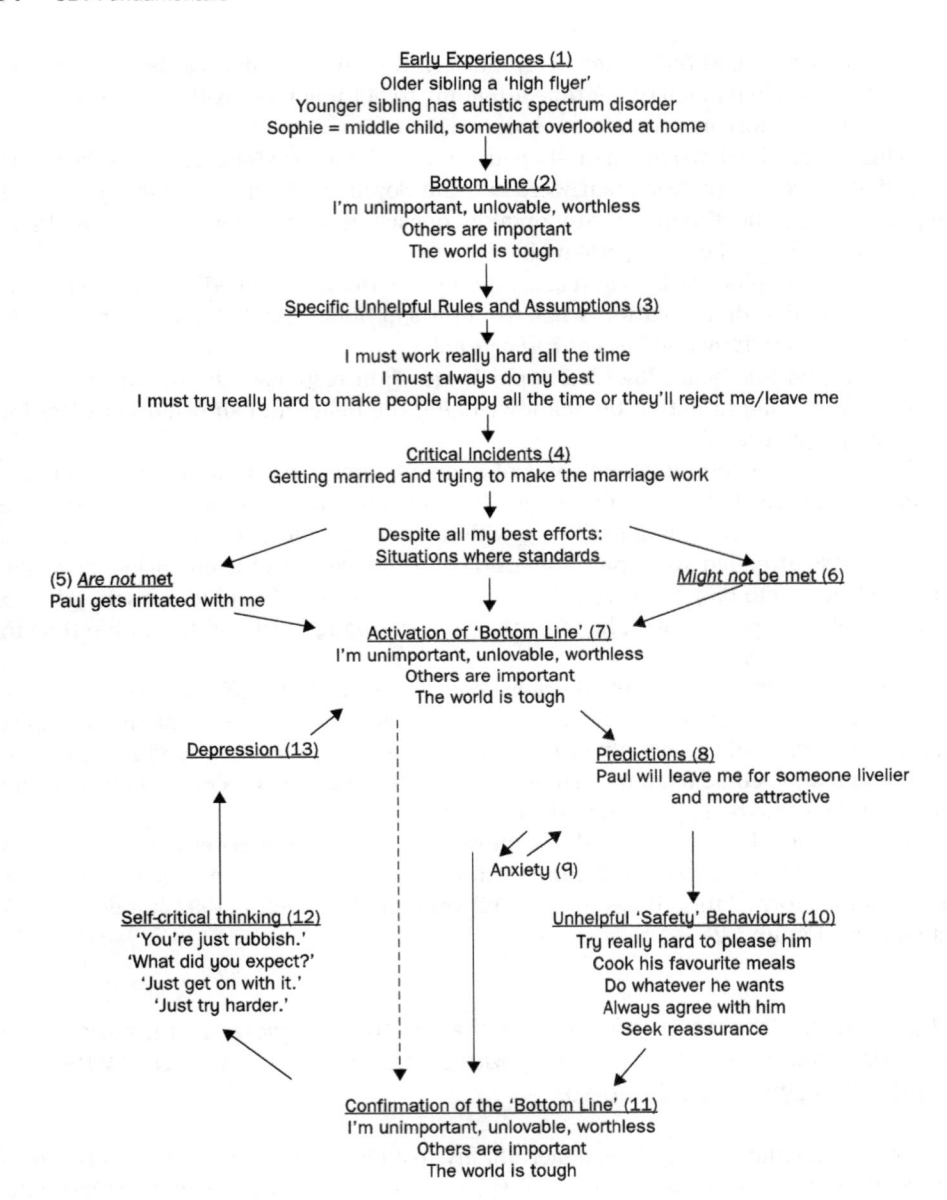

```
                          Early Experiences (1)
                          Older sibling a 'high flyer'
                  Younger sibling has autistic spectrum disorder
                 Sophie = middle child, somewhat overlooked at home
                                    ↓
                              Bottom Line (2)
                      I'm unimportant, unlovable, worthless
                              Others are important
                              The world is tough
                                    ↓
                   Specific Unhelpful Rules and Assumptions (3)
                                    ↓
                      I must work really hard all the time
                           I must always do my best
       I must try really hard to make people happy all the time or they'll reject me/leave me
                                    ↓
                             Critical Incidents (4)
                 Getting married and trying to make the marriage work
                                    ↓
                          Despite all my best efforts:
                          Situations where standards
    (5) Are not met                                         Might not be met (6)
    Paul gets irritated with me                             
                          Activation of 'Bottom Line' (7)
                      I'm unimportant, unlovable, worthless
                              Others are important
                              The world is tough

         Depression (13)                                    Predictions (8)
                                                    Paul will leave me for someone livelier
                                                         and more attractive

                                 Anxiety (9)

    Self-critical thinking (12)                    Unhelpful 'Safety' Behaviours (10)
      'You're just rubbish.'                           Try really hard to please him
      'What did you expect?'                           Cook his favourite meals
      'Just get on with it.'                           Do whatever he wants
      'Just try harder.'                               Always agree with him
                                                      Seek reassurance

                          Confirmation of the 'Bottom Line' (11)
                      I'm unimportant, unlovable, worthless
                              Others are important
                              The world is tough
```

Figure 5.2 Formulation based on Fennell (1997)

would get irritated with her, or (6) she feared her standards might not be met, both of which activated her bottom-line beliefs (7) about being unimportant, worthless and unlovable. This led into her original 'loop system', which the therapist modified slightly in accord with Fennell's original model to include her predictions (8) leading round the anxiety loop (8–9 and back again), resulting in a variety of safety behaviours (10), which only confirmed her bottom-line beliefs (11), leading her to think self-critically

(12) which made her depressed (13), further confirming her bottom line beliefs (13–7), thus the cycle was perpetuated.

However, the therapist chose not to share this complete, hypothesised version of the formulation with Sophie at the outset of therapy, as even briefly discussing her beliefs and assumptions had lowered her mood during the initial assessment and working with these in such detail would prove counter-therapeutic at this stage.

The therapist would keep this larger formulation in mind and only present it to Sophie if it became appropriate to do so after progress had been made on her anxious predictions. It could then be presented as a working hypothesis, checking out if it made sense and adjusting it to fit as new information came to light.

Goals and measurement

What could make goal setting difficult for someone with low self-esteem?

Sophie found it difficult to establish personal goals for treatment as she was unused to thinking about what *she* wanted out of situations. Initially she just wanted to feel more confident in her relationship with Paul, so in order to establish specific, measurable, achievable, realistic and time-scaled goals the therapist encouraged her to think about what this would be like in behavioural terms. Sophie identified that she would like to:

1. Get on with her life confidently without the need to keep asking Paul for reassurance
2. Cook meals that she preferred at least twice a week
3. State her opinion, even if it is different from Paul's, and expect it to be considered and valued in an equal way.

Sophie thought these goals looked 'selfish', which the therapist normalised, given how unused she was to thinking about her own needs and desires. Sophie agreed the goals were not unreasonable.

Sophie had completed both the Patient Healthcare Questionnaire (PHQ-9: Kroenke *et al.* 2001) and the Robson Self-Concept Questionnaire (Robson 1989), as this scores attitudes and beliefs that people hold about themselves and is particularly relevant for people with low self-esteem. Sophie's initial score on the PHQ-9 indicated that she was moderately depressed and her score on the Robson Self-Concept Questionnaire indicated that she was experiencing below average self-esteem.

Course of therapy

Where might treatment start and how can the therapist encourage collaboration?

Considering the initial formulation together (Figure 5.1), the therapist asked Sophie where *she* thought it would be most helpful to 'break into' the 'loop'. Sophie chose her

Table 5.1 Completed anxious predictions record

Date/time	Situation	Feelings/body (give % rating)	Anxious prediction (give % strength of belief rating)	What I did to prevent it happening
Saturday	Watching TV after work, Paul was taking care of the livestock.	Anxious 80–90%. In my stomach and throat.	Paul thinks I'm boring. I should be out there showing some interest or he'll get fed up with me and find someone else.	I dragged myself out to help, but it didn't go well and I still felt anxious.

anxious prediction that 'Paul will get bored with me and leave', as this occurred often and distressed her most. The therapist encouraged participation by asking Sophie to write down these details in the format shown in Table 5.1. This promoted teamwork and helped her to take responsibility for the task.

Sophie's anxious predictions had been triggered while she was tired and watching TV after work. Paul had been in the garden caring for the chickens and ferrets. At the time the strength of belief in her thought had reached 80–90% which made her feel anxious, physically in her stomach and throat.

To prevent the anxious prediction from becoming a reality she had dragged herself away from the TV and gone to help Paul with the animals. However, because she was exhausted, their conversation hadn't gone well and her prediction started to look even more realistic, despite her best efforts to counter it.

The formulation was out on the table while Sophie talked this scenario through, and she was quick to spot that she had been caught up in a slightly different version of the same 'loop system' again (see Figure 5.1).

How could the therapist help Sophie stand back from her anxious predictions and start to question them?

For homework Sophie was encouraged to monitor and keep a record each time she found herself making anxious predictions, noting them down in columns as they had in the session, which she now felt confident enough to do independently. On her return she commented how seeing the predictions written down and talking about them helped her to be more detached and curious about them. She clearly identified themes, which were a fear of not being good enough and being rejected as a result. In each case she responded by trying harder to please the other person.

To build on this, the therapist suggested developing the record to include two extra columns, one for 'alternative predictions' and another headed 'experiment'. Sophie drew this out and together they started to think about what she might put in each column for the following weeks' homework.

To encourage curiosity the therapist asked Sophie if she always accepted her predictions as the truth of the matter or if she ever came up with alternative explanations. Using the original anxious prediction as an example to work with, the therapist taught Sophie how to question her predictions by looking at evidence both for and against them and then coming up with a more likely, alternative prediction based on this. Using this strategy, Sophie came up with a more realistic alternative prediction: 'Paul loves me and would understand I'm tired. He wouldn't mind seeing to the livestock on his own. I could tell him what was on the news and he'd be interested. He would be unlikely to leave me based on this.'

Although Sophie could see this fitted the evidence better and was a more realistic prediction, it did not 'feel right' and her strength of belief in it was quite weak (30%). Thus her **propositional** or intellectual understanding conflicted with her **implicational** understanding or 'felt sense' of things (see Chapter 2).

How could Sophie be encouraged to apply behavioural techniques to provide implicational learning, in line with her alternative prediction?

Again, to encourage curiosity, the therapist asked Sophie how she might build confidence in her new prediction by testing it in real life. This brought them to the next column on the record, 'experiment'. Sophie realised her behaviour sometimes fed into the problem, and she decided to experiment by staying on the sofa and letting Paul attend to the livestock the next time she was tired. This way she could test her old predication, 'Paul will leave me', against her alternative prediction, 'Paul loves me and will stay'.

Thinking the details of the experiment through together, Sophie concluded that the absolute *worst* that could happen would be Paul leaving her, which she considered really unlikely based on one event. The *best* thing would be that her new prediction proved true and Paul would ask if she was tired and show interest in what she had seen on the news. *Realistically*, she thought something in the middle might happen and Paul would find it strange and comment that she did not help. If this happened she decided to tell him she was tired and hoped he did not mind that she did not help this once, which she thought he would be fine with. As they had planned things thoroughly in the session, Sophie felt confident to experiment and record her findings for homework. She had a clear understanding of the rationale for the experiment including how it would target her 'felt sense' of things and how it fitted with the formulation.

In response to Sophie's experiment, Paul *had* thought it was unusual for her not to help and had asked if she was tired. His tone of voice had implied concern rather than criticism and the evidence supported the prediction that Paul loved her and would stay. She re-rated her strength of belief in this much higher now, at 65%.

> **Check-in**
>
> This might be a good point to reflect on your original time commitment for reading this chapter and make adjustments. Again, it would be helpful to record any new plans here:
>
> Looking back at the aims of the chapter, take time to note the key points you have learned and how you can practically apply them.
>
> -
> -
> -
>
> If there are still points that you hope the chapter will clarify, make a note of them here to refer back to at the end.
>
> -
> -
> -

The next few sessions were spent questioning more of Sophie's anxious predictions and devising and carrying out behavioural experiments to test her more realistic alternatives for fit and accuracy, all in line with Sophie's goals for treatment. For example, she introduced a number of meals that she preferred and was surprised to find that Paul really enjoyed the variety. She also expressed a preference to watch period dramas on TV occasionally rather than documentaries, which Paul also enjoyed for a change. Over this period Sophie found that their relationship improved and her need to seek reassurance lessened. Objectively she appeared happier and more confident, which was confirmed by her scores on the PHQ-9 and Robson Self-Concept Questionnaire.

What might influence the decision whether to continue working with Sophie on deeper levels of cognition?

At this point they agreed on a consolidation session to draw together Sophie's learning from therapy and collaboratively plan the best way forward. Sophie had met her original goals and made a number of changes, but her mood was still inclined to drop when things went 'wrong' or she thought she had made a mistake. She worked as a healthcare assistant and often felt put upon by both staff and patients because she would 'go the extra mile' to help others, and this had now become expected from her as the 'norm'. Looking at the formulation in light of this, Sophie recognised that again her needs felt unimportant as she was constantly trying to please others to be accepted.

In order to generalise Sophie's learning to other areas of her life, eight more sessions were agreed in which they would focus on Sophie's tendency to self-criticise and on her deeper-level assumptions and beliefs. Sophie set the following goals:

1   To express my own needs, especially at work, including which shifts I would prefer to work
2   To say no to requests that I think are unreasonable
3   To take the breaks I am allowed, including half an hour at lunchtime, without interruption
4   To remain relatively confident if I make a mistake or am criticised. This would mean not crying about the mistake or apologising more than once.

From the full formulation (see Figure 5.2), which aspect of the problem would you target to help Sophie with her depression, and how might you begin working with this?

At this point the therapist introduced the full formulation (Figure 5.2) as it highlighted Sophie's tendency to be self-critical as well as her assumptions and beliefs. Sophie related to the formulation straight away, describing it as, 'a map of my life', although her anxious predictions 'loop' at the bottom of the formulation now concentrated on people at work rather than on Paul.

As Sophie's tendency to self-criticise could affect her mood for days, they decided to start with this. To raise self-awareness, for homework Sophie was encouraged to monitor any instances of being self-critical, recording examples on a modified version of the anxious predictions record that they devised in the session (see Table 5.2).

Following this they decided to work with a situation that cropped up frequently (see Table 5.3). To generate compassionate alternatives to her self-criticism and help her 'feel' the difference, the therapist engaged her in a brief experiential role-play exercise. First, the therapist role-played being Sophie's work colleague, who was upset because she had not been able to help Sophie with a patient:

> Colleague: 'I'm so sorry, I'm really, really sorry that I let you down.'

Table 5.2 Self-critical thoughts record

Date/time	Situation	Feelings/body (give % rating)	Self-critical thoughts (give % strength of belief in them)	Behaviour/Outcome

Sophie's automatic response to her colleague in this situation was:

> Sophie: 'Don't worry, I understand, it's really difficult here, you'd have helped if you could. There's no need to apologise, the same thing could've happened to any of us. If anything, it was my fault because I didn't think through how difficult the task would be. The patients are OK, there was no risk, please don't worry. You're a good colleague and good at your job.'

The therapist commented on how, as Sophie's colleague, this had felt really compassionate and supportive and how it had made her feel better about herself in that situation.

Next, she asked Sophie to role-play the situation again, only instead of being compassionate to her colleague, to read out the comments from the completed self-critical thoughts record that she made to herself in the same situation (Table 5.3,

Table 5.3 Completed self-critical thoughts record

Date/time	Situation	Feelings/body (give % rating)	Self-critical thoughts (give % strength of belief in them)	Behaviour/Outcome
Wednesday	My line manager asked me to help Angie with a patient. I didn't get there in time to help because I was hoisting another patient.	Guilty (100%) Ashamed (100%) Terrible (100%) In my chest and throat.	'I wasn't good enough' (100%) 'I must try harder' (100%) 'Angie won't forgive me' (90%) 'My line manager will be mad at me' (95%)	I tried to help Angie later with other patients; I kept checking she was OK (reassurance seeking). I kept apologising to her and to my line manager. They told me it was OK but I still felt terrible.

column 4). Sophie flinched as she read out her own critical self-talk in response to her colleague's apology,

> Colleague: 'I'm so sorry, I'm really, really sorry that I let you down.'
>
> Sophie: 'You weren't good enough, you must try harder. I won't forgive you. Your line manager will be mad at you.'

Sophie immediately understood the point of the exercise. She recoiled at the thought of saying these things to someone else, viewing it as the verbal equivalent to 'kicking someone when they're down'. She felt shocked to realise this was how she 'speaks' to herself and it became clear why she felt so bad in these situations.

Again, to promote curiosity, the therapist asked Sophie *why* she thought she did this to herself, given that it was against her nature to be like this. After some thought, Sophie identified her assumption that 'being self-critical prevents me from becoming complacent'. This provided an opportunity to test whether treating herself more compassionately in the face of difficulties and shortcomings would make her a more sensitive and caring person, or make her complacent and uncaring.

She kept an 'alternative to self-critical thoughts record' (see Table 5.4). The outcome of this behavioural experiment demonstrated that practising self-compassion

Table 5.4 Alternatives to self-critical thoughts record

Date/time	Situation	Feelings/body (give % rating)	Self-critical thoughts	Alternative compassionate perspective (what would I say to friend?)	Outcome
Friday	Got to work late because Paul needed a lift.	Afraid (90%) Ashamed 80%) Guilty (80%)	This isn't good enough. You should have got up earlier. You're letting others down. The manager will be mad and others will feel resentful.	This is a one-off. I haven't been late in months. Paul needed a lift, I'm glad I offered. I couldn't have known his car wouldn't start, so couldn't have got up earlier. It's normal not to like being late and others will understand that. These things happen.	The others were surprised I was late and asked what had happened. They were sympathetic and told me not to worry. Angie filled me in on the handover. I felt OK and only apologised once.

improved both her mood and how she felt and behaved in relation to others as it reduced her need to keep apologising and seek reassurance, which had unhelpfully perpetuated her belief system. This change to a more compassionate self-stance marked a real turning point in therapy for Sophie.

How can Sophie be encouraged to choose alternative, more flexible rules and assumptions for herself?

Sophie had already identified the following relevant rules and assumptions and their childhood origins:

- I must work really hard all the time.
- I must always do my best to get noticed.
- I must try really hard to make people happy all the time or they will reject me.

For homework she was asked to monitor these assumptions to increase her awareness of their influence on her daily life, noting any situations they cropped up in, her strength of belief in them, how she felt and how she behaved, as well as their impact on outcomes.

Sophie noted that her assumptions were in operation at work, where she worked harder than others and felt the need to make everyone happy by meeting their needs. Examples of this included making drinks and washing up for others, asking if they needed help and offering to run errands for patients outside of work hours. She found it hard to rate her strength of belief in the rules and assumptions, experiencing them as something that 'just *is*, it's me'.

The outcomes of this behaviour were not always as she hoped. For example, she had gone to the shops especially to get something for a patient, who had then complained and expected her to exchange it next day. This left Sophie feeling put upon and resentful; nevertheless she had returned the item as requested. Sophie noted mixed emotions when she responded to her rules, while obeying them made her feel wanted and needed, she could also feel worthless and unimportant when people took her for granted.

The therapist encouraged Sophie to consider what, if anything might be better or worse for her if the rules were to change in some way. Sophie looked at the rules, considering them carefully. After a few moments she laughed and said it would be better if people liked her anyway, then she would not need the rules at all. She then observed: 'I'd probably end up doing my best in any case, but it wouldn't feel so hard.' On closer inspection Sophie concluded that it was their 'always' and 'all the time', nature that made them rules rather than choices, along with the 'or else' threat that people would reject her if she did not obey them. She found analysing the rules objectively in such detail very interesting.

Sophie decided to risk adjusting her rules to make them more flexible:

- I have a choice whether to work really hard.
- I can choose when and when not to do my best.

- People can sometimes take responsibility for their own happiness; they might prefer *me* to take responsibility, but they are unlikely to reject me if I don't.

Why would it be helpful to continue using behavioural experiments when working with Sophie's assumptions?

Behavioural tasks play a key role in reinforcing new learning and are a powerful method of addressing cognitions at all three cognitive levels (James *et al.* 2001; Bennett-Levy *et al.* 2004). As Sophie felt confident with behaviour experiments, they decided to test her new modified rules and assumptions for fit. She could see *logically* how the old rules reinforced her beliefs but they still *felt* real, which meant that experimenting with the new rules was anxiety provoking.

She undertook a series of experiments to test whether others would reject her if she let them take responsibility, including letting colleagues make their own tea, reading a magazine during her break instead of washing up after everyone, and suggesting that visitors fetch things rather than offering to run errands for patients. Her learning from these experiments was that by automatically doing things for others it paradoxically made her 'invisible' over time, feeding into her belief that she was unimportant, worthless and unlovable. By choosing when to do her best for others she felt more respected.

Finally, Sophie tested not doing her best for others by requesting a change in her shift pattern, which meant that others had to take shifts they did not particularly like. She initially felt uncomfortable about this, but did get some Saturdays off as a result. This made Paul happy as they had more time together, which to Sophie meant he loved and wanted to be with her.

In conclusion, Sophie decided to keep her new rules as they made her feel more worthy, important and lovable. Working to build new assumptions had undermined her bottom-line beliefs, and Sophie and her therapist agreed to conclude their work at this point. The extra sessions had consolidated and generalised her learning, making relapse less likely. To prepare Sophie for continuing therapy independently they completed a continued improvement plan (see Table 5.5).

Table 5.5 Continued improvement plan

What have you learned from these sessions?	I have learned that my thoughts, assumptions and beliefs are really my opinions rather than facts. My opinions about myself have been unnecessarily harsh and negative and I have learned to think about myself in a kinder tone, as if I was my own best friend. I have also learned that I am important, worthy and lovable, but others will take advantage of me if I let them and this will make me lose my sense of being of value.

(Continued)

Table 5.5 (Continued)

What strategies have you found most helpful?	Role-playing talking to someone else as I talk to myself! Learning to be kinder and more compassionate in the way I relate to myself. Standing back from my thoughts and taking an objective look at them. Experimenting to find the reality of the situation rather than assuming I already know this.
What do you need to do to maintain/extend change?	Make sure I think carefully before I launch in working hard and doing my best. Think: am I just doing this to please other people and make them like me? Keep experimenting with my new assumptions to build confidence in them (and myself). Notice what I'm thinking and how I'm feeling and pay attention to my own needs.
What might lead to a set back?	Being criticised or making mistakes.
How would you recognise this?	By my feelings. I would start to feel terrible about myself and guilty and I would apologise too much and seek reassurance that the person still liked me.
Can you identify skills you have learned, resources, people and agencies that could help manage this set back?	I can look at the formulation again and see where the problem fits with this and what I need to do. I have my therapy notes to refer to, to remind me of what to do if I have a setback. I can go back to doing anxious prediction charts and come up with alternatives to test out. Think about the assumption that is causing me problems and come up with an alternative to test.

Client Name .... Therapist Name .... Date ....

Treatment outcomes/measures

Table 5.6 PHQ-9 scores

	Week 1	Week 7	Week 13
PHQ-9 score	19	9	4

Table 5.7 Robson Self-concept Questionnaire scores

	Week 1	Week 7	Week 13
Robson Self-Concept Questionnaire score	77	105	148

By the end of treatment Sophie's PHQ-9 scores suggested she was no longer depressed (Table 5.6) and her score on the Robson Self-Concept Questionnaire had reached the mean total score for the 'normal' population (Table 5.7). In practical terms she had met all of her goals and reported feeling more confident in her relationships with others. Her new self-compassionate stance had impacted significantly on her mood and she felt more self-assured as a result.

Reflection

A turning point for Sophie had been learning to relate to herself as a compassionate friend, rather than as her own worst enemy. This had enabled her to take behavioural risks as she could shrug things off more easily if they didn't go well, rather than harshly criticising herself and becoming depressed.

Starting with building alternatives to her anxious predictions then testing these using behavioural experiments had gently undermined her assumptions before working with them directly. Behavioural experiments had allowed her to let go of the **compensatory** behaviours demanded by her rules and to develop new assumptions and beliefs that she was worthy, important and lovable.

Conclusion and consolidation of your learning

Explain the term 'trans-diagnostic'.

Name three key elements of Fennell's (1997) model.

1

2

3

CBT Fundamentals

> What strategies would you use to work with each of these?
>
> 1
>
> 2
>
> 3
>
> At what point in therapy would you consider it appropriate to start working with assumptions and why?
>
> 1
>
> 2
>
> 3

Homework

To gain an appreciation for developing a self-compassionate self-stance you may wish to watch 'The Space between Self-esteem and Self-compassion, Kristin Neff at TEDxCentennialParkWomen' on YouTube at http://www.youtube.com/watch?v=IvtZBUSplr4, and read Fennell (2006).

Feedback

Think about your experience of reading this chapter and note any feedback for the authors here:

At the end of the book you may wish to collate the feedback together to forward to the following address: nick.wrycraft@anglia.ac.uk

6 Panic disorder with agoraphobia

Reader's agenda

Consider and make a note of any experience you may have of panic and/or agoraphobia, whether this involves personal experience, or experience in the role of carer. From this, what would you say are the main features that impressed on you?

Take a few moments to consider your own agenda or reasons for reading the chapter and make a note of them here:

-
-
-

The aim of this case study is to:

- Identify the salient features of panic disorder and agoraphobia
- Raise awareness of how panic disorder and agoraphobia can impact on friends and family, and how their responses might, in turn, impact on the problem
- Illustrate some of the difficulties inherent is treating this disorder and how treatment might proceed in light of these difficulties.

Managing your time

Take a moment to consider how long you plan to spend reading this chapter, and make a note here:

There will be a reminder later in the chapter to check whether you have kept track with this.

Introduction

Mary is a 62-year-old woman, referred by her GP for cognitive behavioural therapy for both panic disorder and agoraphobia. Until her husband's death 6 months earlier, she had managed to avoid the most distressing aspects of the problem by relying heavily on him. However, since his death her son and daughter-in-law had been more involved and the full impact of the problem had gradually become apparent. She visited her GP at the insistence of her son, following a particularly distressing panic attack while being taken supermarket shopping by him.

Mary had a fear of panic attacks and over the past 15 years or so had changed her behaviour significantly by remaining within the safety of her home in order to prevent them. However, things had changed since her husband's death and she had once again started to experience recurrent and unexpected panic attacks during which she feared passing out and being carried off to hospital against her wishes. She was now persistently concerned about having further attacks. This indicated to the GP that Mary met the criteria for both panic disorder and agoraphobia (American Psychiatric Association 2013).

The GP had medically screened Mary as suitable for CBT. This was important in order to eliminate the possibility that Mary had actual physical problems, for example, epilepsy, heart or breathing problems.

It was agreed that Mary would be seen for six weekly sessions in the first instance, with the possibility of extending treatment by another six sessions if necessary. She was seen by a second-year student on a placement with her local GP surgery, and who was being supervised fortnightly by an experienced CBT therapist at the same practice.

What are the main characteristics of panic disorder and agoraphobia?

Panic attacks are characterised by intense fear or terror that comes on suddenly and often with little warning. Although they may pass within 5–10 minutes, panic attacks can leave the person feeling unsettled and exhausted for hours afterwards.

Panic disorder can coexist with agoraphobia, and in this case the person can experience repeated panic attacks accompanied by fear and avoidance of going places where it would be embarrassing to escape from or be difficult to get back from quickly in the event of a panic attack. Examples of this might be waiting at checkouts, on public transport, in the car when there is heavy traffic, in lifts, in queues, crowds, the cinema or theatre, in waiting rooms or even being alone indoors. Panic disorder and agoraphobia are separate disorders but can often occur together.

Many severely agoraphobic individuals are unemployed and as a result may experience lower socio-economic status. They often suffer in silence for many years, preferring to live with the problem rather than seek treatment. They may feel ashamed or guilty about seeking help, and to take the edge off of their symptoms may self-medicate with drugs or alcohol. Dependence usually needs to be treated by a specialist before the panic disorder or agoraphobia can be successfully addressed.

A formula that helps to make sense of panic disorder and/or agoraphobia is widely known as the 'anxiety equation':

$$\frac{\text{Overestimation of threat and dangerousness of the situation}}{\text{Underestimation of one's personal resources to cope and of the availability and willingness of others to provide help}}$$

Diagnostic criteria for panic disorder and for agoraphobia (American Psychiatric Association 2013)

Criteria for *panic disorder* include:
1. recurrent unexpected panic attacks
2. at least one of the attacks has been followed by 1 month (or more) of one (or more) of the following:
    (a) persistent concern about having additional attacks
    (b) worry about the implications of the attack or its consequences (e.g., losing control, having a heart attack, "going crazy")
    (c) a significant change in behaviour related to the attacks

Criteria for *agoraphobia* include avoidance or anxiety related to open spaces or any place outside of one's home or safe zone.

Endorsement of fears has to come from two or more different agoraphobia situations (as this distinguishes agoraphobia from specific phobias).

Special considerations

Prior to the assessment, Mary's daughter-in-law, Amy, telephoned to ask if she could sit in with Mary for the assessment. She explained that Mary would be unlikely to come unless she could be accompanied, and that both she and her husband were very keen for Mary to attend.

What advantages and disadvantages might you weigh up when deciding whether to agree to Amy's request?

The student therapist initially thought that agreeing to this request would be unhelpful as it could be viewed as **colluding** with Mary. However, she discussed the request with her supervisor, who suggested they look at the advantages and disadvantages of Amy's request together. It was clear that Mary's explicit personal consent would need to be obtained before the therapist could agree to Amy's request.

Potential advantages. Engaging Mary in therapy was crucial to successful treatment. She was coming at the request of her son rather than through personal choice, which made it particularly important to form a collaborative working alliance with her as quickly as possible.

When working with panic disorder and/or agoraphobia it can be very helpful to have another trusted person involved who is prepared to support the individual in learning and implementing treatment strategies between sessions. This is particularly the case at assessment when the individual may be experiencing high levels of anxiety in the unfamiliar environment, making it difficult for them to take in and retain information (Marchand *et al.* 2007).

Potential disadvantages. It is often acknowledged that speaking to a stranger about a problem can be easier than speaking to someone who is familiar, and there may be a tendency to 'sanitise' details in front of someone who knows us well. With regard to panic disorder and/or agoraphobia, a particular difficulty could be that while women frequently adopt avoidance behaviour, it is more common for men with agoraphobia to use drugs or alcohol to calm their symptoms, which can lead to dependence over time. If a friend or relative is present at assessment it may be embarrassing or shameful to talk about dependence openly, which is clearly unhelpful (Hawton *et al.* 1989).

On balance, after discussion with her supervisor, the therapist decided that if Mary was happy for Amy to be present for assessment and/or some of the sessions, it would be useful to have her as a co-therapist for Mary, to support and encourage her between sessions.

What ingredients of a collaborative therapeutic relationship are particularly important while working with Mary (and Amy) on this problem?

Mary's agoraphobia had led to a lack of autonomy. At assessment she expressed fear about what she might be asked to do in therapy, which made it particularly important to adopt a collaborative, team-working approach to treatment.

From the outset, the therapist made it clear to Mary that she would be encouraged to make choices and to take responsibility throughout the process of therapy, and that nothing would happen that she had not agreed to. It was explained that the therapist could provide needed structure, support and encouragement, but would not seek to take over or control what happened. Mary and the therapist would be seen as collaborative partners, jointly 'putting their heads together' to think through helpful approaches to therapy, with Amy as an additional collaborator, occasionally coming in for parts of the session when Mary and the therapist thought this would be helpful and providing support for any work that they might agree to between sessions. Mary expressed appreciation for this openness as it helped to alleviate some of her fears (James *et al.* 2001).

Assessment and formulation

Amy accompanied Mary for the assessment. Mary appeared nervous and chose to keep her coat on throughout the interview, which indicated that she might not feel 'at home'.

The therapist suggested that Amy might want to sit in for the first half an hour of the assessment, and that if Mary felt comfortable enough by then, she might agree for Amy to leave during the remaining 20 minutes. Mary expressed apprehension, but agreed to reconsider this after half an hour.

What are important questions to ask during CBT assessment of agoraphobia and/or panic disorder?

In order to generate a detailed description of Mary's problem to build the formulation on (Figure 6.1), the therapist asked a series of information gathering questions known as the '4WFINDS' (see Chapter 2). This enabled the therapist to understand the exact main features of the problem. It also helped to establish a baseline from which to measure progress and outcomes.

What? For her main problem, Mary explained that since her husband had died she did not go out of the house except to put the bins out and to go shopping once a week with her son and daughter-in-law. This was because she experienced panic attacks when outside her home, in particular going shopping with her son and daughter-in-law. She would prefer it if her son brought the shopping to her, but he insisted that she got out of the house once a week as he thought it unhealthy for her to stay at home so much.

The attacks started when the supermarket trip was due (1) starting with negative **automatic thoughts** such as 'What if I panic?' (2), leading to her feeling anxious and panicky (3). Physiologically, she began to feel shaky and hot as her heart beat faster, her mouth became dry and she felt dizzy and 'unreal'. On occasions she would cry, but realised that this embarrassed her son, so tried very hard not to let this happen (4).

The panic would then escalate in response to her body sensations as she misinterpreted these as signs she was about to pass out. Her main fear was that she would be taken off to hospital and left there on her own, abandoned (5).

Where? When her husband was alive she had been able to avoid having the attacks by always going to the same small supermarket and keeping tight hold of her husband's arm. However, since her husband's death she had been taken by her son and daughter-in-law to a larger supermarket nearer to their home, which she found confusing.

When? The first two or three of her recent attacks had happened when her son had left her on her own for a moment in the supermarket and again while they were standing in the queue for the till where she felt trapped and unable to escape easily. Now she was beginning to fear when the next attack would come and had started to experience them on the build-up to the weekly shopping trip (1). This sometimes stopped her going out altogether (6).

With whom? She thought her son was embarrassed by her when she panicked, which made the situation worse for her. However, she felt safer with Amy and would hold her arm, which made her less likely to panic (6), but Amy was not always available to go shopping.

Frequency? The panic attacks tended to cluster around going out once a week (1).

Intensity? Mary described them as sudden, intense and very frightening. She rated their intensity as 10/10 at the time of the attacks (10 being high).

Number? She estimated that she was currently having about three or four attacks a week.

Duration? The attacks lasted between 5 and 10 minutes, but left Mary feeling exhausted for a couple of hours afterwards, and she usually went to bed to recover.

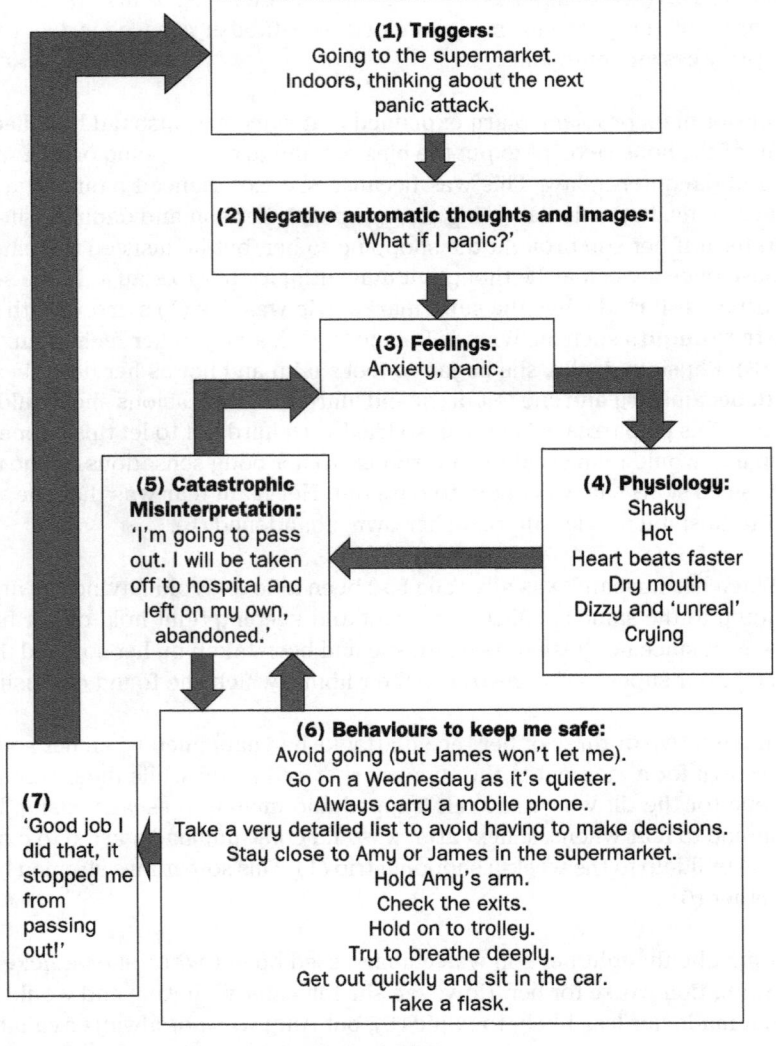

(1) Triggers:
Going to the supermarket.
Indoors, thinking about the next panic attack.

↓

(2) Negative automatic thoughts and images:
'What if I panic?'

↓

(3) Feelings: Anxiety, panic.

(4) Physiology:
Shaky
Hot
Heart beats faster
Dry mouth
Dizzy and 'unreal'
Crying

(5) Catastrophic Misinterpretation:
'I'm going to pass out. I will be taken off to hospital and left on my own, abandoned.'

(6) Behaviours to keep me safe:
Avoid going (but James won't let me).
Go on a Wednesday as it's quieter.
Always carry a mobile phone.
Take a very detailed list to avoid having to make decisions.
Stay close to Amy or James in the supermarket.
Hold Amy's arm.
Check the exits.
Hold on to trolley.
Try to breathe deeply.
Get out quickly and sit in the car.
Take a flask.

(7) 'Good job I did that, it stopped me from passing out!'

Figure 6.1 Formulation (based on Wells 1997)

Sense? Although at the time Mary believed the symptoms meant she was about to faint, she felt embarrassed to be taking up the time of professionals. The sense she made of the panic and agoraphobia was that she lacked self-control and was a bit weak as a person.

How would you explore Mary's key cognitions?

Although she thought it sounded silly saying it to the therapist, at the time of the panic, Mary thought that she would pass out. When asked what she saw in her mind's eye at the time of panicking, Mary was able to identify a picture of herself as a teenager passing out when a friend had left her in a crowded dance hall. She recalled feeling herself 'going', and the 'unreal' sensations she currently experienced during panic attacks reminded her of that feeling. At that time someone had called an ambulance and she recalled feeling embarrassed and afraid when she came round to find the paramedics had been called.

Intrusive images related to past memories are common in panic disorder, although it is interesting to note that individuals rarely mention them unless they are directly asked about them (Hirsh and Holmes 2007). Part of Mary's current fear when she felt faint was that she would be taken off to hospital against her will and abandoned there alone, although she realised on another level that this was 'illogical' (5).

How specifically do behavioural responses (safety behaviours) maintain the problem?

When asked what had stopped her from passing out until now, Mary was clear that this was because she had held either onto Amy's arm or onto the shopping trolley, as well as trying to breathe deeply.

When asked what other things she thought were helpful in either stopping the panic or preventing her from fainting, she identified a range of behaviours that she adopted to stop these things from happening. These included going shopping on a quiet day of the week, making a very detailed list to avoid having to make decisions (which tended to increase her panic), checking exactly where the exits were on arrival, as well as being aware of which checkout staff were the quickest to get through on.

If she started to feel panicky she would ask James or Amy to go outside with her to the car, where she kept a flask of sweet tea, and she would sit and drink this while she waited for them to finish the shopping. She kept her mobile phone on at all times so she could phone if they were taking longer than she expected (6).

Since Mary believed that the only reason she had not passed out was because she adopted these behaviours, they prevented her from disconfirming that the catastrophic thoughts were not accurate and that she would not pass out if she did not do them (7). The reduction in her anxiety when she adopted the safety behaviours **negatively reinforced** the problem, maintaining it in the longer term, leading her back to (1).

The formulation (see Figure 6.1) was based on Well's (1997) model of panic as this included Mary's catastrophic thoughts about the meaning of her body sensations (5), as well as demonstrating how the safety behaviours she adopts (6) feed back into the cycle at (5) and at (1 via 7), preventing disconfirmation of her catastrophic thoughts.

Given the long-standing nature of Mary's problem, what would you consider to be realistic goals for treatment?

Mary's goals for treatment needed to be realistic due to the long-standing nature of her difficulties and the number of sessions available. At assessment Amy had agreed to help Mary with treatment, which led to appointments being spaced fortnightly to allow plenty of time for working between sessions. With support from Amy it was envisaged that progress could continue to be made beyond the end of therapy. Therefore, Mary was encouraged to think of short-, medium- and long-term treatment goals. Her short-term goals were established as follows:

- To go shopping with her son and daughter-in-law without having a panic attack
- To let go of the shopping trolley/Amy's arm for 3 minutes
- To stay in a shopping aisle on her own for 3 minutes, not holding on
- To stay in the supermarket for the whole of the shopping trip
- To go shopping on a different day of the week and do all of the above.

Her medium-term goals were:

- To hang the washing out on the line on her own
- To walk to her local library and back accompanied
- To walk to her local library and back unaccompanied.

Her long-term goal was to go to her local shop independently.

In order to establish a baseline to measure treatment against, the student employed the Agoraphobic Cognitions Questionnaire and the Body Sensations Questionnaire (Chambless *et al.* 1984). Mary scored 40 and 56 respectively on these at assessment. It was agreed to re-rate these after six sessions.

Check-in

Now might be a good point at which to look back on your original objectives for reading this chapter. Which, if any, have been met and which are still outstanding?

It will help to summarise what you have learned so far here:

-
-
-
-

Does your original time plan still look realistic, and if not, how will you adjust it? Make a note here:

What other factors might contribute to long-standing agoraphobia, and what factors might motivate change?

The student was curious about why Mary had come for treatment now and not while her husband had been alive, and so enquired how Mary's relationship with her husband had been. Mary was surprisingly clear about how her husband had played a big part in establishing and maintaining her difficulties. She explained how he had taken pride in looking after her so well, protecting her from harm and generally allowing her to, in her own words, 'get away with not having to face all of this'.

It appeared that her husband had derived his self-esteem from being Mary's carer, and because of this Mary had not been encouraged or felt inclined to deal with the problem while he was alive. Once her husband had died, Mary and her family were left with the problem and the need for change became evident. While she remained terrified of going out because of the panic attacks, Mary was ashamed at how much difficulty she was causing James and Amy and wanted to improve the situation for them.

What is it important to establish before discussing psycho-education about panic attacks?

One factor that the student and her supervisor considered together at the outset was whether Mary *had* ever passed out while panicking. This is relevant because research by Green *et al.* (2007) indicates there are a very small number of people who *do* experience the physical catastrophes that they fear, such as fainting, vomiting or becoming incontinent during panic attacks.

While this is rare, it is nevertheless important to ascertain whether the person's fears *do actually* materalise, because this will influence the content of psycho-education, with the emphasis then being placed on de-catastrophising the consequences of the feared physical events rather than on strategies designed to help the person learn that the events are unlikely to occur.

The only time that Mary had actually passed out was in the dance hall as a teenager, which she acknowledged had probably been because she was unaccustomed to drinking and it was hot. She had never passed out again since.

What physiological changes occur during a panic attack, and why is it helpful to provide psycho-education about this at the outset of treatment?

The first stage of treatment was to educate Mary about the physiology of panic. The therapist explained how negative automatic thoughts and images about fainting and its feared consequences send 'threat signals' to the brain. The body tries to protect the individual from the perceived threat by producing powerful hormones, including adrenaline and cortisol, which prepare the individual to either run away or defend themselves.

In response to the hormones, the person's heart rate and blood pressure rise to increase blood supply and thus oxygen to the muscles. Breathing becomes faster to provide needed oxygen and the person may feel dizzy as a result of changes in carbon dioxide levels in the blood. Increased heart rate produces heat, so the body perspires to lower and regulate temperature. The liver releases sugar for quick energy and nonessential functions such as digestion and saliva production slow down, causing dry mouth and a feeling of 'butterflies' or even nausea. Sphincter muscles contract.

Under actual threat conditions these symptoms are really helpful, but in situations that are harmless they can be problematic and anxiety provoking in themselves.

Once Mary realised that fainting is the body's way of getting blood to the brain in the event of low blood pressure and that raised blood pressure would not and perhaps could not, cause fainting, she was surprised that she had not thought of this before. This realisation started to cast doubts on her original catastrophic thoughts about fainting during panic attacks. This moment of realisation is often referred to in CBT terms as an 'aha moment'.

What are the potential benefits of keeping a panic diary?

In order to develop her curiosity about this further, Mary was encouraged to keep a diary of her panic attacks over the next 2 weeks, including the time and date of any attacks, the situation that the panic attack occurred in, her symptoms, her catastrophic misinterpretations of these, and (as catastrophic thoughts are central to the distress) she was encouraged to try to come up with an alternative response to the idea that she was about to faint (Table 6.1).

Keeping a panic diary is particularly helpful because in order to reduce anxiety it is important for the individual to be able to generate believable alternative, less catastrophic explanations for the anxiety responses in the moment. It is also helpful to practice keeping this record in the moment rather than retrospectively, because it is in the moment that the alternative explanation is most helpful.

Table 6.1 Panic diary

Date	Situation	Anxiety response	Catastrophic misinterpretation	Alternative explanation

Based on Young (2007).

As Mary already had a new idea about what was happening physiologically during panic, she found she was able to come up with an alternative fairly readily, which she found helpful and reassuring, and which lessened the intensity of the emotion in the moment. She was still acutely attentive to her bodily sensations, but these were beginning to take on a new meaning: 'My heart is beating faster, so it's unlikely I'll faint. It must be a rush of adrenaline.' The fact that these alternative thoughts reduced her panic feelings lent weight to their believability.

In order to increase Mary's curiosity still further and to build on her findings so far, the therapist's supervisor wondered with the student how they might proceed from here. Referring to the formulation, it was clear that Mary needed to test her thoughts about the saving abilities of her safety behaviours. The supervisor therefore suggested carrying out some *in vivo* work involving exposure and response prevention with a cognitive focus, going out together with Mary and Amy to the supermarket to test the behaviours. 'In vivo' is a Latin term that means something occurring in a natural setting, in this case, a behavioural experiment that is taking place outside of the therapy room, in a 'real-world' setting.

How might the therapist's reservations about working experientially be turned to advantage?

The student initially experienced some catastrophic thoughts of her own about this and felt a rush of adrenaline, which she later thought was quite funny in the circumstances. She reported having images of Mary fainting in the supermarket, a big fuss being made, and of herself being held responsible and 'struck off' the training course because things had all gone wrong.

The supervisor noted how helpful it was that the student had experienced similar catastrophic thoughts, images and feelings to Mary, as this would make her more sensitive about setting up the exposure exercises. She suggested that the student might write a personal thought record to identify her unhelpful thinking (catastrophic/all-or-nothing thinking/making predictions), and that she might use the *in vivo* therapy sessions as a behavioural experiment to test her own catastrophic thoughts at the same time (see Chapter 2).

Before suggesting anything to Mary, the student made a trip to the nearby supermarket where the proposed experiment would take place. This was so that she would know what to expect and to get a clearer idea about things. She noted that this was probably a safety behaviour as she was feeling anxious about working *in vivo* for the first time, and the visit reassured her. This brought home how difficult it is not to employ safety behaviours, and therefore helped her to take Mary's concerns seriously.

What impact might working in vivo have on professional boundaries, and how might these be negotiated?

While the boundaries of the therapeutic relationship had been made explicit at the outset of therapy, new issues can arise when moving therapy from the environment of the consulting room to outside it. Things may become more conversational when travelling between venues and the line between personal and professional can easily blur. The student discussed this with her supervisor and decided that it may be helpful to talk with Mary and Amy about this before the undertaking, as she could imagine Mary asking her some well-meaning personal questions out of interest. She also wanted to discuss with Mary how she would want to manage the situation if either party met someone they knew while out, as this could potentially threaten confidentiality.

What might you include when collaboratively setting up a series of behavioural experiments with Mary, incorporating exposure and response prevention?

Mary had started to develop a real curiosity about her panic symptoms and was quite prepared to take part in the experiment, as long as Amy could come too. The rationale for exposure and response prevention, as well as how to set up behavioural experiments, was explained and she demonstrated her understanding of these principles by explaining them to Amy when she came in for the last 10 minutes of the session (something they had agreed from the outset so that Amy could be involved with homework assignments).

The experiments involved Mary's first two goals:

1   To let go of the shopping trolley/Amy's arm for 3 minutes.
2   To stay in a shopping aisle, on her own, not holding on, for 3 minutes.

Mary's original target cognition was 'if I let go of Amy's arm or the trolley I will wobble and faint'. In order to move towards her goals rather than away from her feared consequence, Mary reworded this: 'if I let go of Amy's arm or the trolley, my anxiety will go up, I will feel wobbly but will not fall over or faint, it is just a feeling'.

The experiment involved them all going to the supermarket and Mary standing next to Amy independently in the aisle without holding on for 3 minutes, or until her anxiety subsided. If she was successful in this, a number of graded steps were planned, including Mary moving away from Amy in stages until she could stand at the other end of the aisle on her own without holding on for 3 minutes or until her anxiety subsided. An hour and a half was allowed for each of the *in vivo* sessions to allow time to return to the consultation room and 'unpack' and thus maximise the learning from the experiments using Kolb's (1984) learning cycle (see Chapter 1).

The experiment went as planned. Mary's anxiety 'spiked' each time she attempted more independence by first letting go and then moving further away from Amy, dropping her safety behaviours little by little. She rated her anxiety throughout and her strength of belief that she would pass out, and although she did feel wobbly, at no time did she actually fall over or faint. She noticed that as she focused more on her body sensations she began to feel worse, and as she focused more on the experiment itself, her anxiety lessened, which she found interesting. Within 40 minutes the experiments were complete and Mary had reached the first two of her goals.

Mary's learning, using the learning cycle (see Chapter 2), was that although the safety behaviours quickly reduced her anxiety, they kept her in the belief that she needed to do them to prevent fainting. By tolerating the anxiety she had found that fainting didn't happen, 'at least this time'. She still thought that having Amy and the therapist nearby had made a big difference, and that on her own things would have been very different. This indicated that although some implicational learning had taken place, more was needed. The homework was to repeat this with Amy and/or James between sessions on at least four occasions before they next met in a fortnight, when they would plan the next experiments. Mary returned next session, stating how pleased she was with herself. The new learning from the homework was duly unpacked again and it was decided to build on this further with another experiment.

The next experiment involved testing what actually *does* happen when someone faints in the supermarket. Although by now Mary's beliefs about fainting had diminished, her prediction 'if I faint, people will take me to hospital and leave me there, abandon me' was still alive and well. Although she realised logically that James and Amy were very unlikely to abandon her, at points of high anxiety she still had a strong sense that this was what would happen. The next experiment was again designed to match her **implicational** understanding with her **propositional** understanding (see Chapter 2) and was agreed collaboratively, although the student did experience some strong undisclosed reservations about the next experiment.

The experiment involved Mary and Amy watching from a 'safe distance,' while the student acted out 'fainting' in a prominent part of the supermarket, so that Mary could see first-hand how others reacted. Mary's alternative prediction was, 'If someone faints people might take care of them and make sure they get home safely,' although her strength of belief in this was only 4/10. The plan was for the student to see the experiment through to the end and to meet Mary and Amy in the car afterwards before unpacking the learning back in the consulting room.

Despite discussing this experiment in great detail with her supervisor and even practising 'fainting' in supervision and at home, the student found her anxiety peaking at around 8/10, with sweating palms and shaking as she entered the supermarket, with Amy and Mary following at a discrete distance. The thought crossed her mind to run away, avoid, escape, anything but going through with the feared experiment, but she had a personal prediction to test: 'I will pretend to pass out, make a bit of a spectacle, someone will come over, it will all be over quickly and both Mary and I will learn something really important'.

The student had discussed with her supervisor how she would reassure the person who came to her aid in the supermarket, without biasing the results of the experiment. The experiment again went well: the student 'fainted' spectacularly; a supermarket first aider was called, and once the student had been taken care of and 'recovered', the first aider had offered to call for a cab to make sure she got home safely. The student declined and met up with Mary and Amy for the return journey.

The learning from these experiment(s) was unpacked (twice), once with Mary following the experiment, and later when the student discussed her 'personal' experiment in supervision.

Both Mary and Amy thought the student 'fainting' had been worthy of an Oscar. Mary had been surprised that the first aider had offered to get a cab for the student; it supported her alternative prediction that 'someone would take care of you if you faint and make sure that you got home safely'. Her strength of belief in this prediction increased from 4/10 to 8/10. Mary said she had found it difficult not to laugh when the student had 'fainted'. Laughing was something she would not have dreamed of doing in a supermarket before, which indicated she was feeling more relaxed.

By this point Mary was well on her way to meeting her goals. By the sixth session she had begun to consider hanging some of the washing on the line in the garden on her own.

The student used part of this session to discuss how they would end therapy. Both Mary and Amy thought that another two sessions, spaced out fortnightly as before, would be really helpful to consolidate things and to write out a 'continued improvement plan' to take things forward, and this was agreed (see Table 6.2). A further follow-up session in three months' time was also arranged to ensure that any lapses had been dealt with successfully.

The scores on the Agoraphobic Cognitions Questionnaire and the Body Sensations Questionnaire had steadily decreased over time (Table 6.3). This seemed to reflect the fact that treatment had been undertaken steadily and progressively, with regular homework exercises conscientiously undertaken with Amy as supporting 'co-therapist'.

Table 6.2 Continued improvement plan

What have you learned from these sessions?	That if my heart rate goes up it's a sign I'm unlikely to faint.
	That I can stand the anxiety if I go slowly and wait for it to go down.
	That some things I do are unhelpful safety behaviours. They reduce anxiety in the short term but keep it all going really. So stop them!
	That I can manage many things on my own.
What strategies have you found most helpful?	Practising being independent in small stages, stay with my feelings rather than avoid them.
	I can use safety behaviours at any time if I feel overwhelmed, but I need to stop them in the end.
	Test out things to see if what I think will happen is true.
What do you need to do to maintain/extend change?	Plan with Amy how to get to the library.
	Ideas: First walk with Amy to the library (don't have to go in).
	Go again with Amy and go in to the library.
	Go again and go in with Amy. Get Amy to show me how to check books in and out.
	Plan to do parts of the trip on my own (with Amy following behind).

	Go on my own and meet Amy in the library. Check book out. Go on my own without Amy and check book back in. Phone Amy and tell her!
What might lead to a set back?	Another panic attack. Feeling overwhelmed.
How would you recognise this?	I'd have a panic attack. I'd feel all of the physical sensations again. I'd be afraid of fainting again.
Can you identify skills you have learned, resources, people and agencies that could help manage this set back?	Remember that my heart rate has gone *up* not down. Remember the experiments. Look at this sheet of paper and do what it says. Talk to Amy about my fears and plan some more experiments with her.

Client Name .... Therapist Name .... Date ....

Table 6.3 Measurement and treatment outcomes

	Agoraphobic Cognitions Questionnaire	Body Sensations Questionnaire
Assessment	40	56
12 weeks (6 sessions)	21	25
16 weeks (8 sessions)	16	20
38 weeks (follow-up)	12	15

Mary had made a number of lifestyle changes. By the follow-up session three months after the end of therapy she had reached all of her goals, including going to both her local library and shop independently. She had wanted to come to the final therapy session on her own as a mark of her success, but thought it would be 'lovely' for Amy to be there for the final session, so they had come together.

Reflection

The student reflected on the case with her supervisor using the learning cycle. First, she reflected on her own catastrophic thoughts and panic feelings in connection with the *in vivo* work, and was encouraged to draw parallels between her own catastrophic thoughts and feelings and Mary's catastrophic thoughts and feelings, and to consider how this had impacted on the treatment.

The student concluded that being encouraged by her supervisor to try something that took her outside her comfort zone was very similar to Mary being encouraged by her to do something that caused her great anxiety.

The student had not felt able to undertake the assignment without the use of a safety behaviour (going to visit the supermarket beforehand) as it would have been too stressful. In a similar way, Mary had initially employed safety behaviours (holding onto and then gradually letting go of Amy's arm) to enable her enter the situation to start with. On the other hand, if the student had run away from the situation at the last minute (as she had wanted to in the face of her strong anxiety), neither she nor Mary would have been able to learn as much.

Without this anxiety-provoking experience, the student thought she would not have appreciated or understood Mary's difficulties as well, and it was possible that she may have unhelpfully tried to go too far too fast without this insight. She concluded that she would definitely use *in vivo* work again.

Reflecting on why the treatment had been so successful for Mary despite the long-standing nature of her problem, the student identified having a supervisor who really encouraged her to try new things as paramount. Other significant factors included Mary's readiness to change now that her husband had died. She had wanted to move on with her life without being a burden to James and Amy.

The most important features of therapy were perceived as empowerment through collaboration, going at Mary's pace and having a reliable, motivated and kindly co-therapist in Amy.

Although relatively simple, the psycho-education had produced an *'aha'* moment for Mary that brought about a small change in cognition which they were then able to build on by using the behavioural experiments combined with exposure and response prevention.

Conclusion and consolidation of your learning

In order to consolidate your learning from this chapter it would be helpful to return to the original case study aims set out for the chapter and to reflect on what you have learned about these.

- Identify four salient features of both panic disorder and of agoraphobia.

1

2

3

4

- What impact can panic disorder and agoraphobia have on friends and family, and how might their responses in turn impact on the problem?

- What difficulties may arise during treatment of this disorder?

- How might treatment proceed in light of these difficulties?

Homework

Using the principles of behavioural experiments and exposure and response prevention, try approaching a situation that you would normally avoid because it would cause you anxiety; stay in the situation long enough for your anxiety to subside and for you to learn something from the experience. Keep notes.

Examples of this might be standing at the top of a tall stairwell and looking over, or you might try a new therapy strategy under the guidance of your supervisor.

Further reading: Hackmann (2004).

Feedback

Think about your experience of reading this chapter and note any feedback for the authors here:

At the end of the book you may wish to collate the feedback together to forward to the following address: nick.wrycraft@anglia.ac.uk

7   Social anxiety disorder

Reader's agenda

Social anxiety is a normal reaction that most people experience at times in their relations with others. However, social anxiety disorder goes beyond this to the point where it causes persistent and significant distress and interferes significantly with the person's life.

Thinking about any difficulties you may have experienced with social anxiety, either personally or in connection with someone you know, take a few moments to consider your own agenda or reasons for reading the chapter and make a note of them here:

-
-

The aim of this case study is to:

- Help you recognise the identifying features of social anxiety disorder
- Apply one well-recognised CBT model for social anxiety
- Understand which central features of the disorder it is most important to target in treatment.

Managing your time

Take a moment to consider how long you plan to spend reading this chapter, and make a note here:

You will be reminded of this later in the chapter to help you keep track of your timing.

Background

Ailsa is a 45-year-old, single, Scottish woman who has been employed in the financial sector for the past 15 years. She has always been socially anxious, but this anxiety has become evident more recently in connection with her work, where she has been promoted to a position which entails giving short monthly presentations to colleagues and senior management. Socially she prefers to stay in the background to avoid becoming the centre of attention and feels anxious in groups of more than two or three people. When accepting the promotion she thought she would manage the presentations as they were brief, but as the time approached she became more and more anxious and eventually took time off sick, arranging for a colleague to stand in for her. Ailsa thought her career might be at risk and so made an appointment to discuss the problem with her GP, who referred her for CBT.

A degree of anxiety when giving presentations is normal and even helpful. How would you recognise when a person's anxiety meets the criteria for social anxiety disorder?

Most people who are not familiar with giving regular public presentations are likely to be nervous at the prospect of doing so, but are also likely to recognise that their nerves are an uncomfortable necessity for a focused delivery on the day. However, individuals with social anxiety disorder experience unreasonable and disproportionate fear or anxiety in situations where they think others might judge them negatively, for example, when exposed to social situations involving contact with people they do not know, or if called on to give a presentation or speech.

These situations trigger fear of acting in a manner that will cause embarrassment, shame or humiliation and are therefore avoided wherever possible, or managed by employing a range of behaviours designed to make the situation feel safer. The anxious anticipation, avoidance and distress involved interfere significantly with the person's normal routine in social settings, at work or school or during other everyday activities. The individual may or may not recognise that their response is excessive or unreasonable (American Psychiatric Association 2013; Veale 2003).

Exercise

Remember a time when you were called on to give a public presentation of some sort, whether a formal presentation to a group of professionals, a wedding speech, or reading aloud in front of your peers at school or college. Close your eyes for a few moments and recall the event.

Prior to the event, what were your key concerns?

> What did you do to prevent your concerns from materialising?
>
> If they did materialise, how did you manage?
>
> After the event did you move straight on, or did you spend time thinking about your presentation? If you did, what specific parts of the presentation did you focus your thoughts on and how did this make you feel?
>
> If you have never given a public presentation of any kind, what are the reasons for this?

CBT assessment and formulation

From the above description of social anxiety disorder, what might make it difficult to establish therapeutic rapport with your client and what might help the process?

> The core of social phobia appears to be a strong desire to convey a particular favourable impression of oneself to others and marked insecurity about one's ability to do so.
>
> (Clark and Wells 1995: 69)

Given that the therapist's ability to form a good relationship with the client is crucial to therapy (James *et al.* 2001) and that social anxiety is fundamentally an interpersonal disorder which tends to affect relationships negatively (Alden 2005), it is important to pay particular attention to establishing therapeutic rapport from the outset when assessing for social anxiety disorder.

Socially anxious individuals commonly feel insecure about their ability to engage in therapy and may fear being exposed by the therapist as inadequate in some way. Ailsa's therapist therefore aimed to build trust from the outset by showing appropriate levels of empathy and warmth in both her verbal and non-verbal manner. At the same time she adopted a genuine and straightforward therapeutic style which involved acknowledging any difficulties that might arise during the assessment because of the social anxiety (James *et al.* 2001).

During the assessment Ailsa spoke quickly and quietly in a strong Scottish accent, which made her both hard to hear and to follow. The therapist recognised that speaking quickly and quietly was likely to be a behaviour that Ailsa was adopting to try to keep herself safe socially. **Safety behaviours** are employed by socially anxious people in an attempt to reduce their anxiety in situations they find difficult (see Chapter 2). Unfortunately these behaviours tend to be paradoxical in nature and often contribute to interpersonal difficulties by contaminating them in an unnatural way, unhelpfully bringing about the very consequence that the person is trying to avoid.

In Ailsa's case her safety behaviours of speaking quickly (so as to get the situation over as quickly as possible) and speaking quietly (so as not to draw attention to herself) meant the therapist could not hear properly, so the behaviours ended up prolonging the assessment and drawing more attention to Ailsa, while also preventing effective, meaningful communication.

Safety behaviours are an important feature of social anxiety which the therapist was watching out for from the outset. Rather than let Ailsa continue unheard, the therapist gently fed back the difficulty she was experiencing, asking if Ailsa would mind slowing down and speaking louder. Ailsa blushed very slightly but responded more slowly and loudly that people often found her difficult to understand. The therapist fed back how much clearer it was when she spoke more slowly and loudly as she really wanted to hear and understand so they could work together to make life easier for Ailsa. Ailsa said she appreciated having this discussion at the outset.

How does social anxiety often develop?

Ailsa had much in common with other's who experience social anxiety disorder. She had been quite a shy child at school and had been taught to put others' needs ahead of her own; however, this often resulted in her being overlooked in favour of pushier children, whom she found difficult to deal with or stand up to.

During adolescence she became increasingly anxious among her peer group, which resulted in few meaningful relationships developing and little contact with members of the opposite sex, hence she was still single. During her teens she suffered from depression but immersing herself in work had given her a sense of purpose and accomplishment which eventually lifted her depression. Once she was in full-time employment and respected by her work colleagues for her abilities, things had improved still further, although she still remained socially anxious.

While low self-esteem can often be a common problem associated with social anxiety, Ailsa's problem had not 'fitted' with the self-esteem model as she was neither overly self-critical not particularly depressed, which are both associated with low self-esteem (Fennell 2009).

What is the central feature of Clark and Wells's social anxiety disorder model, and how do the various elements of the model link to maintain the cycle?

The therapist asked Ailsa to describe in detail what happened when she was given the presentation to do at work. This in-depth analysis provided explicit information about Ailsa's thoughts, feelings, physiology and behaviour in this specific situation. As Ailsa described what had happened, the therapist jotted the details down, writing each element in the positions they appear within Clark and Wells's (1995) model of social anxiety. She shared and clarified the **conceptualisation** of the problem as they went along, with Ailsa adding in the various connections once they had been collaboratively agreed (see Figure 7.1).

The connections included (1) the triggering social situation (being asked to give a presentation) which activated (2) Ailsa's assumption that 'If I put myself forward others will see I'm inadequate and reject me'. This assumption led to Ailsa's perception of social danger (3) that others would see her looking anxious and not coping (trembling, blushing, sweating, shaky voice, etc.) and would not want to know her afterwards based on this.

This sense of social danger led her to adopt various safety behaviours (3–4). These included using PowerPoint so people would look at the screen rather than at her, spending hours preparing the presentation to get it just right, writing out word for word what she would say, practicing reading her notes aloud, speaking quickly and quietly to get through as fast as possible and so that people could not hear any mistakes she might make, keeping her head down so her hair fell forward covering her face when she blushed and so she could avoid any eye contact, as well as wearing dark colours and keeping her arms down to hide any possible tell-tale signs of perspiration.

Ailsa also described how, if she had been able to give the presentation, she would certainly have gone back over the whole event looking for any mistakes or socially inept things she might have had said or done during the presentation. This post-event **rumination** involved rerunning negative aspects of the presentation in her mind's eye from an **observer perspective**. Ailsa finally phoned in sick to avoid giving the presentation altogether (4).

From past experience, Ailsa knew that both her sense of social danger (3) and the behaviours she adopted (4) would also result in (5) various physiological symptoms of anxiety, including trembling, turning red, perspiring, an unsteady voice and feeling panicky which included an increase in heart rate, shallow breathing and the possibility of her mind going blank.

All three elements, her sense of social danger (3), the safety behaviours (4) and the anxiety symptoms (5), fed directly into an overwhelming sense of self-consciousness (6), which included images of herself from an observer perspective standing before the audience looking, red, sweaty, shaky, inept, voice trembling, and as Ailsa saw and described it, 'looking a complete fool' in front of others. This image of herself sustained her sense of social danger (6–3), further fuelled her safety behaviours (6–4) and stepped up her anxiety symptoms (6–5), forming a continuous feedback cycle which maintained her social performance anxiety.

```
                    ┌─────────────────────────────┐
                    │  (1) Social situation:       │
                    │  Being asked to give a       │
                    │  presentation                │
                    └──────────────┬──────────────┘
                                   ▼
                    ┌─────────────────────────────────────┐
                    │  (2) Assumptions activated:          │
                    │  'If I put myself forward others     │
                    │  will see I'm inadequate and         │
                    │  reject me.'                         │
                    └──────────────┬──────────────────────┘
                                   ▼
                    ┌─────────────────────────────────────┐
                    │  (3) Perceived social danger:        │
                    │  Negative automatic thoughts:        │
                    │  'Others will see I'm not coping     │
                    │  and won't want to know me.'         │
                    └─────────────────────────────────────┘
                                   │
                                   ▼
                    ╭─────────────────────────────╮
                    │  (6) Self-focused attention: │
                    │  Image of self, shaking      │
                    │  badly, going red and        │
                    │  looking out of control.     │
                    ╰─────────────────────────────╯
```

(4) Safety behaviours:
Use PowerPoint so people won't look directly at me.
Prepare thoroughly.
Practice reading from notes, word for word.
Speak quickly to finish quickly.
Speak quietly so mistakes aren't noticed.
Keep head down to avoid eye contact.
Wear dark colours and keep arms down to hide perspiration.
Go over the presentation in my head afterwards looking at all the mistakes I made from an observer perspective.
Avoid the presentation.

(5) Anxiety symptoms:
Trembling.
Going red.
Perspiring.
Unsteady voice.
Panicking.
Shallow breathing.
Mind going blank.

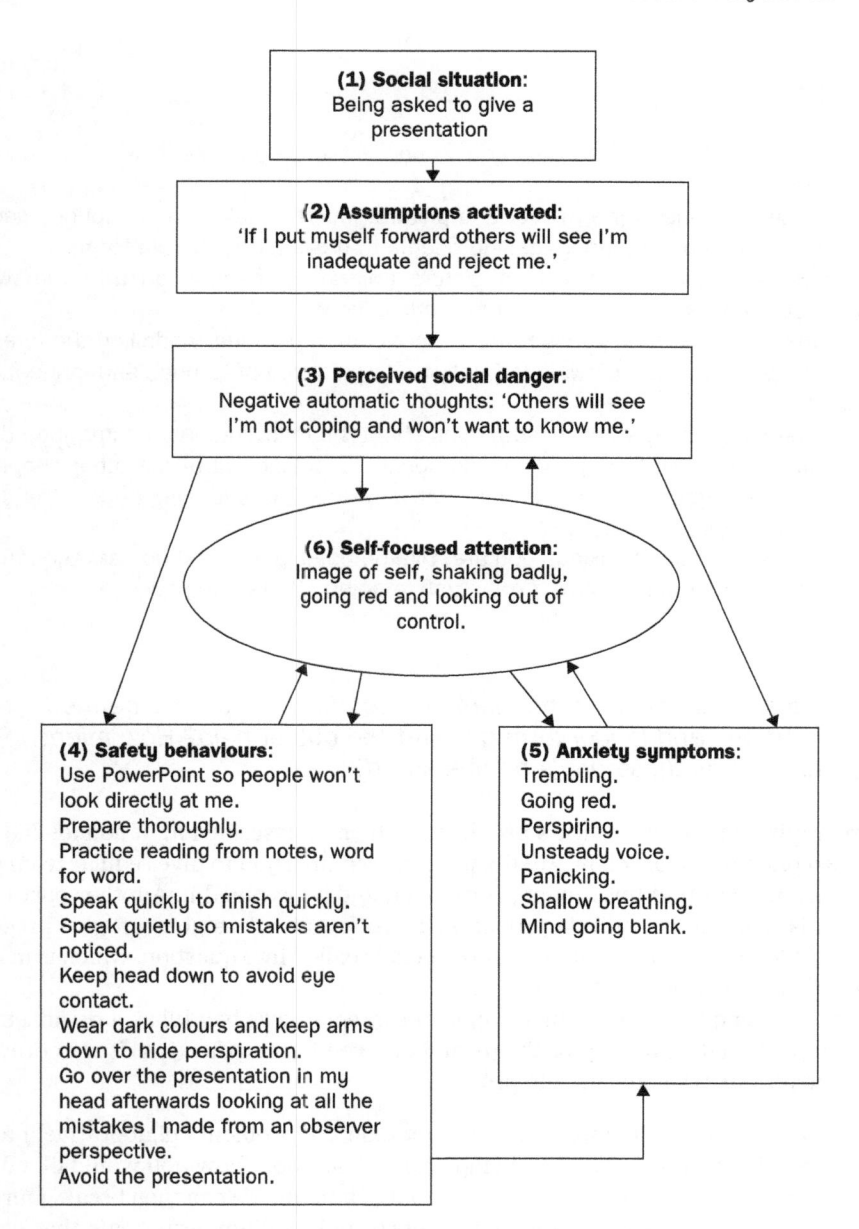

Figure 7.1 Formulation of social anxiety, based on Wells (1997)

> **Exercise**
>
> This imagery exercise may help you to understand the concept of self-focused attention.
>
> Close your eyes for a minute and picture yourself making an announcement over the underground tannoy, asking people to move along the platform.
>
> Now take another minute to picture yourself appearing on a well-known televised 'dance-off' final in front of an audience of millions.
>
> Finally, repeat the exercise, this time picturing yourself modelling the latest fashion garments on a catwalk in front of a large crowd of famous and influential people.
>
> After these imagery exercises, think about the following. In your imagery, did you picture yourself from your own perspective, looking out at the other people, or did you see yourself from the perspective of the others looking at you, that is, from an observer perspective?
>
> The more socially anxious you are, the more likely it is that you saw yourself from an observer perspective, i.e. as you imagine others see you.

How does summarising the problem and establishing clearly defined short-, medium- and longer-term goals at the outset help? How might progress towards these goals be measured?

The therapist summarised Ailsa's problem as she had described it: 'It sounds like you have two parts to the problem. Firstly, your job requires you to give regular team presentations, but you find this anxiety provoking and so avoided it. Another part to the problem is that you are still on probation at work and unless you can give presentations it could mean your suitability for the post is called into question, which is making you even more anxious. Is that right?'

Summarising the problem in a couple of sentences was helpful as it demonstrated the therapist's understanding of things and allowed for clarification. It also provided the foundation for the goal-setting process.

> This makes it important for us to tackle the problem collaboratively and it would be good to start by being really clear about how you would like things to be different so we have a clear goal to aim for. We can then break your goal into smaller pieces, so we have short- and medium-term goals that can be tackled one step at a time.

For homework Ailsa was encouraged to define her goals in behavioural terms. The goals she returned with were, in the short term:

1. To explain to my line manager that I'm having difficulties and to get support.
2. To be able to raise points and give answers in team meetings without having to repeat myself because I haven't been heard properly.

In the medium term:

3   To give a 10-minute presentation to colleagues and my line manager.
4   To ask the audience if they have questions at the end and to answer these without blushing or my voice sounding quiet and shaky.

And in the longer term:

5   To be confident giving regular presentations at work, i.e. taking a maximum of 1 hour to prepare for these.

Ailsa considered it would be normal to expect a moderate level of anxiety about the presentations (a subjective rating of 4–5/10 instead of her present 10/10) and wanted not to feel (overly) self-conscious. It was agreed that they would check in every week to see how therapy was going in relation to these goals.

The Social Anxiety Scale (Heimberg et al. 1999) was used as a measurement tool to establish a baseline to compare treatment results against. This is a well-established measurement tool relevant to Ailsa's problem (Veale 2003). At the outset of therapy Ailsa's score indicated that she was severely socially anxious.

Treatment

What key areas are important to focus on when treating social anxiety disorder?

Working collaboratively on the formulation had socialised Ailsa to the rationale for treatment, and from this she understood the three key areas hypothesised to be maintaining the problem in the 'here and now':

1   The shift of her attention to self-focusing whenever she believed she could be in danger of negative judgement by others.
2   The safety behaviours she adopted which prevented her from disconfirming her fears.
3   Her anticipatory and post-event processing which focused on her emotional responses and self-constructed images about the event.

Both Ailsa's goals and the formulation were referred to each session throughout treatment to make sure that therapy did not 'drift'.

Why is self-monitoring helpful in the first instance?

From the outset Ailsa was encouraged to monitor and collect data from the situations that caused her anxiety (see Table 7.1). The task of self-monitoring is valuable but takes effort; therefore the therapist made sure that this was prioritised

Table 7.1 Form for monitoring the features of social anxiety

Situation or event	Negative thoughts	Anxiety (0–10)	Physiological symptoms	Behaviour

at the start of each session to ensure Ailsa treated it as important (James *et al.* 2001).

This exercise yielded valuable information about different aspects of Ailsa's life that were affected by her social anxiety and helped her to become better at observing her own thoughts, feelings and behaviours. From this, unhelpful thinking habits that are common to people with social anxiety disorder were identified, including mind-reading, **emotional reasoning**, catastrophising and selectively attending to negatives. However, because Ailsa's problem was long-standing the therapist chose to focus most of the therapeutic work on implicational learning, including behavioural experiments for maximum therapeutic impact (see Chapter 2).

How can the therapist encourage Ailsa to shift her focus of her attention from internal to external events, and how might she learn from this?

In session Ailsa took part in two brief experiments to find out how self-focusing compared with focusing outwards. The first experiment involved giving an informal three-minute 'presentation' about her work to the therapist while increasing her internal self-focus, including monitoring her physiological status and how well her safety behaviours were working. The second experiment involved giving the same presentation but this time deliberately focusing outwards, that is, watching and being curious about the therapist's reaction to her delivery (Butler 2008).

Although Ailsa could see logically from the formulation that focusing outwards might be helpful, her prediction was that if she did not concentrate on monitoring herself she would say something stupid and there would be big gaps in her delivery. However, she was able to come up with an alternative prediction to test, which was that 'trying to monitor myself as well as giving a delivery will be difficult and focusing on the other persons' reactions could be easier'. She agreed to be filmed on her mobile phone so to compare the two presentations objectively afterwards, rather than relying on her usual method of subjectively going over things in her own mind's eye.

After the experiments they used Kolb's reflective cycle to 'unpack' the findings from the recordings (see Chapter 1). When Ailsa self-focused she noticed she made little eye contact with the therapist and did not pick up that she was not being heard clearly. As a result she considered the presentation look 'weird'. During the presentation she had visualised herself from an observer perspective glowing red and perspiring profusely, trying to hide this behind her hair. However, from the recording it was clear that her anxiety about this was based on emotional reasoning, as in reality she had occasionally flicked her hair back, making it clear that although she appeared a little self-conscious, she was not glowing red or noticeably perspiring. Her anxiety rating for the self-focused presentation had also been 9/10.

In the second presentation Ailsa was surprised at the difference the outward focus made to how she appeared. The recording provided feedback that she looked much more confident when focusing outwards. Making even brief eye contact meant she could see whether or not she was being heard and was able to respond by slowing down and speaking louder. Her anxiety rating for focusing outward had dropped to 5/10.

Analysing these findings alongside the formulation, Ailsa's confidence in (and understanding of) the social anxiety model deepened; she now appreciated first-hand the maintenance role that self-focused attention played. Her learning from the experiment was that although she had thought self-focusing was a helpful thing, she could now see that it was a maintaining factor in her anxiety. She planned to take this learning forward for homework by experimenting some more with concentrating on how others were *actually responding to her*, rather than focusing on her *imagined construction* of how they were responding.

Check-in

Are you keeping to your original time management plan? If you want to adjust your timing it may be helpful to make a note of this here:

What has been your main learning from this chapter so far?

What learning outcomes are still outstanding from the original agenda?

How might Ailsa experiment with her safety behaviours, including anticipatory and post-event processing, so as to find out more about the role they play in the problem?

From the experiments and the homework she had undertaken, Ailsa was beginning to realise the extent to which her own behaviour could be influencing social situations and could well be making her feel more rather than less anxious.

To find out more about the role of her safety behaviours, Ailsa and the therapist collaboratively devised another behavioural experiment, this time to test Ailsa's new hypothesis that dropping her safety behaviours (including inward focusing) would result in her feeling less anxious and therefore able to give a more effective presentation. Again, the experiment involved Ailsa giving two brief presentations, the first time using as many of her safety behaviours as possible, and the second time behaving in opposite ways to those safety behaviours. Data were collected as before on her mobile phone camera.

Before the first presentation, Ailsa thought long and hard about what she would say, scripting out her three-minute presentation word for word. During the presentation she read from this quietly, so the therapist would not hear any mistakes and quickly, to get the presentation over with. She kept her head down so as to avoid eye contact and kept her arms by her sides so that if she got anxious any perspiration would not show. After the presentation she went over the experience of giving the presentation, critically picking through in her mind's eye for any mistakes she had made and reviewing how 'rubbish' she had looked from the therapist's point of view.

In contrast, the second presentation involved Ailsa speaking extemporaneously about her work and making eye contact with the therapist rather than reading from notes. She spoke louder and more slowly in response to any external cues she was picking up from making eye contact. Instead of keeping her arms down, she lifted them to gesture and to draw an illustration on the whiteboard. After the presentation she resisted negatively sifting through the experience in her mind's eye for embarrassing faults to dwell on, instead using the camera recording to learning more objectively from the experiment.

Again, a comparison of the two recordings revealed surprises for Ailsa. For example, when reading her presentation word for word she noticed how 'flat' she sounded and how she had lost her place a couple of times, which she considered off-putting to watch. Her presentation was hard to follow because of how quickly and quietly she spoke, and she considered her lack of eye contact made her look timid and uncertain. During the presentation she had noticed how keeping her arms down to hide any perspiration had ironically made her warmer and therefore more likely to perspire; watching herself afterwards, she realised that keeping her arms by her sides made her presentation look oddly 'wooden'.

By contrast, the second presentation looked altogether more natural and confident. Not spending time on anxious thoughts pre- and post-presentation reduced her anxiety considerably. Her speech and manner had an enthusiastic flow when she spoke about what interested her rather than reading from pre-scripted notes. Her eye contact with the therapist allowed for 'feedback', and Ailsa could see when the therapist was following along and when she did not appear to understand so well and make adjustments accordingly. Gesturing and writing on the whiteboard had also livened things up considerably. Ailsa was surprised to see how confident she actually appeared.

She concluded that the experiment upheld her new hypothesis that 'dropping my safety behaviours (including inward focusing) enables me to give a more effective presentation because I feel less anxious about it'. Ailsa would definitely *not* recommend using safety behaviours to anyone else and planned to take her learning forward by practising outside of the session focusing outwards and doing the opposite of her safety behaviours for homework. Together they planned more experiments in a graded way for Ailsa to undertake between sessions.

Ailsa's assumption that if she put herself forward others would see she was inadequate and reject her had, until now, fed into the problem. How might working with this assumption reduce her perception of threat and reduce the likelihood of a relapse?

The next session was used to consolidate Ailsa's learning so far, review her goals, and plan a way forward. Ailsa reported that the in-session experiments had increased her confidence in the formulation and she had subsequently begun to question a number of aspects of the model that she had previously assumed were true. Because she had found her safety behaviours to be unsafe (4), and her internal focus had made matters worse rather than better (6), she was now routinely experimenting with focusing outwards and dropping her safety behaviours outside of the sessions.

With regard to the formulation, she was now wondering about her long-standing assumption that 'If I put myself forward others will see through me and reject me'. As a result of the experiments so far, this was already beginning to feel less absolute and Ailsa was curious to find out more about this. She was keen not to relapse and as she had worked well in therapy so far, another six sessions were agreed to experiment further with this assumption.

How might Ailsa be encouraged to test her assumption within the therapy session itself, and why might this be beneficial?

The 'if . . . then . . .' nature of assumptions makes them ideal for testing by means of behavioural experiments. Ailsa's old assumption had already been undermined by her experiments so it was now time to start building her belief in a new, more helpful assumption. The therapist therefore encouraged her to devise an alternative, more flexible and therefore more functional assumption to test and eventually adopt (Bennett-Levy *et al.* 2004). Ailsa tentatively suggested the alternative 'if I put myself forward others are unlikely to judge me harshly and may enjoy what I have to offer'. Although she thought this assumption sounded possible, she only rated her strength of belief in it as 40% at this stage.

To test and potentially build confidence in the new assumption, Ailsa decided she wanted to give the next presentation that was due at work in a week's time. A benefit of doing this at short notice was that she would not have too long to (over)prepare and thus develop unnecessary anticipatory anxiety.

The therapist considered this was the appropriate stage in therapy for Ailsa to be experimenting with the actual presentation but used her creativity and resourcefulness to suggest that Ailsa might want to experiment with a trial run of presenting the information within the session in front of a small audience, suggesting that if she wanted to spend 10 minutes or so preparing something brief to present on the same topic, she, the therapist, would muster up three or four other people (two receptionists and two colleagues) who could be Ailsa's audience for the 10-minute presentation. They could record the presentation as before to provide objective feedback about the new assumption for Ailsa (James et al. 2001).

Based on the previous experiments, Ailsa thought this would be a good idea, but worried that the subject of pensions would be boring and that the audience would see she was inadequate and perhaps talk about her afterwards together (negatively). She would then have to face the humiliation of seeing them on reception each week.

The therapist pointed out to Ailsa how fears related to her old assumption were creeping back in as the possibility of it being proved true suddenly felt imminent. She normalised this experience and pointed out how Ailsa would now be prepared if this happened again on the actual day. She reminded Ailsa of her new assumption, 'if I put myself forward others are unlikely to judge me harshly and may enjoy what I have to offer', which she said was helpful.

In her (limited) preparation for the presentation, Ailsa jotted an agenda on the whiteboard (much as the therapist did each week for their sessions) and made a few bullet-point notes under each item as prompts, but apart from this made no further preparation as she was already quite familiar with what she needed to present.

She wrote out a cue card to refer to with the new assumption written on one side and on the reverse were reminders to look up, speak up, slow down, and focus on the audience.

Ailsa presented the information on pensions clearly and enthusiastically. She dropped her safety behaviours and went slowly, making sure that all in the audience were following, and used the whiteboard to demonstrate sources of income that could still be liable for tax once a person was receiving a pension. After the presentation she asked if anyone had questions, and was surprised when the questions went on longer than the presentation.

Once the audience had gone they reviewed the recording together; the results of the experiment clearly supported Ailsa's new assumption. Despite the slightly odd arrangement for the presentation, all five people in the audience fed back to Ailsa that they had found it useful. Two people were approaching retirement age, another was considering taking out a personal pension, and the other two had parents on a pension, so everyone had found the topic relevant and interesting. They had wanted to 'pick her brains' afterwards, viewing her as an expert they would not normally have access to.

Ailsa re-rated her strength of belief in the new assumption now at 75%, and was encouraged to write the outcome of the experience in a **'positive data log'** which would help to correct the self-prejudiced unhelpful thinking habits she had formed until now (Padesky 1994).

A follow-up session was arranged after the actual presentation, and Ailsa reported that things had gone better than expected. Being prepared for her old assumption to become triggered as the presentation approached had been really helpful as it meant she was not taken by surprise. The presentation had not been recorded, which made it hard for Ailsa to resist mulling it over afterwards in her head and she decided to postpone this until the next therapy session where they could 'unpack' things more constructively. She received positive feedback from both her peers and her line manager, and added all this information to her ongoing positive data log.

The remaining sessions were spent devising and undertaking more behavioural experiments to build Ailsa's strength of belief in her new assumption, and finally completing a 'continued improvement plan' to enable her to take therapy forward independently (see Table 7.2).

Table 7.2 Continued improvement plan

What have you learned from these sessions?	How to learn by using experiments to test out what I had previously taken for granted about myself. To focus externally in social situations. That doing the opposite of my safety behaviours is actually safer for me and more productive socially. That people seem less likely to reject me than I thought.
What strategies have you found most helpful?	Noticing and correcting thinking biases, including emotional reasoning and jumping to conclusions. Switching to an external focus so I can pick up on social cues and respond appropriately. Using experiments to test out different behaviours in a logical and methodical manner.
What do you need to do to maintain/extend change?	Continue with being more self-aware and noticing when I'm feeling inclined to revert to old behaviours. I need to be (a) aware and (b) prepared to respond by doing what I don't feel inclined to do in that moment (i.e. drop any safety behaviours).
What might lead to a setback?	If I didn't cope well with a social situation and someone seemed to reject me because of that.
How would you recognise this?	I'd recognise I was having negative images from an observer perspective again. I'd feel embarrassed and ashamed in the first instance. I'd want to hide (probably behind my hair to start with). I'd have a strong urge to leave the situation.
Can you identify skills you have learned, resources, people and agencies that could help manage this setback?	Yes. Instead of leaving I could retreat temporarily to consider what would be best to do next. I would need to focus outwards and do the opposite of my safety behaviours. This could even involve approaching the individual concerned and talking to them about things (if I was very brave). I could refer to the 'continued improvement plan' and decide what to do next. If things really relapsed I could book a 'top-up' therapy session.

Client Name .... Therapist Name .... Date ....

Treatment outcomes

Table 7.3 Liebowitz Social Anxiety Scale (1987)

Date	Fear score	Avoidance score	Combined score
Week 1 Assessment	56/72	54/72	110/144
Week 5	45/72	42/72	87/144
Week 9	32/72	28/72	60/144
Week 15 Final session	26/72	15/72	41/144

Ailsa's score at the start of treatment indicated she had very severe social anxiety; by the end of treatment her score indicated little or no social anxiety. This improvement reflected how hard Ailsa had worked in treatment (see Table 7.3). She had met both her short- and medium-term goals, and planned to complete her longer-term goal independently after formal treatment had ended.

Therapist reflections

Reflecting on the case, the main focus of their work had been on **implicational** rather than **propositional** learning (see Chapter 2; see also Teasdale and Barnard 1993).

Working implicationally with behavioural experiments in session had the advantage of ensuring that the experiments were set up and carried out effectively and that any experiential learning from them was maximised and used to plan, using Kolb's reflective cycle. Adhering to just one main therapeutic strategy gave Ailsa practice and confidence in using behavioural experiments, making it more likely that she would remember and use them independently in the future.

Explicitly and clearly focusing on three main areas in therapy had been helpful. Firstly, the central feature of social anxiety, self-focused attention (6), was targeted. Self-focused attention maintains other features of the problem, including Ailsa's perception of social danger (5), her use of safety behaviours (4) and her symptoms of anxiety.

Like many other people with social anxiety, Ailsa was actually quite socially skilled but came across unnaturally because of the safety behaviours she adopted; therefore the second main focus of therapy had been dropping, and even doing the opposite of, her safety behaviours (Veale 2003; Butler 2008).

The third focus of therapy had involved the anticipatory and post-event processing she engaged in, as this focused on her emotional responses and self-constructed images about the event. These involved the habits of mind-reading, emotional reasoning, catastrophising and selectively attending to negatives.

As Ailsa's social anxiety had been long-standing, the extra sessions to build and test a new central assumption were likely to help prevent later relapse. Ailsa had been well motivated at this point in her life to deal with her social anxiety, and the therapist reflected on how it is often not until people reach a crisis in their lives that they present for therapy.

The therapist also reflected on Ailsa's goals and considered that she might have focused more explicitly on Ailsa's short-term goal to 'raise points and give answers in team meetings without having to repeat herself because of not having been heard properly'. This goal had been achieved in a rather 'random' fashion, and while Ailsa had been pleased when she had done this, unpacking her learning from this more clearly and explicitly might have yielded more learning for her to build on.

Otherwise therapy had progressed relatively smoothly and uneventfully, with Ailsa's work colleagues proving supportive of her endeavours. Had things been more problematic – for example, if Ailsa's work colleagues had challenged her proficiency – it may have been necessary to teach assertiveness skills to help her defend herself against criticism. Looking back, the therapist realised that this omission could potentially lead to a relapse in the future and might be considered a potential weakness of therapy in this case. However, in assertive defence of herself, the therapist reflected that she had not treated this because it had not been a problem at the time (Padesky 1997).

Homework

To gain insight into how difficult social anxiety can be you may wish to watch the film *Little Voice*.

Suggested further reading: http://www.cci.health.wa.gov.au/resources/infopax.cfm?Info_ID=40

Conclusion and consolidation of your learning

To consolidate your learning it would be helpful to reconsider the initial aims set out at the start and reflect here on what you have gained from reading the chapter.

- State the identifying features of social anxiety disorder.

- What problems of engagement are common?

- How might these be managed?

- What is the central feature of social anxiety disorder according to Wells and Clark's (1997) model?

- What other aspects of the disorder does this central feature maintain?

- What three key areas are important to focus on when treating social anxiety disorder?

Feedback

Think about your experience of reading this chapter and note any feedback for the authors here:

At the end of the book you may wish to collate the feedback together to forward to the following address: nick.wrycraft@anglia.ac.uk

8 Obsessive compulsive disorder

Reader's agenda

Take a few moments to consider your own agenda or reasons for reading this chapter and make a note of them here:

-

-

The aim of this case study is to help you:

- Understand the nature of OCD
- Assess someone experiencing OCD and engage them in the process of therapy
- Develop an appropriate formulation
- Understand how therapeutic strategies for OCD might be employed to good effect.

Managing your time

Take a moment to consider how long you plan to spend reading this chapter, and make a note here:

There will be a reminder later in the chapter to check whether you have kept track with this.

Please consider how long you have to invest in reading this chapter and make a note of your intended timeframe here:

Introduction

Obsessive compuksive disorder (OCD) is a complex disorder with many variations which can make it difficult to understand and to treat. The many types of OCD include checking, washing and cleaning, ordering and the need for symmetry, 'pure' obsessions with distressing aggressive or sexual thoughts, as well as scrupulosity OCD with concerns about moral and religious rectitude (Hyman and Pedrick 1999).

Presentations can involve more than one type of OCD and, to complicate things further, **obsessions** and **compulsions** can change during the course of therapy, with one type of compulsive behaviour quickly being replaced by another. Regardless of the type of OCD, the principle on which sufferers invariably operate is one of 'better safe than sorry', leading to excessive efforts to make certain of things (Veale and Willson 2005).

OCD tends to be a chronic and disabling condition, and sufferers often come for treatment only after many years of debilitating symptoms, which become normalised as a way of life over long periods of time. Family members are frequently drawn into the OCD way of life by providing excessive reassurance or by engaging in extreme or odd behaviours themselves to relieve the anxiety of their loved one. Indeed, it is often only when a partner refuses to participate in the OCD rituals any longer, or they threaten to leave, that the sufferer eventually acknowledges there is a problem and comes for treatment. It can be helpful, with client consent, to invite relatives in or to provide them with some written information, so they are aware of how to support the person without inadvertently contributing to the problem (Veale and Willson 2005).

OCD also tends to overlap with other problems, including low self-esteem and depression, generalised anxiety disorder and perfectionism; over time it can even become an entrenched part of a person's personality. In order to avoid the potential for confusion and to make clear the basic principles of treatment, this chapter presents a relatively straightforward case of checking OCD. Chapter 9 builds on the complexity of OCD by introducing further aspects of the disorder and the treatment of it.

Exercise

List five factors that can make OCD a difficult disorder to understand and treat.

1

2

3

Background

Gail is a 36-year-old single mother who has suffered from OCD since her mid-teens. The OCD involves obsessional thoughts about safety, followed by a strong desire to compulsively check to make sure that everything is completely secure before she goes to bed or leaves the house; she has noticed that the problem gets worse when she is under stress.

Recently her compulsive checking has increased to the point that she is making the children late for school by up to an hour, resulting in a complaint from the children's head teacher. Gail is conscientious about her children's education and was therefore very upset about the complaint, which increased her stress levels and OCD symptoms still further. As a result, the school head suggested she should see her GP, who referred Gail for a CBT assessment, as recommended by the NICE (2005) guidelines.

> **DSM-IV-TR criteria for OCD**
>
> According to the American Psychiatric Association (2000), the criteria for OCD include:
>
> - The presence of either obsessions or compulsions.
> - At some point during the course of the disorder the person has recognised that the obsessions or compulsions are excessive or unreasonable.
> - The obsessions or compulsions cause marked distress, are time-consuming (take more than 1 hour a day), or significantly interfere with the person's normal routine, occupation or functioning.

Assessment and engagement

Because of the relatively straightforward nature of Gail's case, it was assigned to a second-year student therapist called Tom, who was being closely supervised. Although this was Tom's first experience of treating OCD, he had sat in on treatment sessions with a more experienced therapist before and therefore had some 'real-world' understanding of the nature of OCD and how to apply relevant therapeutic strategies.

What is important in the assessment and engagement of someone with OCD and which might be particularly relevant in Gail's case?

Impact of the disorder

At initial assessment Gail was asked about the impact of the OCD on her life. She described the main impact on the children, getting them to school on time because of her obsession with safety and the need to compulsively keep checking that the windows, gas, plugs and doors were all completely safe every time she left the house. She would repeat this routine again before going to bed at night, which could take up to an hour and a half, often leaving her tired the next day.

Initially Gail did not disclose the impact that her reluctance to turn on the gas was having on the family diet. She would only turn on the gas hob once a day as it provoked anxiety and because of the time her rituals took to turn it off 'properly'. Tom found it curious that Gail did not mind having the boiler on, despite it having a pilot light; Gail explained this was because she was not responsible to turn it on or off, which at least meant the family had hot water and could keep warm.

Gail found the TV plug particularly anxiety-provoking and only switched on the TV at weekends. For recreation the family played games together during the week, which the children enjoyed and which seemed to impact favourably on their school work, which was generally above average.

Details about the disorder

Tom's supervisor explained how the well-known saying 'The devil's in the detail' is particularly true with regard to OCD, and how the specific details necessary to treat the problem can be difficult to elicit because the sufferer is so normalised to what is happening that they may no longer notice. To complicate matters, sufferers tend to be over-inclusive when describing their problems because of their need to make certain that the therapist has understood everything perfectly, but unfortunately the details they provide are often not the most relevant ones (Veale and Willson 2005).

Tom had noticed this when observing other therapists assessing OCD clients and how sometimes it seemed best just to just let them 'tell their story' in assessment if it seemed they needed to. This made sense to Tom as people with OCD have often suffered in silence and this might be their first opportunity to speak about the difficulty in years.

It was agreed for Tom to complete the assessment over two sessions to allow him adequate time. The supervisor explained how using closed questions might be helpful to slow things down at times and elicit the relevant information.

The relevant information that Tom gathered included:

- Triggers to the problem (leaving the house or car and going to bed at night).
- Deficits and excesses in behaviour (avoiding going out, postponing going to bed, avoiding turning on the gas or electrical appliances, checking between three and six times per plug until it 'feels right', which could take up to 10 minutes for each appliance, returning to check again, and constantly asking her children for reassurance that she had secured things properly).
- How Gail went about her checking behaviour. (Gail found this difficult to explain, so Tom asked her to demonstrate using his windows, plugs and door.

It took almost 5 minutes for her to demonstrate the door alone. At this point Gail mentioned how, ironically, her door handle at home had begun to work loose because of all her tugging on it to make sure it was safe. Interestingly, Gail does not experience obsessions and compulsions about other people's property as she does not feel responsible for it.)
- What it was that Gail was trying to prevent by employing the checking behaviour. (Again, Gail initially found this difficult to say, so Tom asked if she had any 'images in her mind's eye' of what she thought might happen if she did not check. This provoked mental images of the house burning to the ground and her getting the blame for it, and of returning home to find that burglars had 'trashed everything' and it being all her fault.)

Normalising the problem

As Gail demonstrated her checking rituals to Tom, she commented on how stupid she felt about having to do all this 'palaver', and about the impact it was having on everyone's lives. She also felt ashamed telling Tom that she only cooked for the children once a day, fearing he would think she could not care for them properly and that he would report her to Social Services to have the children taken away.

Tom explained compassionately and non-judgementally that this type of concern was 'normal for people with OCD', and how keeping the family together was paramount; he stressed that they would take their time and work together in therapy to improve the situation. Gail fed back how Tom's compassionate tone and accepting manner would help her to be open and honest in therapy.

Following this discussion, Tom took a family history in which it became clear that Gail's mother also had OCD symptoms of checking. Rates of OCD are increased among first-degree relatives (Billett et al. 1998), and as a child Gail felt responsible for helping to prevent bad things from happening by ritualising for her mother and stopping her becoming overly anxious. Again, Tom 'normalised' Gail's current problem in the context of her family history, explaining that it was understandable she was having these difficulties in these circumstances.

Involvement of others

OCD can be demanding on family members, who often respond by colluding with the individual concerned, participating in OCD rituals rather than face the upset it will cause if they refuse. Gail's children were clearly involved in reassuring Gail that she had checked things properly, and at times they would check for Gail.

Risk

Tom's supervisor pointed out the importance of minimising any risk to either Gail or her children, which could be as a result of their education being compromised. Although the children's head teacher was aware of the situation, Gail said she would inform her that she was now having a course of therapy for her OCD.

During assessment Tom enquired more generally about the impact of Gail's checking on the children's welfare and found that both children were involved in making sure that everything was safe before leaving in the morning and considered the hour-long checking routine to be 'normal'. As OCD can be a learned behaviour it is often passed down through generations; because Gail's children were already taking responsibility for reducing her anxiety, Tom discussed his concerns about them with his supervisor (Veale and Willson 2005).

Gail was cooperative about treatment and keen to make changes, so it was decided not to involve Child and Adolescent Services, although this remained an option if the children had problems once Gail's OCD was successfully treated. Tom was glad to discuss this with his supervisor as he was anxious not to overlook anything important, especially where children were concerned.

Another area of risk that Tom's supervisor raised was the potential for Gail to drop out of treatment. People with OCD often experience extreme anxiety about having to face their fears, and unless treatment is approached gently, going at the client's own pace and ensuring a safe environment in therapy, there can be a significant risk of drop-out. As it had taken Gail years to approach services and children were involved, it was particularly important to build a strong therapeutic alliance with Gail so she could engage well with the process of therapy from the outset. Therefore, Tom agreed to take two sessions for the initial assessment to allow enough time to develop his understanding of the problem from Gail's point of view.

Another potential area of risk that Tom enquired about was depression, which is common in OCD sufferers. While Gail was frustrated with the OCD and cross with herself for getting the children to school so late, she was not particularly depressed and said she had a lot of enjoyable things in her life, including caring for her children and looking after her elderly mother, which brought her satisfaction. Had Gail been severely depressed or suicidal, Tom would have focused on raising her mood before treating the OCD.

Motivation
As is true in Gail's case, therapy for OCD is often initiated following complaints from someone else, rather than being entered into willingly by the person themself. This makes assessment of motivation an important consideration, and Tom thought about using a cost–benefit analysis to enhance Gail's motivation and to see if she was ready to make changes. This would involve listing both the short- and long-term advantages and disadvantages for Gail and her children if she (a) addressed or (b) did not address the problem now. However, Tom found this unnecessary as Gail clearly wanted to sort the problem out before it impacted any further on her children; she was ready and motivated to make changes, despite her fear of what therapy might involve. Tom made sure that it was a good time for Gail to start treatment and that she was not overcommitted in other areas of her life and could prioritise treatment over the next 2–3 months.

Gail could remember life before the OCD started, around the age of 9 or 10, and how she had not been worried very much at all about safety then. In fact, looking back, she thought she must have been quite complacent, but concluded it was because her mother had been responsible for the checking at that time. Nevertheless, the memory helped her to see that life without OCD was possible, which further helped to motivate her.

Measurement
Gail could not identify any other areas in which the OCD affected her. However, in order to measure treatment outcomes and because OCD behaviour can become so normalised, Tom asked her to complete the Revised Obsessive-Compulsive Inventory (Foa *et al.* 2002). While this is not a diagnostic tool, it is a **validated measure** and can

help to assess a range of areas in which OCD might be problematic. Gail scored highly on checking and 'a little' on ordering, but as ordering was not bothering her and her score was low it was decided to focus on the checking. They agreed to repeat the measure at monthly intervals throughout treatment.

Realistic goals

Gail was clear about her goals for treatment, which were:

1. To get the children to school by 8:50 a.m. each day. This would involve getting up at 7:00, undertaking all the necessary chores, locking up and checking *just once* that the house was secure and then leaving promptly at 8:30. Her goal included not going back to check when she started to doubt if she had done things properly.
2. To get to bed regularly at 10:30 p.m. after securing things *just once*.

Tom thought these goals might be achievable within 3 months, although it was agreed there was scope to adjust the timescale as things progressed.

> List and summarise the eight points mentioned here that are important to consider when assessing and engaging someone in the process of therapy for OCD:
>
> 1
>
> 2
>
> 3
>
> 4
>
> 5
>
> 6

Case formulation

What is maintaining Gail's OCD and how might you formulate this to make sense of the problem?

Between them, Gail and Tom **formulated** the difficulty adapting a traditional 'fear and avoidance' model to include obsessive thoughts and images (Figure 8.1).

The triggers (1) to Gail's checking behaviour were leaving the house or car unattended and going to bed at night. This would trigger obsessive 'what if . . .' thoughts (2) about the various catastrophes that might happen if she did not secure things properly, and how she would be held responsible and would not be able to cope. These catastrophic thoughts produced vivid pictures in her mind's eye of her worst fears coming true. These thoughts and images produced strong feelings of fear and anxiety (3) from which Gail reasoned (4) that if she felt anxious, there must be something to be anxious about. This in turn reinforced her obsessive thinking (2). In further response to her fear and anxiety (3), Gail felt compelled to engage in numerous checking behaviours (5) to make sure that her oven, hob, plugs and appliances, windows and doors were all safe and secure. If for any reason she could not check she could sometimes 'block' her feelings which enabled her to get on with things. This checking and blocking reduced her anxiety in the short term (6), **negatively reinforcing** the problem. However, in the medium and longer term (7) more doubts and uncertainty would arise about whether she had checked properly, leading back to more anxiety (3) and the desire to reduce this by (5) more checking behaviours. The long-term consequence (7) of constantly repeating this cycle was to reinforce Gail's need to respond in the same way to triggers in the future (7 back to 1). Her repeated checking behaviour prevented her from learning that the house would not burn down or be burgled if she did not repeatedly check, as well as from gaining confidence to manage things without the OCD behaviour.

Gail found the links between each part of the formulation revealing and could see clearly how treatment was going to involve dropping the behaviours that she had been relying on to make herself feel safe.

Obsessive compulsive disorder

1. Trigger/stimulus:
Leaving the house or car
Going to bed at night

2. Obsessive thoughts:
'What if there's a fire...?'
'What if there's a burglary...?'
'It will be my fault.'
Images of the house burning down/being trashed and of the car being stolen and being unable to cope.

3. Feelings:
Fear and anxiety

4. Emotional reasoning:
If I feel anxious, there must be something to be anxious about...

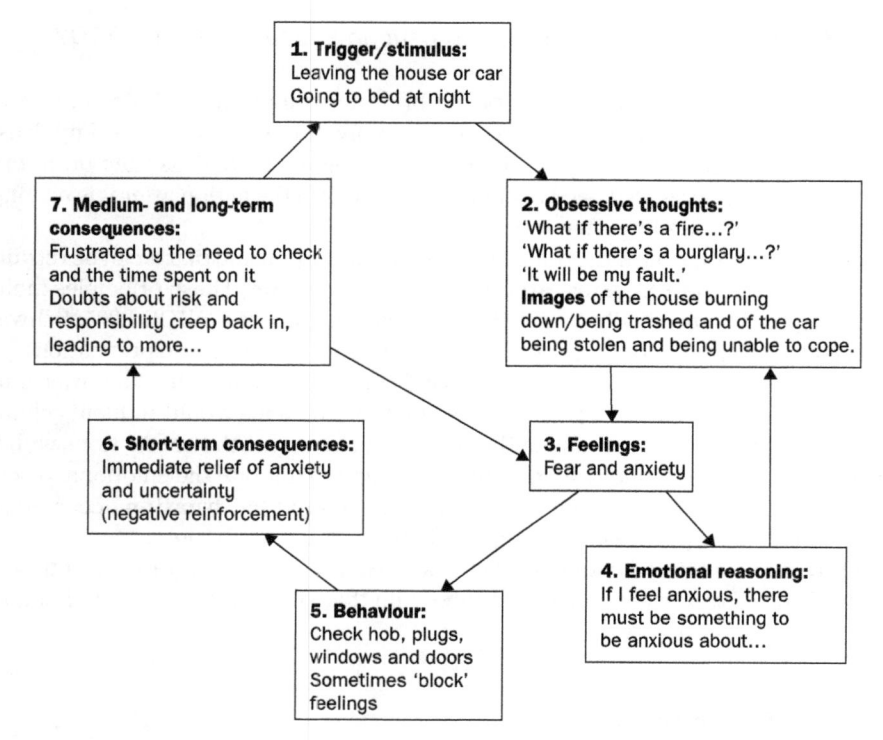

5. Behaviour:
Check hob, plugs, windows and doors
Sometimes 'block' feelings

6. Short-term consequences:
Immediate relief of anxiety and uncertainty
(negative reinforcement)

7. Medium- and long-term consequences:
Frustrated by the need to check and the time spent on it
Doubts about risk and responsibility creep back in, leading to more...

Figure 8.1 Formulation

Summary

OCD is negatively reinforced by behaviours which reduce anxiety and distress in the short term. Emotional reasoning often plays a part in the problem, with compulsive behaviour being repeated until things 'feel right' to the individual.

Check-in

At the start of the chapter you were asked to think about the time you had available for reading this chapter. As this is mid-point in the chapter it is a good place to consider how you are doing in relation to your original plan.

Are you on track? If your original timing no longer looks realistic you may wish to consider adjusting things here. Make a note to help you keep on track.

What information might you include in psycho-education about OCD?

Tom explained to Gail how a region of the brain including the orbitofrontal cortex, thalamus and caudate nucleus appears to be involved in OCD and how impulses to perform a particular action do not diminish in people with OCD as they do in other people. Hence, the perceived need to continue to perform the action after it is no longer necessary to do so (see http://www.ocduk.org).

Tom also explained how the brain is a very flexible organ and that it can be retrained using the principles of **exposure and response prevention**. These principles include overcoming fear by gradually facing the thing causing anxiety (NICE 2005; Schwartz 1996; see also Chapter 2 for an explanation of exposure and response prevention).

Tom noted that in the session logically Gail could see that her checking was unnecessary but when she was trying to leave the house her feelings would suddenly change, overwhelming any logic. The task in therapy would be to match her emotions with her logic within the 'OCD moment' by gradually learning to tolerate the emotional discomfort until it diminished and finally went away altogether as **habituation** occurred (see the discussion of propositional and implicational learning in Chapter 2).

Before commencing treatment, Tom asked Gail if she had any further questions about OCD or its treatment, and she assured him that she would ask if she thought of any as treatment progressed.

Treatment interventions

In order to enhance Gail's sense of safety and keep her engaged in therapy, where might Tom start?

For homework between the two assessment sessions Tom asked Gail to buy a notebook in which to record things that she did in therapy as well as any activity between sessions. To start with, her homework was to monitor and gather data about the problem and to record this in the notebook. The data she was asked to record included (1) triggers, (2) ratings of how strong the urge was on a 1–10 scale (with 10 being high) before, during and after each time she checked, as well as (3) how quickly she responded to the urges, (4) what happened if she was prevented from responding to the urges and (5) how she managed this. He also asked her to record the same information with regard to her reassurance-seeking behaviour.

Although there was a lot of information to collect, Gail was aware that just recording data was unlikely to provoke much anxiety and joked that Tom might be trying to lull her into a false sense of security with this first homework assignment. Tom smiled at this and just nodded. This gentle use of humour suggested that a good therapeutic relationship was starting to develop between them (James *et al.* 2001).

The relatively non-threatening and simple nature of this first homework assignment was designed to engage Gail in treatment by increasing her curiosity about the checking behaviour and to help her to 'stand back' from it rather than get bogged down in it, as she normally did. The data would be used as a basis for developing a hierarchy of difficult situations to work with later on in treatment.

How can working with a hierarchy of feared situations reduce anxiety for both client and therapist?

From the data gathered (see Figure 8.2) they explored the things that made Gail very anxious and the things she coped with better. Tom's supervisor suggested they work

Date	Friday 02.11.12					
Trigger	1. Bedtime	2. Thinking about leaving the house	3. Shutting the door	4. Locking the car	5. Leaving to collect the children	6. Bedtime
Urge pre %	90%	80%	100%	100%	70% but blocked it	90%
Urge mid	50%	70%	Made it stop	Arguing with myself 70%	0%	90%
Urge post	0% (but rises again with 'what if' doubts)	80% (fluctuates until I actually go)	0%	30% then 75% when doubt thoughts came back	60–70% Thought returned as I walked away, couldn't keep blocking	20% then 90% again
Response speed	1 min	1 min	Immediate	Immediate at first then couldn't go back so immediately asked for reassurance	Didn't respond	1–2 min
Prevented?	No	No	Yes, I needed to get the kids to school	Not at first but post I didn't have time to go back and check again	Yes. *Had* to collect the girls on time	No
How I managed	N/A	Keep checking	Just told myself to do it. Didn't think, blocked it all out	Asked the girls for reassurance	Reassured myself it would be OK, we'd be back in 10 minutes, but anxious all the time and we ran back	Urge returned so I checked twice more

Figure 8.2 Gail's homework (one typical day out of the seven she completed)

with this information to build a hierarchy of feared situations in order of difficulty to work with in treatment (see Box 8.1; see also Hyman and Pedrick 1999). Having an ordered list that Gail had designed herself helped with treatment collaboration and allayed her fears of what would be asked of her next, as things were planned in advance.

Box 8.1 Gail's hierarchy of feared situations

Key: *10 = most feared situation,*
1 = least feared situation
(Number in brackets = estimated distress level)

10   Locking the door when I'm going to be out for a long time (100%)
9   Checking the appliances just before leaving the house if I'm going to be out for a long time (95–100%)
8   Checking the gas hob after I've cooked (95–100%)
7   Going to bed at night (90–95%)
6   Locking the car door when I'm going to be leaving it for a long time (90%)
5   Locking the front door when I know I'll be returning soon (80–90%)
4   Checking appliances and plugs when I know I'll be returning soon (70–90%)
3   Locking the car door when I know I'll be returning soon (60–80%)
2   Not having anyone to reassure me (increases anxiety in all cases by up to 10–20%)
1   Putting appliances on/off if I'm in on my own (50%)

Engagement in therapy can be enhanced by developing a safe environment in which the client knows and has agreed to what is going to happen next.

What are the benefits of working 'in-vivo' with the client and what might stand in the way of this?

Tom's supervisor was keen for Gail to make early gains in therapy as this would increase her confidence in CBT and enhance her engagement. The supervisor also knew that early gains would do the same for Tom, boosting his confidence in both CBT as a treatment for OCD and in his ability to deliver it effectively. Therefore she suggested that this case would be a good opportunity for him to gain some experience of using ***in vivo*** work for OCD, suggesting that as Gail came for treatment in her car, later on they might consider practising unlocking and locking the car in the car park and then leaving it to go back to the therapy room without checking or giving reassurance, thus practising exposure and response prevention together within the session.

This suggestion concerned Tom as he was not sure just how anxious Gail might get or how he would manage if she panicked; in fact, he had a picture in his mind of Gail shaking and crying and of him standing by feeling responsible for her distress and not knowing how on earth to react. Initially he did not mention his concerns for fear of looking inadequate as a student therapist. However, knowing that he usually learned a lot from his supervisor's ideas, he would likely raise the suggestion again at a future meeting.

In the next therapy session Tom and Gail worked together to devise an exposure task for Gail to do at home, involving her turning the kettle on and off without checking (number 1 on her hierarchy). She would measure her distress level on a chart at five-minute intervals to measure how long it took to reduce (see Figure 8.3).

Following this session, Tom returned to supervision with a question about what to do next. The supervisor suggested that Tom might introduce a cognitive element to the exposure work by including hypothesis testing. This would involve Gail testing her original fear, 'if I don't check the kettle something dreadful will happen' (hypothesis A), against an alternative, 'if I don't check the kettle *I will become really anxious that something dreadful will happen*' (hypothesis B).

This hypothesis testing would strengthen their exposure and response prevention work by providing an alternative, more helpful, cognitive explanation for Gail's distress which she would not otherwise be able to come up with in the situation (Bennett-Levy et al. 2004).

Following this, the supervisor again mentioned the idea of the *in vivo* work as the next exposure task on Gail's hierarchy (number 3). This time Tom was prepared to discuss his concern and they decided that the best way for Tom to learn how to manage his feared situation would be to role-play it with the supervisor.

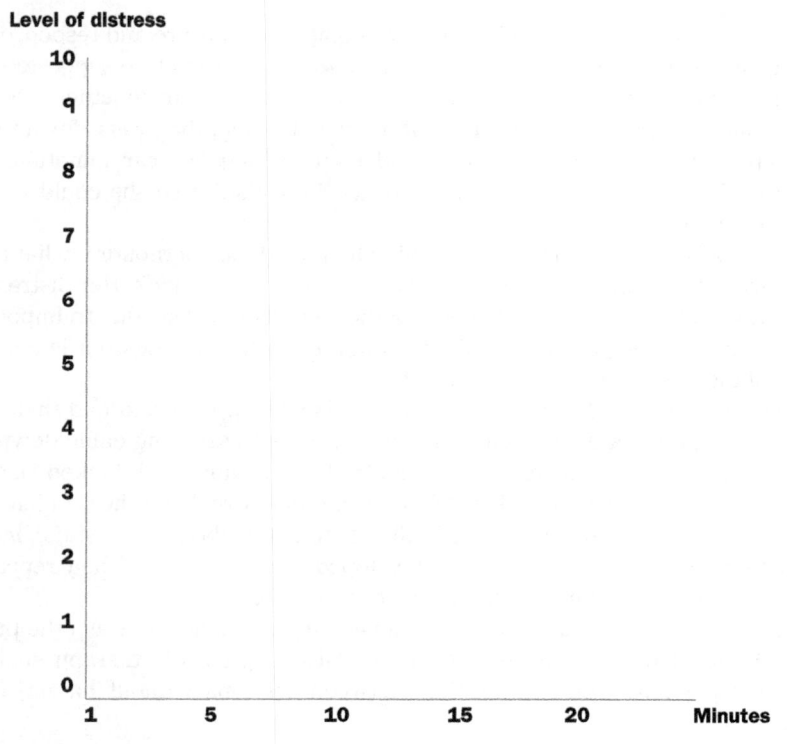

Figure 8.3 Gail's distress level chart

Firstly, they agreed to role-play Tom's feared situation *in vivo* using Tom's car outside. In the role play the supervisor (acting as therapist) asked Tom (as Gail) to lock the car door and walk away without checking straight off. Tom role-played his worst-case scenario of Gail becoming highly distressed, shaking and crying. The supervisor (as therapist) responded to this by gently suggesting to 'Gail' that this exercise had been too difficult and that if she wanted to, she could return and check and they would approach things much more slowly next time. As Tom (role-playing Gail) returned to check, he could imagine her distress levels subsiding and how this would reduce his own fear about managing the situation.

From this role play Tom learned that the exposure exercise needed to be sensitively planned and carried out and that if distress levels did rise too far they could be managed by 'backtracking' and approaching things more cautiously.

The supervisor noted how the use of safety behaviours is not unique to clients and how Tom's catastrophic fear had resulted in him avoiding the *in vivo* exposure exercise in order to keep himself 'safe'. Tom found the role play empowering in helping him to overcome his catastrophic fear about Gail's potential level of distress, as well as his own feelings of inadequacy about being unable to cope if the worst happened. Tom found the therapist's modelling of a calm approach was helpful.

The following week Gail returned to therapy having turned the kettle on and off easily without checking (hierarchy item number 2). On investigation Tom found that she had managed by exchanging one safety behaviour (checking) for another (blocking her emotions).

Gail explained that she would be happier doing the exposure and response prevention with someone else around, at least to start with. Tom therefore suggested moving to hierarchy item number 3, unlocking and locking her car together, which Gail thought would be very helpful. After collaborative planning, they went down to the car park where Gail started by unlocking and then locking her car mindfully, paying attention to the sight and sound of the door as she locked it so she could visualise it clearly in her mind.

This visualisation was helpful to recall when the doubtful thought 'what if it's *not* locked?' arose the moment she turned away and wanted to check. Her distress rating rose to a tolerable 60% and Tom asked whether the distress was due to hypothesis A, 'the door is not locked', or hypothesis B, 'I am *really anxious* the door is not locked', Gail thought it was probably hypothesis B.

After standing with her back to the door visualising it locked and then walking away and standing at a distance for 5 minutes, her distress rating came down to 50%. During this time Gail kept asking Tom 'is it alright?' (meaning 'is it locked?'), to which Tom only once responded 'yes, it's OK', before quickly realising he'd fallen into her 'reassurance-seeking trap'. They were both able to laugh about his mistake, indicating a sound therapeutic relationship had developed between them. They repeated the exercise twice more until her rating came down to 35%.

This *in vivo* exercise gave Gail confidence by helping her to grasp the principles of what she needed to do and how to do it. This early gain in therapy enabled her to work independently on the problem between sessions without having to block her emotions.

> **Summary**
>
> Working *in vivo* can promote early gains in therapy, providing confidence for the client that they have 'got it right', as well as highlighting any subtle safety behaviours (client or therapist!).
>
> Hypothesis testing introduces a cognitive element, providing a reasonable alternative explanation to consider.

How might therapy progress, and what are the benefits of consistently using the same therapeutic strategies throughout treatment?

Staying with exposure and response prevention and hypothesis testing as the main therapeutic strategies helped Gail to grow in confidence that she could use them independently of Tom and that they worked.

In the next session they repeated the exposure and response prevention exercise in the car park with Tom standing further and further away from the car until Gail could eventually lock the car on her own without checking and return to the therapy session for the final 20 minutes and tolerate her anxiety level. She learned that the less she checked, the less she felt the urge to check. The car was always locked on her return, which strongly supported hypothesis B.

The next ten sessions were spent continuing methodically with exposure and response prevention and hypothesis testing in various situations on the hierarchy. Between sessions Gail worked on reducing her checking and reassurance-seeking behaviour at home. The girls enjoyed helping by noting down her anxiety levels and by refusing to offer reassurance or join in the checking, which they made a game of with Gail. They enjoyed being allies against the OCD with their mum and liked getting to school on time as well as Gail's reducing stress levels (Veale and Willson 2005).

The final sessions of treatment were spaced fortnightly and then monthly. By session 16 Gail had managed to achieve all of her goals, although she was still not confident leaving the house for long periods, and planned to continue working on this independently over the next few weeks.

The final session before follow-up was used to develop a blueprint or continued improvement plan (Beck 1995; see Table 8.1). This was based on Gail's learning from CBT so far and could be used to refer to over the following weeks and months. She marked fortnightly 'self-therapy time' in her diary for the next 3 months, when she would take half an hour to reflect on how things were going and what she needed to do to take things forward. Having a plan gave her confidence that she could cope without Tom's input until the follow-up session in 3 months' time.

The supervisor suggested having a three-month follow-up. Tom worried that treatment might not have worked properly and that by follow-up the OCD would have returned; the follow-up therefore provided an opportunity for a behavioural experiment to test Tom's anxious prediction.

Table 8.1 Gail's continued improvement plan

What have you learned from these sessions?	To test whether scary things are actually going to happen or whether I am just afraid they are going to happen.
	To do things gradually so I can manage without having to block my feelings.
	Not to check or ask for reassurance because it only increases my uncertainty.
What strategies have you found most helpful?	Hypothesis testing.
	Exposure and response prevention – don't check – stay with the uncomfortable feeling until it dies down. If I need to, I can do this with someone else around at first.
What do you need to do to maintain/extend change?	Plan in my diary for fortnightly self-help therapy sessions to make sure I'm still on track.
	Three times a week for 2 weeks I'm going to leave the house without checking and stay out for at least 2 hours. After that, make sure I keep this up at least once a week.
What might lead to a setback?	If I get really stressed I might start to check again or to block my feelings. I might just forget and slip back into old ways.
How would you recognise this?	I would start checking again. The girls would probably notice and tell me I'm asking for reassurance again.
	Everything would take a lot longer because of this.
Can you identify skills you have learned, resources, or people that could help you manage this set back?	I have my notebook of what we did in therapy to refer to. The girls know and could remind me not to ask for reassurance.
	Don't check!
	I have a follow-up session in 3 months that I could bring forward if necessary.

Client Name .... Therapist Name .... Date ....

How might Tom manage if Gail does have a setback and his feared outcome happens?

At follow-up Gail explained how, a week before, her purse had been stolen while out shopping. She had subsequently started regularly checking that her new purse was safe, which involved new OCD rituals.

Tom was not sure how to handle this setback at first, but decided to use Kolb's learning cycle (see Chapter 1) in conjunction with her continued improvement plan to reflect together on how she had coped with the situation. Gail said she had been surprised at how well she coped, logically thinking through who to contact, cancelling her store and debit cards in methodical order. She did not think it had been her fault, as her bag had been zipped up and as safe as could be in the circumstances. No one had blamed her either; even her mother had been sympathetic and bought her a new purse.

Reflecting now with Tom, she saw her return to checking like an old habit returning, and recalled how much better life had been since she had stopped checking. They used the session to look through Gail's therapy notebook, starting with her original motivation to change, through her hierarchy and anxiety ratings at each step of the way. From this she devised a new hypothesis to test in her current situation: 'my purse will be stolen again if I don't keep checking' (hypothesis A), against 'I'm really anxious my purse will be stolen again if I don't keep checking, but it's only happened once in all of my life, so it's not probable if I take reasonable care in the first place' (hypothesis B).

By the end of the session Gail was confident that she could take things forward independently. On reflection, she considered having her purse stolen had been helpful for the OCD as it had tested her coping ability in a difficult situation and she had managed well. At the end of the follow-up it was agreed that Gail could contact Tom again within the next 2 months if she needed to; after that her file would be closed.

Exercise

Briefly explain how consistently using the same treatment principles throughout therapy helps the client if they have a setback.

Treatment outcomes

Gail's final rating on the Obsessive-Compulsive Inventory (Foa et al. 2002) indicated measurable success (see Table 8.2). She no longer checked things more than once or

Table 8.2 Gail's scores on the Revised Obsessive-Compulsive Inventory (Foa et al. 2002)

Date	Washing	Obsessing	Hoarding	Ordering	Checking	Neutralising
01.11.12	0	1	0	6	12	0
29.11.13	0	1	0	6	12	0
03.01.13	0	1	0	6	9	0
31.01.13	0	1	0	6	6	0
14.03.13	0	0	0	4	3	0
11.04.13	0	0	0	2	0	0

obsessed about things, and although she still liked order her need for this had lessened as her stress levels reduced.

Gail had achieved all of her therapy goals, although she remained quite anxious about leaving home for extended periods. Despite her recent setback she had a plan to take things forward over the next few months and felt more confident about handling setbacks now.

Reflection on the case

On completion of therapy, Tom and his supervisor took time to reflect on the case in depth. One of Tom's personal experiments as a student had been the follow-up session, which tested his predictions about Gail relapsing because therapy had not been adequate. On reflection he recognised his catastrophic thinking, so made a plan to undertake regular thought records until he could spot this thinking habit in the moment and adopt a more reasonable approach. His supervisor agreed to check in with him how this was going from time to time.

Tom had also learned the value of talking about his emotional reactions and fears in supervision, and how helpful this had been to overcome his difficulty with the *in vivo* work. The *in vivo* work had been significant in helping both Tom and Gail to grasp how to go about treatment in the first few weeks and he could see how, if he had not addressed his own problem, Gail would not have made such good progress.

Also he now understood from experience the need to go about exposure and response prevention in a gentle, graded way, by offering to do the exposure exercise with Gail at first, which had enabled her to stay with the situation without 'blocking' emotions or needing to escape.

All in all, both Tom and his supervisor were pleased with his learning and felt he was now ready to take on a more complex case of OCD.

Conclusion and consolidation of your learning

Answer the following questions:

1. What is it about the nature of OCD that can make engagement in therapy difficult for some individuals?

2. Why is engagement in therapy for OCD so important, and what might you do to enhance this?

3   What maintains OCD?

4   What are the main principles of treatment for OCD?

5   What details of the case stand out in your mind?

6   How might you use your learning to take your own practice forward?

7   What questions from your original agenda do you need to explore further?

8   When and how do you plan to do this? (Homework)

Feedback

Think about your experience of reading this chapter and note any feedback for the authors here:

At the end of the book you may wish to collate the feedback together to forward to the following address: nick.wrycraft@anglia.ac.uk

9 Obsessive compulsive disorder – mental compulsions

Reader's agenda

While most people are aware of OCD compulsions such as cleaning and checking, they may be less aware of covert mental compulsions that are equally as debilitating and time-consuming for the individual concerned. Can you think of any compulsive behaviour that might take place *mentally* rather than *physically*? Make a note of your ideas here:

-
-

Bearing in mind the principles of exposure and response prevention (see Chapter 2), make a note of any questions about mental obsessions and compulsions that you hope the chapter will address:

-
-

Take a few moments to consider your own agenda or reasons for reading this chapter and make a note of them here:

-
-

The aim of this case study is to help you to:

- Apply Wells's (1997) cognitive OCD model to a clinical case
- Understand the concept of meta-cognitive thinking and how to work with this in treatment

- Become familiar with the role of thought–action–fusion (TAF) and its connection with magical thinking
- Identify and work with avoidant and neutralising safety behaviours in therapy.

Managing your time

Take a moment to consider how long you plan to spend reading this chapter, and make a note here:

There will be a reminder later in the chapter to check whether you have kept track with this.

Background

Lang-hao is a 27-year-old Chinese mature student who came to England 6 months previously to study engineering. He visited his GP on the advice of his university lecturer, who was becoming increasingly frustrated by Lang-hao's problematic time keeping. Lang-hao had felt obliged to confide some aspects of his problem to the lecturer, who advised him to see his GP. Lang-hao found the doctor's appointment reassuring and agreed to be seen by a student cognitive behavioural therapist called Tom who was connected to the medical practice.

Tom had successfully treated one other person for checking OCD (see Chapter 8). He had no prior experience with mental obsessions and compulsions and no experience of working with people from a Chinese cultural background.

Given that 'empathy and genuineness' are key ingredients of any effective psychotherapy, what might Tom consider prior to assessment of this client?

When discussing the suitability of taking on the case with his supervisor, Tom acknowledged that he knew little about Chinese culture and expressed his fear of coming across as either insensitive or, worse still, patronising. He imagined that Lang-hao would be more familiar with Western culture than he (Tom) was with Chinese culture, and while he did not want to overestimate the potential for misunderstandings, he was also aware that there could be some.

Tom's supervisor thought the case would be particularly suitable for him to take on because of his level of self-awareness, and suggested that he should be open in acknowledging his concerns with Lang-hao, asking him to explain any aspects of Chinese culture that might be relevant as they went along. This openness would likely strengthen the therapeutic alliance, encouraging disclosure of information that might otherwise seem difficult to talk about (James et al. 2001).

In view of his concerns and relative inexperience with treating OCD, Tom decided to take a couple of sessions over the initial assessment so he could take time to understand the problem from Lang-hao's perspective and build rapport.

Why might therapy for mental obsessions and compulsions require a particularly trusting therapeutic relationship, and how might this be facilitated during assessment?

Mental obsessions are **ego-dystonic**, that is, they do not fit with the person's actual desires or personality traits. It is the meaning or sense that the person makes of the obsessive thought – for example, that they are a 'bad' person for having the thought – which is so problematic. This meaning makes it feel shameful or even dangerous for the individual to talk about the thoughts, hence the need to explore them sensitively (Veale and Willson 2005; Northumberland, Tyne and Wear NHS Trust 2013).

At assessment Tom found Lang-Hao's reluctance to describe the details of his problem somewhat frustrating. Lang-hao referred only to having 'bad' thoughts that he had to supress or 'cancel out', but would not talk about the content of these. Tom valiantly (but unhelpfully) tried to explore the content, but eventually had to give up, recognising this **therapeutic impasse** as a problem to take to supervision.

What could Tom do to enable Lang-hao to feel safe enough to explore his frightening thoughts?

Tom started to think negatively about how the therapeutic relationship was going and could not imagine how he would ever be able to do **exposure and response prevention** work with Lang-hao, as he was so afraid to talk about the thoughts and fears that he would need to expose himself to. Rather than make the situation worse, Tom decided not to explore things further at this point and instead to introduce some psycho-education about OCD (Swinson et al. 1998).

Tom started by 'normalising' Lang-hao's experience, explaining that 'odd' or 'unusual' thoughts are quite common among the general population, and how it is the sense or meaning that the person makes of the thought that can be problematic (Northumberland Tyne and Wear NHS Trust 2013). He explained how two people having the same unusual thought might react quite differently to it, and then asked Lang-hao what he thought might account for the difference. Using the ABC model Tom illustrated how (A) the odd thought, could result in (C) feeling OK or perhaps ashamed, depending on (B) the thought the person had in between A and C. He demonstrated it thus:

first person:
(A) 'I could steal that purse' (odd thought)
↓
(B) 'Good job I'm honest' (thought about the thought)
↓
(C) Feel OK/good about self (resulting feelings)

second person:
(A) 'I could steal that purse' (odd thought)
↓
(B) 'That must mean I *want* to steal it' (thought about the thought)
↓
(C) Feel shame/bad about self (resulting feelings)

Discussing the ABC model in relation to someone else's potentially shameful thoughts seemed to take the pressure off of Lang-hao. He followed along attentively, nodding that he understood and commented that drawing things out on paper was helpful (Hawton *et al.* 1989).

Although he still did not mention (A) the content of his original 'bad thought', using the model did allow Lang-hao to talk about (B) his 'thought about his thought', which was 'Having the bad thought means I will do it, I am a bad person'. He also described (C) feeling 'bad-shame' about the type of person this must mean he is.

Tom empathised, but thought better of questioning the content of the original thought (A) again that session, having decided to discuss this in supervision first. He also decided not to explain the principle of exposure and response prevention (ERP) at this point, as the prospect of the treatment could feel overwhelming and Lang-hao may not return if this proved to be the case.

Thought–action–fusion

Thought–action–fusion (TAF) is a common type of cognitive bias in obsessional thinking where thoughts and actions become fused in the persons mind. It can take two forms:

- Probability TAF, in which intrusive thoughts are believed to increase the likelihood of the negative thought actually happening; thus, a thought could cause, or may have already caused, the content of the thought to happen in real life.
- Morality TAF, in which the person believes that having the intrusive thought is morally equivalent to carrying out the prohibited action.

The concept of TAF is closely linked to the idea of **magical thinking**, where a person believes they have special (unwanted) power to influence things negatively.

Both types of TAF involve an exaggerated sense of responsibility. This motivates behavioural or cognitive responses to neutralise the thoughts and thus avoid the considerable feeling of guilt that would otherwise result (Salkovskis and Westbrook 1989; Rachman and Shafran 1999).

Exercise

To illustrate the concept of thought–action–fusion take a few moments to think about the following sentence and then complete the blank space by writing the name of someone you really care about in it. 'I hope that in the next half an hour _____ is involved in a horrible accident and has to be taken to hospital.'

No problem? Many people (but by no means all) find this exercise, and particularly writing it down, somewhat uncomfortable. Understandably, people prefer not to think about bad things happening to people they care about, and may experience an almost 'superstitious' sense that this could be a dangerous thing to do, or that if something actually did happen, then they would be responsible.

Culturally, Lang-hao is unused to discussing his feelings. How might Tom help him explore and identify these?

As Tom continued with the assessment he again found Lang-hao's non-specific replies, this time when discussing his emotions, rather frustrating. For example, Lang-hao often just described feeling 'bad', so Tom asked him to specify what sort of 'bad' he meant; Lang-hao struggled with this and then explained that he was not accustomed to describing his problem aloud or putting his feelings into words, which he found difficult. Tom found this openness helpful and asked if people tended not to talk about their emotions in Chinese culture. Lang-hao said that emotions and mental health problems were not normally discussed, but he wanted to do well in therapy, so would do his best.

To help Lang-hao identify his feelings more accurately, Tom tried naming some alternative emotions for Lang-hao to choose from, at the same time teaching Lang-hao how he could identify feelings by locating them in his body. Lang-Hao picked out feelings in his stomach and abdomen which he picked out as 'guilty-bad' when he had the thoughts, and feelings in his chest and throat which he identified as 'anxious-bad' when he was unable to supress or cancel out the thoughts (Sanders and Wills 2005).

Tom noticed that the therapeutic relationship had started to improve and that they were beginning to make some progress.

How might Tom introduce Lang-hao to the concept of exposure and response prevention?

In supervision Tom asked how he could introduce the concept of ERP to Lang-hao. Rather than answer the question directly, the supervisor first wanted to explore what had happened during the assessment to enable the therapeutic relationship to develop from 'not so good' to 'much better', and whether this had been related to Lang-hao's ability to talk about his **metacognition**, 'thinking this thought means I'll do it, I'm a bad person' (Wells 1997).

Tom explained how the relationship got into difficulty when he kept asking questions about Lang-hao's 'bad thoughts' that he was unable to answer and improved when he switched to talking 'around' the problem in a less direct manner. He also noticed how using someone else's example seemed to normalise things, enabling Lang-hao to open up about his own thinking process. On reflection, he realised that Lang-hao had probably felt safer and more understood at this point, which had allowed him to share scarier aspects of his inner world (Sanders and Wills 2005). The supervisor suggested that Tom should do more talking around the problem, perhaps asking questions like:

'I wonder what makes it so difficult for you to talk about this?'
'What do you fear could happen if you talk about it?'
'What would make it easier?'
'How could I help to make it easier for you?'

The supervisor also suggested that Tom could ask some more **leading questions** which might help to normalise the experience, such as 'Some people with OCD find that . . . / worry that . . . I wonder if you find the same/worry about the same sort of thing?'

Finally, in answer to Tom's question, the supervisor wondered whether Tom might *already be* engaging Lang-hao in the process of exposure and response prevention by gently encouraging him to explore his thoughts and fears about the 'bad thoughts', which was something he would normally avoid. Tom could see that although the principle of ERP had not yet been explained and they had not explicitly planned a hierarchy, Lang-hao was nevertheless beginning to approach his uncomfortable thoughts in a gradual or graded way when he had gently facilitated this.

Following supervision Tom felt more confident and prepared for the second assessment appointment.

Summary

Mental obsessions are generally **ego-dystonic**, that is, contrary to a person's value system. The person may fear what will happen if they talk about the obsessions and may feel embarrassed and ashamed about having them (Veale and Willson 2005). It is therefore helpful to go slowly, normalising things and talking 'around' the problem at first rather than directly asking about the content of the obsessions.

Second assessment session

How might Tom manage his own anxiety about Lang-hao's 'bad' thoughts, and how might his reaction impact on the therapeutic relationship?

Key cognitions are fundamentally associated with emotional distress, so Lang-hao's avoidance of talking about them was understandable. Tom patiently 'talked around' this avoidance in a gradual way, promoting safety for Lang-hao, as rehearsed in supervision. He asked if Lang-hao could say what the thought involved without being too specific, and eventually Lang-hao opened up to Tom that his distressing thoughts and images involved harming other people.

Tom had not been expecting this, as Lang-hao seemed such a gentle person who would be unlikely to have such thoughts. Tom found **automatic**, negative thoughts coming into his own mind:

> 'What if the GP's got it wrong and it's not OCD?'
> 'What if the supervisor's got it wrong as well?'
> 'What if he harms someone?'
> 'What if I get him to think the thoughts and it happens . . . I'll be responsible . . .'
> 'What if he harms me?'

Thus, for a moment, Tom's thoughts started to parallel Lang-hao's (Formica 2009). He managed to maintain his professionalism, acknowledging how difficult it must have been for Lang-hao to talk about this and asking if it was the first time he had ever done so. Lang-hao said he had never mentioned this to anyone before and how it was a relief to tell someone, although he feared that talking about it could increase the likelihood of it actually happening.

Tom thought this would be an appropriate moment to pause things, and asked Lang-hao if he would mind completing an OCD measurement tool, the Revised Obsessive-Compulsive Inventory (Foa *et al.* 2002). This allowed Tom a few minutes to compose his own thoughts and feelings. Because he had recently been using thought records to identify and modify his own **catastrophic all-or-nothing thinking**, Tom had been quick to notice it cropping up again. He was able to think about his fears in terms of a hypothesis test: 'Lang-hao is going to harm someone, he does not have OCD at all and is really a bad person' (hypothesis A) against 'I'm really anxious that Lang-hao is going to harm someone, but actually he has OCD and is really upset about the thought of being a bad person' (hypthesis B).

Tom found having an alternative, more rational explanation for his fear helpful. While he realised there was a *possibility* that hypothesis A could be true, he reminded himself that hypothesis B was *probably* true, after all Lang-hao had not hurt anyone so far and had come for therapy because he was upset about his thoughts. This made hypothesis B seem much more likely (Bennett-Levy *et al.* 2004).

Tom's attention to his own thoughts and feelings was timely. His original automatic negative thoughts were unhelpful to the therapeutic relationship, whereas these more realistic and positive thoughts would facilitate a healthy therapeutic working environment (Sanders and Wills 2005).

Tom used the remainder of the session to gather more data for the **formulation** (see Figure 9.1), including what Lang-hao did to stop himself from harming people. This included a range of avoidant behaviours, thought control, as well as neutralising any 'bad' thoughts.

1. Trigger
For example, seeing girlfriend asleep on the sofa

2. Intrusion
'I could smother her with a cushion or stab her with a knife.'

3. Meta-cognitions
'Thinking these thoughts means I'll do it, I'm a bad person.'

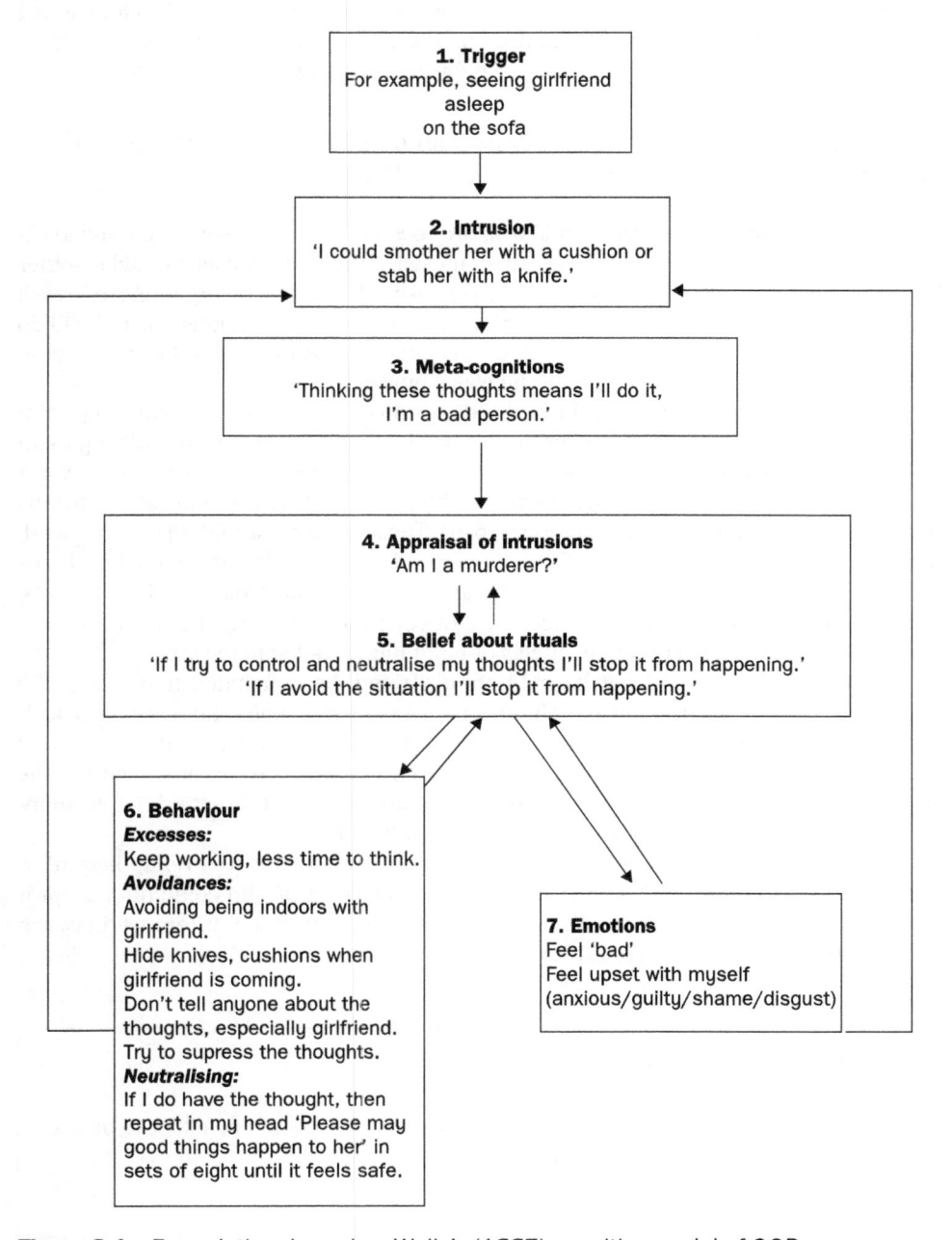

4. Appraisal of intrusions
'Am I a murderer?'

5. Belief about rituals
'If I try to control and neutralise my thoughts I'll stop it from happening.'
'If I avoid the situation I'll stop it from happening.'

6. Behaviour
Excesses:
Keep working, less time to think.
Avoidances:
Avoiding being indoors with girlfriend.
Hide knives, cushions when girlfriend is coming.
Don't tell anyone about the thoughts, especially girlfriend.
Try to supress the thoughts.
Neutralising:
If I do have the thought, then repeat in my head 'Please may good things happen to her' in sets of eight until it feels safe.

7. Emotions
Feel 'bad'
Feel upset with myself
(anxious/guilty/shame/disgust)

Figure 9.1 Formulation, based on Wells's (1997) cognitive model of OCD

What might influence Tom's choice of model for the formulation, and what would be important to include?

After considering the various OCD models that could help Lang-hao make sense of the problem, Tom concluded that Wells's (1997) model would be most helpful as it included metacognitions. He decided to maximise Lang-hao's engineering experience of 'how things work', to encourage him to make the various connections. This worked well.

Looking at the formulation, can you explain how the various elements of Lang-hao's OCD relate to each other and maintain the problem?

The first thing Lang-hao noticed would be a provocative situation, usually involving his girlfriend, that acted as a trigger (1–2) to an intrusive thought such as 'I could smother her with a cushion or stab her with a knife'. From here (2–3) his metacognitions followed: 'Thinking these things must mean something, must be important, it must mean I will do it, I must be a very bad person to be able to be able to harm someone I care about so much.' He would then wonder whether he was a murderer (3–4).

Being a responsible person, he wanted to prevent a murder and came up with rituals that would prevent this, including controlling his thoughts or neutralising them (4–5). However, these rituals only reinforced his belief that he needed to do this because he *was* a murderer (5–4). His beliefs about the rituals led him to engage in various preventative and neutralising behaviours (5–6). These included avoiding his girlfriend, putting all the knives at the back of the drawer under a tea towel, putting the cushions away when he knew his girlfriend was coming, as well as trying to supress his thoughts, or if he actually had the thought, cancelling it out by praying silently in his mind 'Please may good things happen to her' in cycles of eight until it felt safe to stop.

Because Lang-hao had not harmed his girlfriend, he concluded that it was the rituals that were preventing the bad thing from happening, which reinforced his beliefs about them (6–5). His beliefs about the rituals and their role in keeping things safe led to him feeling 'bad' and upset with himself (5–7), which increased his need for the rituals (7–5). Both his behaviours (6) and his emotions (7) led directly back to more intrusive thoughts (2) as they focused his mind on the ideas.

Lang-hao could see the *logic* in the formulation and said it was really helpful to analyse and map it out in this way. However, another part of him could not accept it because it was not how things *felt* for him, thus highlighting the difference between **propositional** and **implicational** learning (see Chapter 2).

> **Summary and check-in**
>
> Reflecting on what has been covered so far, what do you consider to be the therapeutically significant features of this case?

-

-

-

Considering your own agenda for reading this chapter, make a note of any questions that have not been answered so far.

-

-

-

Check and adjust your timescale for reading this chapter and make a note here of any changes:

Psycho-education

How might Tom explain the physiology of the brain to help his client?

Again maximising Lang-hao's engineering interest in how things work, Tom demonstrated what appears to be happening 'mechanically' in the brain by showing him a diagram of the brain which he found on the internet. Using this, he explained how the orbito-cortex (behind the eyebrows) is involved in the initial recognition and response to danger. This picks up threat signals, detecting if something is 'right' or 'wrong' in a fast, decisive, black-and-white manner. This signals to the cingulate gyrus to activate gut-feelings which indicate that something is not right.

The third part of the brain involved is the caudate nucleus, which is basically like an 'on–off' switch: in the 'on' position it indicates that action is needed, and in the 'off' position it indicates that action is no longer needed.

Tom pointed out how constant negative introspection, overthinking, worry and anxiety associated with OCD can overload this mechanism, causing it to malfunction. As a result, the on–off switch (caudate nucleus) can get stuck in the 'on' position, indicating that the threat has not been dealt with satisfactorily. Threat messages then loop back to the orbito-cortex, which again activates the cingulate gyrus, keeping up the gut-feeling of threat and the urge to engage in further (now unnecessary) action. This threat signal loops round and round until the gut-feeling eventually subsides and things start to 'feel right'. The switch can then eventually move to the 'off' position again, until next time (see http://www.bbc.co.uk/science/humanbody/mind/articles/disorders/causesofocd.shtml).

Lang-hao showed great interest in the diagram of the brain and appreciated having the mechanics explained as it demystified things for him, making the problem seem solvable.

Treatment

What are the key elements of treatment for OCD?

Tom had already engaged Lang-hao in five key elements of treatment for mental obsessions:

1 *Building a trusting therapeutic relationship* in which Lang-hao felt safe enough to explore his thoughts and describe his experience. This had been facilitated by going slowly and normalising the problem. The moral tone involved in Lang-hao's obsessional thinking had felt frightening and shameful to him, so it had been helpful to lessen these feelings as quickly as possible.
2 *Focus on the role of metacognition*, that is, the sense that Lang-hao was making of his thoughts (e.g. 'This means I'm a bad person'), rather than their content.
3 *Providing psycho-education* to help Lang-hao stand back from his thoughts and see the bigger, more general picture about OCD.
4 *Formulating or mapping out* the problem together, which enabled Lang-hao to understand how each aspect of his experience was linked. This provided a rationale for treatment and enhanced his engagement in the process.
5 *Exposure and response prevention along with hypothesis testing.* Assessment and formulation of the problem exposed Lang-hao to his fear of talking about his thoughts, while also preventing his usual response of avoiding the subject. Once he had spoken his thought aloud he immediately felt very anxious and wanted to neutralise it, but Tom noticed and asked what was happening.

Tom recognised this emotionally 'hot' moment as an excellent opportunity to access Lang-hao's implicational, or 'felt-sense' system, and asked him to stay with the 'anxious-bad' emotion for a moment without attempting to neutralise the thought. Tom then asked Lang-hao whether he thought that saying the thought aloud made it more likely that he would harm his girlfriend (hypothesis A) or that saying the thought aloud made him very *anxious* that he would harm his girlfriend (hypothesis B).

Adding this cognitive element can strengthen the learning from ERP alone (Bennett-Levy *et al.* 2004). Giving Lang-hao an alternative thought to consider in the 'hot' emotional moment opened up his perspective slightly and he smiled, realising that hypothesis B was actually more logical. However, it still *felt* risky not to neutralise the thought, so he did. Nevertheless, the seed of hope that hypothesis B might be the case had been sown.

Appealing to Lang-hao's engineering background again, Tom asked how neutralising *worked*, and what forces were involved. Lang-hao realised that he neutralised in sets of eight because the number 8 is considered lucky in Chinese culture. He had been brought up with this idea and although he no longer believed in it, acknowledged it had a stronger hold on him than he cared to admit. In the spirit of curiosity Tom suggested that Lang-hao might want to try neutralising in sets of five or seven for a change, to see if this made any difference, and Lang-hao agreed to try this for homework. Although this still involved use of a safety behaviour, it nevertheless encouraged Lang-hao to finish his neutralising at a place that did not feel 'comfortable' or 'complete' (Veale and Willson 2005).

The following session Lang-hao reported that nothing bad had happened, despite only neutralising in sets of five. Tom unpacked Lang-hao's learning from this, asking him what he had been testing, what he had feared, what had happened and what sense he made of the results. Lang-hao half-jokingly suggested that 'Perhaps five is the new number eight?' He decided to change the number again for the following week and see if *any* number worked just as well. By changing the numbers Lang-hao was beginning to undermine his belief in his neutralising system. However, he had been very anxious about harming his girlfriend after talking about it to Tom. Again, Tom asked whether this fitted with hypothesis A or hypothesis B. Lang-hao could appreciate the force of logic (hypothesis B) but said that emotion (hypothesis A) is still powerful (Bennett-Levy et al. 2004).

Tom was curious about *how* thinking or talking about thoughts made them more likely to come true, and asked if this happened to Lang-hao often. Lang-hao was clear that until now he had always been careful to push his 'bad thoughts' away, so no, it had not happened so far.

Applying this concept to a less emotive topic, Tom asked Lang-hao if he could think or talk about other things and make them happen. For example, if he thought or talked about Tom spilling his glass of water, or falling down the stairs, might that happen? At first Lang-hao laughed and thought it would not (20% likely) but when Tom seriously suggested testing this out, the thought started to feel much more likely (80%), making Lang-hao suddenly anxious. This sudden change made him curious and he agreed to think hard about Tom falling down the stairs while he ran up and down several times.

Each time they repeated the exercise and nothing untoward happened, Lang-hao found his probability rating, as well as his anxiety, reducing. After four times, Tom suggested to Lang-hao that perhaps he should try a bit harder by writing on the whiteboard 'I think Tom will fall down the stairs', while he (Tom) ran up and down again. Lang-hao did not see how he could neutralise the thought once it was written down (Veale and Willson 2005). He found this surprisingly difficult to do and thought it would increase the likelihood of Tom falling considerably (90%). Again, Tom asked how that would work, and whether Lang-hao considered that he could harm Tom by writing this on the board (hypothesis A) or that he was *anxious* that he could harm Tom by writing this on the board (hypothesis B).

Again Tom used hypothesis testing at the moment when Lang-hao's anxiety was high to draw his attention to a more logical alternative explanation. When Tom did not fall down the stairs despite Lang-hao's best efforts, Lang-hao again concluded that 'logic wins, hypothesis B appears to fit'. His emotional and probability ratings were lessening considerably (from 90% originally to 30%).

Tom and Lang-hao built on the exposure and response prevention and hypothesis testing over the next few weeks, first using imagery to mentally re-create situations with his girlfriend until he could deliberately imagine trying to harm her without neutralising the thought. It soon became clear that his thoughts were not likely to happen in real life because he did not want to harm her, rather to protect her (Veale and Willson 2005).

Eventually Lang-hao was able to be alone with his girlfriend and when the thought cropped up he did not neutralise it. This initially caused his anxiety and probability ratings to increase (90%), but these quickly subsided as he remembered hypothesis B and his anxiety reduced to 30% within 2–3 minutes. As a result, Lang-hao started to gain confidence in himself once again.

Over the coming weeks he repeated this exposure exercise several more times, 'tweaking' his safety behaviours until he could sit on the sofa next to his girlfriend and eventually leave the cushions out and the knives (although still wrapped in a tea towel) at the front of the drawer.

Tom's supervisor stressed the need to go beyond some of Lang-hao's original goals, as OCD sufferers often drop back once treatment has ended (Veale and Willson 2005). At this point Tom realised that, in his concern about the initial engagement process, he had forgotten to establish goals with Lang-hao. When he did eventually enquire what Lang-hao had wanted to get out of coming it had been to spend time with his girlfriend without experiencing constant obsessional thoughts of harming her, which he could now do.

The only safety behaviour that Lang-hao had not addressed was talking to his girlfriend about the problem, which he thought would be difficult as it was not usual in Chinese culture to talk about things of this nature and she could be frightened. Tom suggested talking about the problem in a gradual way, much as they had done in therapy, mentioning first that he suffered from OCD, then talking around the problem including the sorts of things that bothered him and only gradually getting into specifics as and when it seemed appropriate. Lang-hao thought it would be a good thing if his girlfriend knew, and agreed to try gradually telling her.

Lang-hao returned the following week in good spirits. It had turned out that his girlfriend had a relative with OCD. She was very understanding, if a little upset that he had not confided in her before, as she would have liked to have helped. To Lang-hao's surprise, she had been relatively unfazed by the content of his thoughts, considering them to be mental obsessions, not real possibilities.

Dropping this last safety behaviour had a marked impact on Lang-hao's confidence. Referring back to the formulationn Lang-hao saw the last piece of his 'plan' fall into place as he dropped this final safety behaviour. His girlfriend's reaction had normalised things; she had not seen him as a bad person for having the thoughts, just as a person having thoughts they did not want to be having. Tom, too, was relieved that Lang-hao's disclosure had gone so well.

Lang-hao spent the last few sessions working to build an alternative core belief, 'I'm a good person'. His belief that he was a bad person had already been undermined by the ERP and hypothesis testing, and he was able to gather and record convincing data in support of his new belief. He agreed to carry on with the **positive data log** after treatment had ended. Tom also spent some time reducing Lang-hao's rather polarised ideas about 'good' and 'bad'. Their final session before follow-up was spent consolidating Lang-hao's learning using a continued improvement plan (see Table 9.1).

Treatment outcomes

By the end of treatment Lang-hao's scores on the OCI-R (Foa *et al.* 2002) had reduced dramatically in each of the areas he originally rated, including obsessing, ordering, checking and neutralising (see Table 9.2). Each of these areas had been connected. In

Table 9.1 Lang-hao's continued improvement plan (Beck 1995)

What have you learned from these sessions?	That OCD is not logical. While my obsessive thinking might be possible, it is not at all probable. I do not want to harm anyone and am not likely to. I don't need to hide knives and cushions. I might be really worried about doing bad things, this means I don't want to do them. OCD thinking doesn't mean I'm a bad person.
What strategies have you found most helpful?	Talking about the problem. Standing back from my thoughts and observing them. Gradually staying with distressing situations, I get to find out whether the thoughts are true or not. Hypothesis testing. Changing my 'lucky' number, and finding out I don't need to neutralise at all. Adopting a more playful attitude.
What do you need to do to maintain/extend change?	I need to unwrap the kitchen knives and leave them normally in the drawer. In fact, my girlfriend thinks I should get a magnetic knife holder so they are on display. Perhaps we could put it up together. Continue to collect evidence that suggests I'm a good person. Continue to see things in a less all-or-nothing way.
What might lead to a setback?	Stress. I have exams coming up in June.
How would you recognise this?	I will start to get obsessional thoughts and have strong urges to neutralise them. I may start to avoid things if they cause distress.
Can you identify skills you have learned, resources, or people that could help you manage this set back?	I can talk to my girlfriend now. Stay in the situation until I become convinced that the feared thought is unlikely and my anxiety subsides (ERP and hypothesis testing, see above). I am having a follow-up session in 3 months' time, I can bring this forward if I need to.

Client Name .... Therapist Name .... Date ....

Table 9.2 Lang-hao's scores on the Revised Obsessive-Compulsive Inventory (Foa et al. 2002)

Date	Washing	Obsessing	Hoarding	Ordering	Checking	Neutralising
01.11.12	0	12	0	9	3	12
29.11.13	0	9	0	9	3	9
03.01.13	0	6	0	9	3	6
31.01.13	0	9	0	3	3	6
14.03.13	0	3	0	0	0	0
11.04.13	0	2	0	0	0	0

January his scores had increased slightly while he was transferring his ERP skills to working *in situ* with his girlfriend, but this had been an understandable 'blip' while he continued to make progress overall.

Real-world progress meant that he no longer made sure the knives were in the back of the drawer, his obsessional thoughts had disappeared because he had stopped responding to the compulsive urges to neutralise them; instead he would stay in the situation and let the thoughts remain, seeing how likely they seemed after a minute or so. Seeing himself now as a relatively 'good person' was helpful as it made any obsessional thoughts seem even less likely.

At the three-month follow-up Lang-hao reported that his girlfriend had bought a magnetic strip for the kitchen knives, which were now out on display. He was feeling reasonably confident about his final exams in June, and had started revising for these already. The best news was that he was now engaged to his girlfriend and they planned to marry once they had both completed their degrees and would be in a better financial position. Objectively, Lang-hao appeared much more relaxed and happy.

Reflection on the case

Once Lang-hao had been finally discharged, Tom and his supervisor spent time reflecting on the case. Both Tom and his supervisor had been surprised about the omission to set goals from the outset, and that this had only been noticed toward the end of treatment. Tom had made the assumption (as it happened, correctly) that Lang-hao's goal was to be able to spend time with his girlfriend without being distressed by unwanted thoughts of harming her. However, this goal had not been explicitly set by Lang-hao, which meant that treatment had not been truly collaborative; if Lang-hao's goal been very different from the one Tom had imagined, no amount of collaboration elsewhere would have ensured a satisfactory outcome for Lang-hao. Tom planned from now on to check in regularly with his supervisor: that his client had set specific, measurable, achievable, realistic and time-scaled goals; and that they were keeping the goal sheet on the table each treatment session, and tying their weekly agenda items in with these goals.

Tom thought he had learned a great deal from the case, in particular from dealing with his own unhelpful negative thoughts when Lang-hao had disclosed his obsessional thinking about harming people. He realised that if he had not been using thought records regularly on himself, he might not have noticed his catastrophic, all-or-nothing thinking and would have bought into his thoughts much more easily. This could have had a significant negative impact on the therapeutic relationship. This drove home the benefits of self-therapy and Tom decided to carry this forward by scheduling self-therapy sessions in his diary each week from now on.

Another learning curve had been the therapeutic impasse. It had become clear that directly addressing the feared thoughts had felt unsafe for Lang-hao, whereas talking in a gentle manner 'around' the thoughts had facilitated enough safety for him to disclose them. Tom's experience of creating this safe environment felt indelibly learned (i.e. implicationally learned – see Chapter 2), and he planned to use this in his practice from now on.

Although Tom had expected to find working with a person from a different cultural background challenging, he was surprised at how much easier things had become once the subject of cultural difference was out in the open. Knowing whether difficulties were because of the OCD (e.g. avoidance of his thoughts) or because of cultural difference (e.g. not being able to identify or name his feelings) had been a bit confusing and talking this through collaboratively had been helpful. Lang-hao's willingness to explain things had given Tom confidence to be more open about this in future.

Conclusion and consolidation of your learning

Reflecting on the case study aims for this chapter, answer the following questions:

1   What central feature of Wells's (1997) model of OCD influenced Tom to choose it as a basis for formulating Lang-hao's problem?

2   What do you understand by the term 'meta-cognition'?

3   Can you identify an example of one of your own meta-cognitions?

4   Why is it important to work with meta-cognitions rather than with the content of obsessive thoughts?

5   Briefly summarise the concept of thought–action–fusion.

6   How might you help a person reduce and eventually give up their neutralising behaviour?

Are there still outstanding questions from your own agenda for the chapter? If so, what are they and what do you intend to do to fill these gaps in your knowledge?

When do you plan to do this?

Homework

In order to develop your understanding of OCD you might find it helpful to watch the films *As Good As It Gets* and *The Aviator*, which both give insight into how difficult life can be for people with OCD.

There are also a number of useful OCD websites that you may wish to look at, including:
http://www.ocduk.org
http://whosebrainisit.wordpress.com/category/caudate-nucleus/
http://www.neutoticplanet.com/ocd.php
Finally, it would be helpful to read Schwartz (1996).

> **Feedback**
>
> Think about your experience of reading this chapter and note any feedback for the authors here:
>
>
>
> At the end of the book you may wish to collate the feedback together to forward to the following address: nick.wrycraft@anglia.ac.uk

10 Generalised anxiety disorder

> **Reader's agenda**
>
> A defining characteristic of generalised anxiety disorder (GAD) is chronic, excessive and uncontrollable worry. People with this disorder tend to be distressed by worries across a range of topics and will often describe themselves as having 'always been worriers' (American Psychological Association 2013; Stokes and Hirsch 2010).
>
> You may have come across individuals experiencing these symptoms, either in your capacity as a healthcare professional or in your personal life.
>
> Take a few moments to consider what you already know about GAD, as well as any gaps in your knowledge and understanding of the disorder. It will help to make a note of anything you hope the chapter will address for you:
>
> •
>
> •
>
> Take a few moments to consider your own agenda or reasons for reading this chapter and make a note of them here:
>
> •
>
> •
>
> The aim of this case study is to help you:
>
> - Recognise the salient features of GAD and understand its relationship to other disorders
> - Become familiar with one particular model for GAD
> - Build confidence in applying relevant treatment strategies for GAD.

> **Managing your time**
>
> Take a moment to consider how long you plan to spend reading this chapter, and make a note here:

Introduction and background

Eddie is a 62-year-old self-employed builder. He has strong family values and has always considered himself to be the family provider and protector. Eighteen months ago his granddaughter was involved in a hit-and-run accident which left her hospitalised for 3 months. Although she made an almost complete recovery, Eddie had become very cautious and begun to worry a lot. He was constantly plagued with catastrophic 'what if . . . (the worst thing happens)' thinking and at one point thought he was 'going mad' with worry and decided to visit his GP (see Box 10.1).

> **Box 10.1 Characteristics of GAD**
>
> According to the American Psychiatric Association (2013), GAD is characterised by:
>
> - Chronic, excessive and uncontrollable worry for a period of more than 6 months.
> - Repetitive, intrusive, negative thoughts about the future, which are predominantly in verbal form and relatively non-specific in content.

Eddie described his physical symptoms, explaining how he felt apprehensive and anxious much of the time and how difficult it was to relax. His GP first sent him for a test for hyperthyroidism, which came back negative (Wells 1997).

The GP recognised that although the onset of GAD tends to be insidious, usually starting between a person's late teens and late twenties, it can also come on suddenly after a stressful event in later life, such as Eddie had experienced with his granddaughter. He asked Eddie to complete the Patient Healthcare Questionnaire (PHQ-9: Kroenke *et al.* 2001), which indicated he was moderately depressed, and the Generalised Anxiety Disorder Assessment (GAD7: Spitzer *et al.* 2006), which indicated that he was highly anxious. The GP therefore referred Eddie for a course of CBT (Clark 1989).

Differential diagnosis and measurement

GAD is often co-morbid with other disorders. What differentiates GAD from other disorders and what disorder should you prioritise in treatment? (see Box 10.2)

Box 10.2 Co-morbidity

GAD is frequently co-morbid with other disorders, including:

- Social anxiety
- Panic disorder
- Obsessive compulsive disorder
- Depression
- Dysthymia

If this is the case, treatment may proceed in two stages, treating the primary diagnosis first, followed by treatment of the GAD (National Institute of Mental Health 2013).

A note of interest

Social anxiety can also involve 'what if . . .' catastrophic thinking, but the content is about specific events in anticipation of social embarrassment, whereas GAD involves 'what if . . .' thinking across a wide range of topics (Hirsch and Matthews 2012).

While Eddie described his granddaughter's accident as traumatic for him at the time, he was not experiencing symptoms of post-traumatic stress disorder such as flashbacks or nightmares and did not experience hypervigilance or feel 'stuck in time'. Nevertheless, in view of the accident the therapist decided to employ the Penn State Worry Questionnaire (PSWQ: Meyer *et al.* 1990), which discriminates more precisely than the GAD7 between the independent construct of worry and other disorders such as social anxiety and PTSD. While the therapist noted that Eddie had scored as moderately depressed on the PHQ-9, he scored highly for worry on the PSWQ, indicating that GAD was his main problem; the depression was likely to improve once the GAD had been treated. This was also the GP's assessment of the situation.

Assessment: CBT assessment and models of worry

How might you recognise a typical presentation of someone with GAD?

At CBT assessment Eddie described his main problem as an inability to stop worrying. This was particularly problematic at night as his mind would race, making sleep difficult. He worried about all manner of topics, ranging from what would happen if he could not sleep to what would happen to his family if he died. Eventually he would drop off in the small hours of the morning and was therefore constantly tired and on edge during the day. He found it difficult to concentrate and was irritable with his family due to the tiredness.

> Individuals who experience GAD are often characterised by:
>
> - A strong sense of responsibility
> - An overly nurturing and intrusive interpersonal style
> - Perfectionism
> - Rigidity
> - Issues of control

There are a number of different CBT models of worry. Can you identify the main features of each? (see italics)

On reflection, Eddie recognised that he had always been a bit of a worrier, but never to the point where the worry had concerned him like this. The therapist asked what life had been like before the worry, including what he used to do before that he did not now, and what he was doing now that he did not used to do.

Eddie said he had always been protective of his family, wanting to know what they were up to; however, he had also wanted them to have fun and had encouraged them to go out and about. Since the accident things had changed and he did not want them to go out now. He therefore encouraged more passive behaviour, organising family film evenings and meals in. If family members did go out, either on their own or with others, he wanted to know all the details of where they were going, how they were getting there, who they were with, etc. and would phone, sometimes more than once, *to make certain* that everyone was OK and that their plans had not changed. He would then worry until everyone was home safely, finding any uncertainty difficult to tolerate. While his family put up with his worrying and made allowances, Eddie realised that he was being tiresome but *could not tolerate the uncertainty of not knowing and would worry until he was certain that everything was OK* (Dugas et al. 1998).

In line with Wells's (1997) **metacognitive** model of worry, the therapist explored Eddie's *positive and negative beliefs about worrying*. On the one hand, he believed that worrying about every possible outcome would prepare him for any eventuality; therefore it was good to worry because it would help him to cope. On the other hand, when he felt unable to stop worrying he feared he would go 'out of his mind'.

Eddie was unable to identify any imagery in connection with his catastrophic worry. Imagery is a powerful cognitive process which evokes strong emotions and associated psychological arousal. According to the avoidance theory of GAD (Borkovec et al. 2004), *the largely verbal nature of worry serves as a means to avoid any troubling imagery and the distress this causes. The theory suggests that this avoidance leads to a lack of emotional processing with the person continuing to worry uncontrollably as a result.*

During the assessment Eddie was keen to discuss the content of his many worries with the therapist; however, the therapist enquired whether talking about his worries in such detail had been helpful in the past. Eddie paused to consider, noting that it had not actually solved the worry in the longer term. It was therefore suggested that therapy might be an opportunity to try something different and that instead of talking in detail about the *content* of his worries, they might focus on his *habit of worrying* and the biases in his attention to threat. Eddie had not thought about worrying in this way before and said it made sense to try a new approach (Hirsch and Mathews 2012).

Formulation

What factors appear to be maintaining Eddie's worry?

The therapist chose to use Hirsch and Mathews's (2012) cognitive model of worry as it incorporates aspects of both Wells's and Dugas' theoretical models, as well as taking into account the person's inability to regulate their emotions. The central feature of the model, the habit of attending to threat and of making negative interpretations, appeared to fit well with Eddie's presentation. The formulation was planned collaboratively, with the therapist providing the model and Eddie providing the details from his own experience, synthesising both into an understandable 'map' of the problem (Figure 10.1).

Eddie's worries were usually triggered (1) by something apparently neutral, such as a comment about him retiring, or his daughter saying she was taking the children to the park. A series of thoughts would follow about this (2), starting with something benign such as 'It will be nice to have more time with the family' or 'They'll enjoy the swings', before switching to more negative thoughts (3) such as 'What if I can't provide for them once I've retired?' or 'What if Ellie [his granddaughter] falls off the swing?'

Since his granddaughter's accident, Eddie had begun a habit of attending to threat and making negative interpretations of benign situations (4). The perceived threat (5) 'I won't be able to provide for my family and they will have a hard time' led directly into the worry process (6), where Eddie would focus internally on his worries, catastrophising about all manner of dire outcomes in an all-or-nothing way. In this state, his worrying would move from one topic to another in a rather abstract way and in verbal form (rather than being about specific concrete examples and employing imagery). This worry process fed directly back into his perception of threat (6 back to 5 again), forming a feedback loop.

The worry process (6) also led to a number of symptoms and emotions (7), including difficulty concentrating on what he was doing at the time, as well as feeling tired, on edge and afraid. His fear was of both what could happen in the future, and the worry process itself, in case he could not control the worry and it drove him mad. These fears would only escalate the worry process (7 back to 6) and he would adopt a number of both internal and external behaviours (6 to 8), such as deliberately thinking of all the negative outcomes that could happen, while procrastinating over the task he was currently involved in. He would check for physiological signs of anxiety, and try to suppress the worry (but be unable). These behaviours fed directly back into the worry process itself (8 back to 6) as he continued to focus on the content of his many worries. Thus, the worry cycle was perpetuated and escalated.

Generalised anxiety disorder

```
(1) Situation – e.g. a comment about retiring
                    ↓
(2) Benign thoughts – 'It will be nice to have more time with my family.'
(3) Negative thoughts – 'What if I can't provide for them?'
                    ↓
(4) Habit of attending to threat.
Habit of making negative interpretations.
                    ↓
(5) Perceived threat – not being able to provide for his family and them suffering
                    ↓
(6) Worry process
Internal focus.
Catastrophise.
Move from one negative topic to the next.
All-or-nothing thinking.
Verbal and abstract.
          ↙                  ↘
(7) Symptoms and emotions        (8) Behaviours (internal/external)
Difficulty concentrating on tasks   Deliberately thinking of all the negative outcomes
because of worrying                 and telling others about his worries
Tired and on edge                   Procrastinating
Afraid                              Avoidance
                                    Trying to suppress worry
                                    Checking for anxiety
```

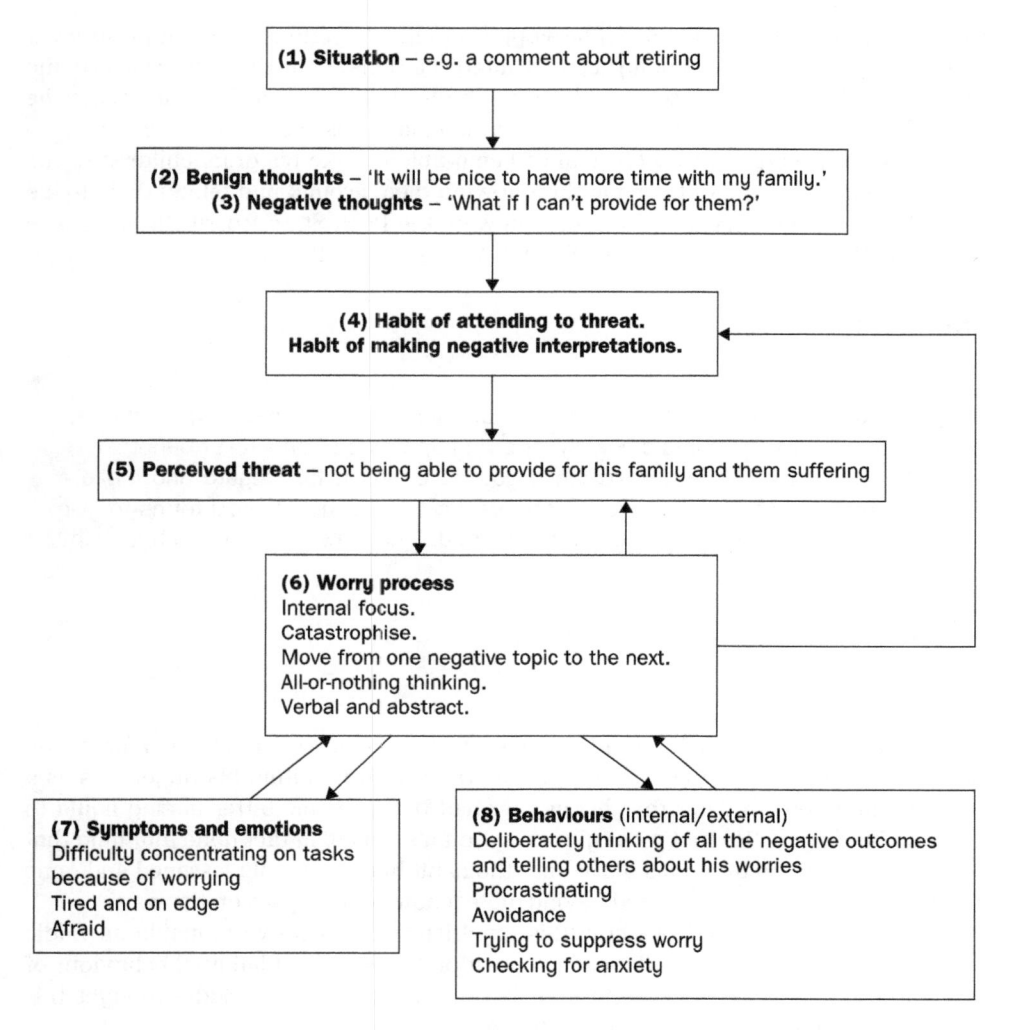

Figure 10.1 Formulation (based on Hirsch and Mathews 2012)

The formulation was developed over two sessions. Eddie considered it made good sense, but felt none the wiser about what to do to break the habit, as once he started to worry he felt unable to stop.

Treatment goals and measurement

Eddie was keen to stop the worrying as it felt out of control and he worried that it would drive him mad. However, his positive belief about worry was that it prepared him and so kept him safe, so he was somewhat ambivalent about breaking his worry habit, fearing that something bad could happen if he stopped (Wells 1997). He could see how his habit of attending to threat and making negative interpretations all the time was central to the problem and how this caused problems for both his family and himself; ideally he wanted to return to the 'normal' level of worrying that he used to experience.

He therefore agreed to set a goal of being able to take his grandchildren to the park as he used to, without constantly following them around and telling them to 'be careful'. The measurement tools employed were the Penn State Worry Questionnaire (PSWQ) (Meyer *et al.* 1990) and the PHQ-9 (Kroenke *et al.* 2001).

Treatment

> Most people have some experience of trying to break a habit, whether biting fingernails, stopping smoking, or giving up drugs of one sort or another.
>
> Think about any experience you have had in this regard and make a note here of what you did in both practical and psychological terms to give up the habit. What support from others did you have and how did this help?

The therapist asked Eddie if he had any past experience of trying to break a habit and how he had gone about this. Eddie remembered giving up biting his fingernails as a teenager and how, to deter this, his mother had bought some bitter tasting liquid to paint on his fingers. He had worn gloves, sat on his hands, in fact done anything that was in opposition to biting his nails, until the habit had eventually lessened and gone away altogether. He remembered having quite a number of lapses on the way.

The therapist pointed out how this experience could prove valuable as Eddie would need to practise doing things in opposition to his current habitual behaviour of attending to threat and of interpreting information negatively. Eddie thought this sounded logical but had no idea where to start.

What can the therapist do within the session to help Eddie reduce his worrying and begin to tolerate a degree of uncertainty and anxiety?

The therapist noted that Eddie was still prone to getting into detailed accounts about the content of his worries in the session. This effectively amounted to using the session as time for worrying; this was therefore a good place for them to start. Together they set up a behavioural experiment to test whether Eddie considered therapy worked more (or less) effectively when he kept going over detailed accounts of the *worry content or* when they concentrated on the *habit* of worrying. Subjectively, Eddie would compare the previous two sessions (where he had talked in detail about his worries) with the next two sessions in which he would give the therapist permission to refocus him each time she noticed this happening.

In line with Eddie's formulation, refocusing him on the *habit* of worrying rather than dwelling on the *content* of it targeted the central feature of worry, that is, the habit of attending to threat and making negative interpretations (4). This reduced his perception of threat (5) and in turn the worry processes itself, including his internal focus and tendency to worry in verbal form (6). This allowed them to focus on changing the habit instead of feeding into it, thus reducing the symptoms of the worry (7) and the behaviour of deliberately thinking about every possible negative outcome (8). It was made clear to Eddie that refocusing on the task was not an attempt to supress the worry but was about interrupting the worry process in the first place by continuing to focus on the task he was already involved in.

Why is it especially difficult to break the habit of attending to threat?

At first Eddie found keeping focused on the task of therapy incredibly difficult to do and could not understand why this should be the case. The therapist explained how the brain is set up to prioritise threat messages as a matter of self-preservation (Gilbert 2009); because the catastrophic contents of his worries were perceived as threatening, his brain prioritised these messages, making it difficult to concentrate on everyday tasks at the same time. This explanation made sense to Eddie, making it easier for him to engage with the therapeutic task.

Self-criticism is common among people experiencing GAD. How might this be contributing to Eddie's problem, and how could it be addressed?

At first, whenever the therapist pointed out that Eddie was introducing a worry topic again, he would be very critical of himself for making a 'mistake'. As self-criticism is also perceived as threatening, the therapist was keen for Eddie to learn how to react to his 'mistakes' in a kinder, more self-supporting manner (Gilbert 2009). Therefore the therapist introduced the concept of compassionate self-talk in the face of setbacks (as opposed to being self-critical), encouraging Eddie to practise silently talking non-judgementally to himself as he would to a friend whenever he experienced a setback within the session (Hirsch and Mathews 2012).

Eddie commented that he was now 'juggling with two balls' in therapy, trying to not get caught up with the content of his worry, as well as trying to relate more kindly to himself when he did. The therapist therefore slowed things down, not introducing anything else new until Eddie had begun to master these skills.

> **Check-in**
>
> Has this chapter answered the questions you asked at the outset? Are there questions that remain unanswered, including any new questions that might have arisen? Make a note here:

-
-

You have reached the mid-point in the chapter and it is recommended that you take time to consider whether or not you are on track with your original timing set at the outset. Make a note here of any adjustments you intend to make.

-
-

How might Eddie be encouraged to control and limit his worry episodes outside the session?

The result of their earlier behavioural experiment indicated that it was more helpful to work with breaking the worry habit by focusing Eddie's attention back onto the task in hand whenever he caught himself beginning to dwell on the content of his worry in the session (Hirsch and Mathews 2012). Therefore, to build on this learning, Eddie was next encouraged to begin scheduling in well-defined 'worry-free times', outside therapy, starting with short periods whenever he was making tea, gradually extending these to longer worry-free periods (Borkovec and Sharples 2006).

During this time he was encouraged to practise an external focus of attention on what was happening around him, becoming absorbed in the task at hand, as opposed to having an internal focus on his worries (6) (Wells 2006). If a worry intruded into this time, Eddie was to acknowledge this non-judgementally in a compassionate tone and try to focus externally again, at least until his defined worry-free time had ended. In this way Eddie was beginning to break the worry habit (4), reducing threat (5) and disrupting the worry process by shifting his focus externally (6) (Hirsch and Mathews 2012).

Eddie found this helpful and was eventually able to extend his worry-free time until his worrying was restricted to the afternoon. He often found that he was less inclined to worry at this time, and learned from this that worrying was less necessary than he had originally thought.

How might the therapist encourage Eddie to make his worries less 'abstract and general' and more 'concrete and specific', and what are the benefits of this?

In order to encourage more specific and concrete content to his worries, the therapist asked Eddie to write down each worry that he noticed, noting only a word or phrase

Table 10.1 Eddie's worry history outcome chart (based on Hirsch and Mathews 2012)

Date	Worry topic (word or phrase)	Feared outcome	Actual outcome (1–5)	How well I coped with the *actual* outcome (1 to 5)
Saturday	Missing the train	Being late, being thought of badly	I was early for the train and arrived on time (1)	Much better than I feared (1)
Monday	Paying at the till in the supermarket	Holding everyone up	I had enough money to cover the bill (1)	Better than I feared (2)
Wednesday	Maureen visiting her mum	She'll have an accident and be horribly injured	She was fine and enjoyed seeing her mum (1)	I worried a lot until she returned and coped better than I feared once I knew she was fine (2)
Thursday	Grandson asked to play for school football team	He'll break a leg or lose a tooth	His first match went well and he made some good passes (1)	Much better than I feared (1)

about the worry rather than all the general details. The important thing was for Eddie to identify and note down his specific *feared outcome* for each worry. Later, when an outcome applicable to that worry came about (whether in an hour, or even weeks later), he would write down the *actual outcome of the worry*, rating this on a scale from 1 to 5 where 1 = much better that I feared, 2 = better than I feared, 3 = as bad as I feared, 4 = worse than I feared, 5 = much worse than I feared. Finally, he was encouraged to record *how well he coped* with the actual outcome on the same 1 to 5 scale. (See Table 10.1 for Eddie's completed worry history outcome chart.)

Eddie was encouraged to continue identifying his specific feared outcomes on the worry history outcome chart. The actual outcomes (and how well he coped) were consistently much better than he feared they would be, which helped him to become more realistic in his appraisals over time.

How might imagery be used to further reduce Eddie's habit of attending to threat and making negative interpretations?

In order to help Eddie specify his feared outcomes even more accurately, he was asked to close his eyes and generate images of them. Initially the images elicited strong anxiety, but the more he imagined the outcomes, the less anxious he became as he could see most of them were extreme and could be dismissed as unrealistic. The imagery also helped him to develop a tolerance for anxiety rather than constantly avoiding it by keeping worry topics verbal and abstract; paradoxically, the more abstract and verbal his worries were the harder to dismiss they were also (6) (Stokes and Hirsch 2010).

Eddie was also asked to generate really clear and vivid images of when the actual outcomes had gone well and he had coped better than expected. Once he was easily able to access these positive images he was encouraged to do this whenever he noticed himself starting to worry. Generating benign or even positive images of alternative outcomes instead of deliberately thinking of all the negative outcomes (8) reduced the worry process (8 to 6) and his sense of threat (6 to 5) as well as his habit of attending only to negative interpretations and threat (5 to 4), thus reversing the habit. Eddie was encouraged to practise this skill each time he caught himself attending to negatives.

How do positive worry beliefs negatively reinforce the problem?

With regard to his belief that worry kept him safe by preparing him for any eventuality, Eddie was beginning to realise he was quite capable of coping with a whole range of outcomes without his (previously perceived) need to worry. In the past when his worries did not materialise he had attributed this to the fact that he had worried, and the next time he would worry again as he assumed it was this that had kept him safe. By stopping worrying he could now see how his positive worry beliefs had been negatively reinforcing the problem, and that worrying was not a necessary prerequisite for safety.

Given that habits are notoriously hard to break and can be easy to return to, what can be done to help Eddie stay 'on the straight and narrow' (his terminology) once therapy ends?

For some time, sessions had been spaced fortnightly and both Eddie and his therapist thought he was now ready to end therapy. The final session was used to draw up a 'blueprint' or continued improvement plan for Eddie to refer to in order to cope independently (see Table 10.2). A three-month follow-up was arranged to make sure that he was coping independently and to iron out any problems that might have arisen in the interim.

Table 10.2 Eddie's continued improvement plan

What have you learned from these sessions?	That attending to threatening possibilities and making negative interpretations of situations has become a habit. It's possible to break the habit, but difficult.
What strategies have you found most helpful?	Having worry-free time, postponing any worries until after then and gradually extending this time.

	Keeping a worry history outcome chart; this makes it clear that the feared outcome of my worries doesn't often come about and that I can cope with it OK if it does. Imagery makes the content of my worries more definite and clearly defined. Using imagery of my feared outcomes helps me see that many of my fears are unrealistic and they are then easier to dismiss. Generating a variety of alternative benign and positive outcomes is helpful as it stops me attending only to threatening outcomes as if this is the only thing that could happen.
What do you need to do to maintain/extend change?	Keep on with the above strategies. Initially plan weekly, then fortnightly, 'self-therapy' sessions in my diary to make sure I'm keeping on track, and make adjustments accordingly.
What might lead to a setback?	If something awful happened.
How would you recognise this?	I'd start to get caught up in 'worry loops' again and wouldn't be able to sleep. I'd start fussing over things and being annoying to others about this, trying to limit their activity.
Can you identify skills you have learned, resources, people and agencies that could help manage this setback?	Yes. I'd take stock, refer to this sheet firstly and try to apply the strategies independently. If I need to I can phone the therapist and bring the follow-up appointment forward. If the setback happens after the follow-up and I can't manage on my own I can ask for a re-referral via my GP for a couple of top-up sessions to get me back on the straight and narrow.

Client Name .... Therapist Name .... Date ....

Treatment outcomes

By the end of treatment Eddie had learned that worry did not keep him safe and would not drive him mad. He had been able to break the habit of worrying and no longer made negative interpretations about everything or attended exclusively to threat. He had gone beyond his original goal of regularly taking his grandchildren to the park and to his surprise had spontaneously taken them on the dodgems at the local funfair. He learned from this that being spontaneous was helpful because it reduced his opportunity to worry beforehand and that getting on with things straight away instead of procrastinating was liberating (8).

His scores on the PHQ-9 and the PSWQ indicated that he was no longer particularly depressed or unduly worried (see Tables 10.3 and 10.4).

Table 10.3 PHQ-9 scores

	Week 1	Week 5	Week 10
PHQ-9 scores	13	9	4

Table 10.4 Penn State Worry Questionnaire scores

	Week 1	Week 5	Week 10
PSWQ scores	67	55	41

The mean score for GAD is 57. Lower scores mean less anxiety (Meyer et al. 1990).

Reflections

The therapist had recently attended a workshop on GAD and this was the first time she had used Hirsch and Mathews's (2012) model in clinical practice. This was therefore a good opportunity to reflect on the strengths and limitations of the model and to compare it with other models that she was more familiar with.

In the past she had experienced limited success with treating GAD, with the problem often only partially resolving following treatment. This time, by targeting the central feature of worry according to Hirsch and Mathews's model (2012) – the habit of attending to threat and making negative interpretations of events – treatment outcomes were more satisfying. In the past she had relied on treatment measurement using the less specific GAD7, whereas the PSWQ had been much more specific and helpful and had clearly indicated that by the end of treatment Eddie was below the cut-off score for GAD (Meyer et al. 1990).

On reflection, the therapist considered that completing the worry history outcome chart over a number of sessions had been a really helpful way of starting to undermine Eddie's habit of making negative interpretations. Drawing together the data from the worry history outcome chart across a number of weeks clarified for Eddie that much of his worry was unnecessary because his feared outcomes did not come to pass, or if they did, he was able to cope much better than he had expected. The therapist considered this work had provided a sound basis for the imagery exercises that followed.

Eddie reported that the imagery had been a turning point for him. Making his catastrophic feared worry outcomes specific and concrete had enabled him to see that most of them were far-fetched and unlikely, making them easier to dismiss. This element of treatment drew on Borkovec's theory that the verbal nature of worry precludes distressing imagery, whereas promoting imagery facilitates emotional tolerance and processing, thus reducing the need for worry in the longer term.

Reflecting on the logical development of treatment, teaching Eddie to deliberately counter his threatening interpretations by imagining a range of benign or positive alternatives had been influential in breaking his habitual tendency to attend only to threatening possibilities. At the time, the therapist had been unsure about how many sessions to spend focusing on this strategy. As the habit was central to the model and because she had not used imagery in this way before, she had decided to spend more rather than less developing the strategy. In future she might experiment with how many sessions to spend on this, taking into account how well the client engaged in the homework exercises in between.

In the past the therapist had always encouraged clients to postpone worries until an allocated short period of 'worry time' in the early evening, which some clients found difficult to do. Instead, by encouraging Eddie to schedule in a short period of 'worry-free time' each day (e.g. while he was making his tea to start with and then his breakfast as well), he was able to gradually extend his worry-free time to the whole morning without too much difficulty. Gradually building up in this way encouraged Eddie to build a new habit of not worrying, rather than just saving worrying up for later.

In conclusion, the therapist considered that Hirsch and Mathews's model had much to recommend it and that she would continue to learn about it by using it over the next few months, drawing further conclusions as her experience developed. She particularly liked that the principles from the older models were by and large incorporated within this new model.

Conclusion and consolidation of your learning

Reflecting on the initial learning outcomes for this chapter:

- Can you now recognise the salient features of GAD and understand its relationship to other disorders?
- Have you become familiar with one particular model for GAD?
- Have you built confidence in applying relevant treatment strategies for GAD?

1. List three characteristics of GAD.

    A.

    B.

    C.

2. Explain how the content of GAD worries differs from the content of social anxiety worries.

3 Identify the primary feature of each of the following models of worry:

(a) Dugas et al. (1998)

(b) Borkovec et al. (2004)

(c) Wells (1997)

(d) Hirsch and Mathews (2012)

Explain in your own words the treatment strategies that you might employ to treat GAD using Hirsch and Mathews's model, and give a brief rationale for your choice.

Now spend a few minutes going through your answers by looking back through the chapter and filling in any gaps in your memory and understanding.

Homework

If you are inclined to worry yourself, try completing a worry history outcome schedule over the next 2 weeks. After this time it is important to consolidate your learning from this. You might then continue with self-practice of CBT, using imagery to break the habit of attending to negative interpretations and threat. Keep a record of everything that you do and apply any learning from this.

If you are not a worrier you might try using Hirsch and Mathews's model to formulate your next client with GAD.

Further reading: Hirsch and Mathews (2012); Stokes and Hirsch (2010). See also the video 'What is Generalised Anxiety Disorder?' at http://behavenet.com/generalized-anxiety-disorder.

> **Feedback**
>
> Think about your experience of reading this chapter and note any feedback for the authors here:
>
>
>
> At the end of the book you may wish to collate the feedback together to forward to the following address: nick.wrycraft@anglia.ac.uk

11 Post-traumatic stress disorder – single episode trauma

> **Reader's agenda**
>
> Post-traumatic stress disorder is frequently mentioned in the media. Briefly outline your understanding of the disorder here.
>
>
>
>
> On a scale of 0 to 10, how well do you consider you understand the condition? (0 = not at all and 10 = completely)
>
> 0 — 1 — 2 — 3 — 4 — 5 — 6 — 7 — 8 — 9 — 10
>
> What gaps in your current understanding of PTSD are you aware of that you would like to understand more clearly?
>
>
>
>
> Take a few moments to consider your own agenda or reasons for reading this chapter and make a note of them here:
>
> •
>
> •
>
>
> The aim of this case study is to:
>
> - Outline the main features of PTSD
> - Demonstrate and explain the application of Ehlers and Clark's (2000) model to a case of single episode PTSD
> - Relate theoretical principles of treatment for PTSD to practice.

> **Managing your time**
>
> Take a moment to consider how long you plan to spend reading this chapter, and make a note here:

Background

Juliet is a 27-year-old healthcare professional who self-referred to a private CBT therapist, experiencing symptoms of post-traumatic stress disorder (PTSD). She chose a female therapist because of the sensitive nature of the trauma, selecting from the British Association for Behavioural and Cognitive Psychotherapists (BABCP) website.

An initial consultation was agreed as part of the assessment process, to establish whether both parties felt comfortable working together. Juliet explained from the outset that she did not want her GP involved, but agreed that in the unlikely event of risk to herself or others he could be contacted.

What gives rise to PTSD in an individual and what are the basic criteria for this?

Diagnostic criteria for PTSD require that:

> The person was exposed to: death, threatened death, actual or threatened serious injury, or actual or threatened sexual violence, either by direct exposure to this, witnessing it in person, experiencing it indirectly through another close person's trauma or by repeated or extreme indirect exposure to aversive details of the event, usually in the course of one's professional duties. (American Psychiatric Association 2013)

What treatment strategies for PTSD are you aware of and under what circumstances might you use each of these?

Interestingly, although anxiety is commonly thought of as the primary emotion involved in PTSD, more recent research indicates that non-anxious emotions are frequently dominant following trauma, such as sadness, anger, guilt or shame.

This is significant because while fear and anxiety are reduced by the exposure component of CBT (reliving the trauma in the imagination), this same treatment is likely to *increase* other emotions involved, such as shame or anger. Therefore **imaginal exposure** on its own may turn out to be contra-indicated as a treatment for non-anxiety based PTSD (Dalgleish and Power 2004; Power and Fyvie 2013).

Research shows that these other emotions tend to respond better to **imagery rescripting**, which allows the person to 'correct' or rescript the original situation within their imagination in line with how they would have preferred to act at the time. This is because trauma situations often severely inhibit the person's preferred course of action, leaving them ashamed and guilty that they did not respond in the manner they imagined they would. Rescripting is empowering and can help to reduce patterns of helplessness, victimisation and passivity (Grey et al. 2001; Holmes et al. 2007; Arntz and Weertman 1999).

Assessment and engagement

How might the therapist increase interpersonal effectiveness using empathy, genuineness and warmth to put Juliet at ease during what might otherwise be a difficult initial consultation for her?

Shame and disempowerment are often a major consideration when working with sexual trauma. For this reason the therapist took care to allow Juliet to set the pace and extra care to develop a therapeutic environment that felt safe enough for disclosure of very personal and sensitive information.

Juliet explained how difficult it was for her to talk about the traumatic event as she found it embarrassing and painful; this was the first time she had spoken to anyone about it. The therapist warmly acknowledged the difficulty and recognised how, despite this, Juliet had decided to come forward and do something about the problem. She suggested that to make things easier, they might talk 'around' the trauma for now, rather than discuss the actual content of it, thus letting Juliet approach the subject gradually and in her own time.

She asked Juliet what she thought would make things easier, and Juliet acknowledged that allowing time for trust to develop between them would be most helpful. In this way the therapist demonstrated interpersonal effectiveness by empathically acknowledging the difficulty, and thinking through with Juliet in a warm, caring manner how they might manage the problem (James et al. 2001).

Exercise

Think for a moment of something you feel embarrassed or ashamed about. This experience is probably not something you talk about often or share with many people. Most of us have some experience of this type of thing; there is no need to think of anything too shaming.

Now imagine meeting a stranger who expects you to talk about this embarrassing event the first time you meet. The stranger proceeds to ask you probing questions about the event, while at the same time taking notes that you are unable to see. How might you feel?

What three things can you learn about engagement and assessment for treatment of PTSD from this brief experiential exercise?

1

2

3

As the assessment progressed, it became clear that Juliet's primary emotions from the trauma itself were fear and anxiety. This meant that an exposure-based form of CBT, **imaginal reliving**, would be the therapist's initial treatment of choice. Juliet's secondary emotions included embarrassment over talking about what had happened and shame that she had not spoken out earlier, as well as anger towards the man involved. These secondary emotions were more likely to benefit from imagery rescripting at a later point in treatment if necessary (Arntz and Weertman 1999).

What aspects of psycho-education about treatment for PTSD would it be important to explain to Juliet and why?

An important aspect of treatment for PTSD is psycho-education, along with a clear explanation of the rationale for therapy. This explanation is part of informed consent and later helps with adherence to treatment.

Being a healthcare professional, Juliet had a good idea about the neuroscience of the brain and understood how in trauma sufferers there is impairment in the interplay between the amygdala, the hippocampus and the prefrontal cortex.

While the neuroscience of trauma is complex and not yet fully understood, very simply, in traumatised people a part of the brain called the amygdala becomes hyperreactive to anything that reminds the individual of the original traumatic event, resulting in a constant state of emotional hyperarousal.

Under non-trauma conditions, the prefrontal cortex and hippocampus would help to inhibit amygdala activity, but disregulation in the frontal and hippocampal systems (lower activity than would be expected in a non-traumatised brain) keeps the amygdala constantly aroused for threat (Taylor 2006). Understandably, this state of hyperreactivity results in the individual trying to avoid anything that might trigger these emotional reminders.

As Juliet was a healthcare professional, the therapist used a physiological metaphor to explain how processing of emotional events needs to take place within the amygdala in a similar way to the manner in which food is digested in the stomach. In this case, the amygdala still needed to process or 'digest' her original emotional memory in order to prevent it from keeping returning to mind. In practical terms, this meant that Juliet would need to work through what had happened to her in an emotional way so that she could process the emotions and begin to put the experience behind her.

Juliet already had an understanding of what to expect in therapy and only a brief explanation of imaginal exposure and rescripting of memories was necessary. It was also explained to her that, like any effective medical treatment, there may be some initial side effects. These were to be expected, particularly around the time of the imaginal exposure work. Side effects may include a temporary increase in re-experiencing, including increased flashbacks and nightmares, as well as hyperarousal symptoms, but this would be a sign that the memories were being processed effectively, rather than being a cause for concern.

The therapist gave Juliet a handout to read on the subject of PTSD which included this information, and she was asked to consider this for 'fit' with her own experience.

When planning trauma work, what practicalities need to be taken into consideration?

Before undertaking work on trauma it is important to establish that the timing of treatment in the person's life is right. Juliet had no major planned events in her life coming up and was able to commit the next ten or so Saturday mornings to meet weekly for 50 minutes, except where imaginal exposure and rescripting work on the trauma would require 90-minute sessions.

The therapist explained how treatment can be unsettling, and it would be important for Juliet to focus on self-care, making sure not to isolate herself following sessions, and to eat and rest sensibly throughout treatment.

Goal setting and measurement

The therapist used the Posttraumatic Cognitions Inventory (PTCI: Foa *et al.* 1999) to measure trauma outcomes. Initially this indicated high scores on 'negative thoughts about the world' and relatively lower scores on 'negative thoughts about the self' and 'self-blame', which made sense of Juliet's safety behaviours with regard to avoidance of other people (see Figure 11.1).

Prior to coming for the initial consultation Juliet had already considered her goals for therapy, which were as follows:

1. To feel safe enough with the therapist to disclose the necessary information
2. To no longer experience unwanted and intrusive thoughts about the event
3. To be able to stay in the same room with a (known) man for 10 minutes without feeling overwhelmed by anxiety and wanting to leave
4. To be able to cry in response to upsetting events, which she could not currently do.

Developing the formulation using Ehler's and Clark's (2000) PTSD model

> **Exercise**
>
> List six symptoms that you might expect a person with PTSD to present with.
>
> 1
>
> 2
>
> 3
>
> 4
>
> 5
>
> 6

Because of the sensitive nature of the problem, the therapist chose to let Juliet tell her story uninterrupted; this meant that rather than **formulate** the difficulty in the session, the therapist would do this independently afterwards. While this was less collaborative, overall it seemed the best option.

Juliet explained how symptoms of PTSD had emerged progressively (see Figure 11.1). The traumatic event (1) had been a one-off incident that had taken place when she was 4 years old. At the time she had been too young to understand the significance of what had happened, although she had found the accompanying threat 'never to tell, or I'll come and get you', so terrifying that until this point in time (she was now 27) she had never told anyone.

At the age of 4 her appraisals of the trauma (2) had been that:

'I must never tell, or he will come and kill me/my mum'
'Not everyone who seems good is good'
'I must be very careful around others'
'Bad things can happen at any time'.

As she grew into adolescence Juliet started to understand the significance of what had happened and her personal appraisals of the event began to include the belief that she should speak out about what happened to stop the man from doing this to other children. However, her *fear* of the threatened reprisals and the embarrassment involved prevented her from doing so.

Negative appraisals (2 to 1) and trauma memories (1 to 2) influence each other because trauma recall is biased by the appraisals made, so that only information that is consistent with the appraisals is recalled. This prevents any contradictory information from becoming available to change the meaning.

Juliet described a current trigger to the trauma memory (linking 1 to 3) involving recent media coverage of a well-known television presenter from her childhood who had been exposed as sexually exploiting children around the same time.

This triggered a sense of current threat (linking 3 to 4) including *intrusive recollections* and *flashbacks* of the trauma event, as well as strong feelings of *anger*, both towards the perpetrator and towards herself, for not speaking out earlier, as well as feelings of *guilt*. She wondered if other children had suffered at the hands of the same abuser because of her perceived omission.

The therapist accepted and validated Juliet's concerns about this, being careful neither to dismiss nor to reassure her too quickly. However, because trauma survivors are often *quick to take the blame* for things that have happened, the therapist used gentle questioning to establish that Juliet had known neither the man's identity nor his whereabouts to report him, then or now.

Feeding into her *sense of current threat* (4) was the initial appraisal of the trauma that she had made (linking 2 to 4), that she must never mention what had happened or she (and her mother) would be killed. Also feeding in was her belief that she needed to be very careful around others, because bad things could happen at any time.

In response to her sense of current threat, Juliet employed a variety of *avoidant behaviours* (linking 4 to 5) to help her feel safer. The most notable of these had started immediately after the incident and was quickly spotted by her mother. Although her mother was unaware of what had taken place, she quickly picked up that Juliet had stopped crying in response to normal everyday things such as grazing her knees; in fact, Juliet had not cried since the trauma for *fear that if she lost emotional control*, she might blurt everything out and the man would come and get them both.

At the time Juliet had been sent to a child psychologist to find out why she had stopped crying and what the matter was. Even in the face of great temptation to tell all, she had said nothing, and so nothing had been established to account for the phenomenon. Therefore things apparently carried on as 'normal' except that, strangely, Juliet no longer cried.

Juliet also tried to *push any thoughts and memories about the experience to the back of her mind*. She behaved very cautiously around men, even those she knew well, never staying on her own with them if she could help it, limiting her friendships to one, or perhaps two, very trusted people. She also *avoided going near where the trauma had occurred* as this provoked emotional memories and feelings of anxiety, shame and guilt.

Although acting as if her fears were true (5) seemed a logical way of reducing her sense of threat (4 to 5), unfortunately it had the paradoxical effect of maintaining the sense of threat (linking 5 back to 4) as it meant she was always *hypervigilant* for danger.

Her behaviour also prevented disconfirmation of her original appraisals (5 back to 2) of the trauma event, that she must be very strong emotionally (never cry) or she might tell all and the man would come and get them, as well as her need to be very cautious of everyone, even if they appeared good, because 'bad things can happen at any time'.

These behaviours also prevented change in the trauma memory (linking 5 back to 1) by not allowing exposure to the feared symptoms, which in turn produced a *sense of being 'stuck in time'*.

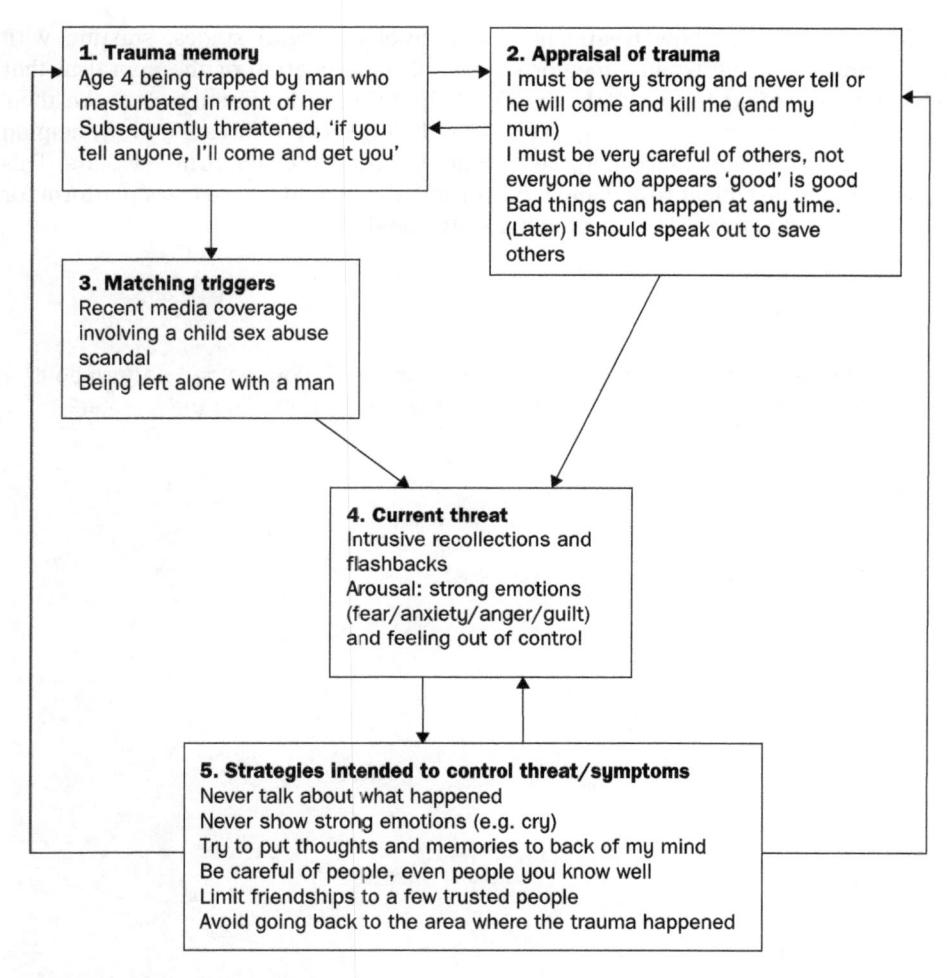

```
┌─────────────────────────────────────┐      ┌─────────────────────────────────────┐
│ 1. Trauma memory                    │      │ 2. Appraisal of trauma              │
│ Age 4 being trapped by man who      │─────▶│ I must be very strong and never tell or │
│ masturbated in front of her         │      │ he will come and kill me (and my    │
│ Subsequently threatened, 'if you    │◀─────│ mum)                                │
│ tell anyone, I'll come and get you' │      │ I must be very careful of others, not │
└─────────────────────────────────────┘      │ everyone who appears 'good' is good │
              │                              │ Bad things can happen at any time.  │
              ▼                              │ (Later) I should speak out to save  │
┌─────────────────────────────────────┐      │ others                              │
│ 3. Matching triggers                │      └─────────────────────────────────────┘
│ Recent media coverage               │
│ involving a child sex abuse         │
│ scandal                             │
│ Being left alone with a man         │
└─────────────────────────────────────┘
```

(Figure: flowchart formulation)

1. Trauma memory
Age 4 being trapped by man who masturbated in front of her
Subsequently threatened, 'if you tell anyone, I'll come and get you'

2. Appraisal of trauma
I must be very strong and never tell or he will come and kill me (and my mum)
I must be very careful of others, not everyone who appears 'good' is good
Bad things can happen at any time.
(Later) I should speak out to save others

3. Matching triggers
Recent media coverage involving a child sex abuse scandal
Being left alone with a man

4. Current threat
Intrusive recollections and flashbacks
Arousal: strong emotions (fear/anxiety/anger/guilt) and feeling out of control

5. Strategies intended to control threat/symptoms
Never talk about what happened
Never show strong emotions (e.g. cry)
Try to put thoughts and memories to back of my mind
Be careful of people, even people you know well
Limit friendships to a few trusted people
Avoid going back to the area where the trauma happened

Figure 11.1 Formulation based on Ehlers and Clark's (2000) cognitive model of PTSD

Ehlers and Clark's (2000) model of PTSD was chosen as a basis for the formulation as it explained the various aspects of Juliet's experience well. The model's central feature is the sense of serious ongoing threat experienced as a result of the trauma.

How would sharing the formulation of the problem socialise Juliet to the therapeutic rationale and provide a shared theoretical overview of the work to be undertaken with respect to Juliet's individual goals?

Juliet found the formulation really helpful as a 'map' for treatment, particularly as it explained how one part of the problem fed into and maintained other parts.

It was explained how treatment would involve several stages, starting with (1) elaboration of the trauma memory itself, (2) modification of the appraisal that Juliet had made of the trauma at the time, (3) helping her to discriminate between 'then' and 'now' when memories are triggered, (4) reducing current threats and (5) helping her to give up her avoidant safety behaviours in order to disconfirm her fears. This explanation made it clear to Julia how the formulation would be used as a platform for treatment, moving towards achieving her stated goals.

Check-in:

This is a detailed chapter. What new points have you learned so far about PTSD in line with your original purpose or aims for reading the chapter?

Recall at least six main features of PTSD.

1

2

3

4

5

6

How long have you spent on this chapter so far?

If this is longer than you intended how can you adjust your timescale to accommodate both your learning needs and your need to finish on time?
Make a note here of any adjusted plans.

Therapeutic strategies

Elaborating the trauma memory: Why is it so important to engage the person emotionally during imaginal reliving of the trauma?

In order to work with the trauma memory, the next stage of therapy was for Juliet to recall the event using imaginal exposure. This involves not merely recalling the trauma memory in a detached, intellectual way, but for the person to relive within their imagination the original emotional experience of the trauma. This allows access to emotions which are still causing hyperarousal in the present, enabling them to be processed or 'digested' properly and stored in the same way as normal memories.

Consent was obtained to record the imaginal reliving so that Juliet could listen back to this daily between sessions, to maximise her exposure to the feared trauma memory. Before starting, Juliet enquired what she should do if she felt like crying during the treatment. The therapist was glad that she asked this question, having momentarily overlooked the difficulty that this might cause her.

Referring back to the formulation, under 'Strategies to try and control the threat (5)' was listed 'Never show strong emotions, e.g. cry'. The therapist pointed out how it would be a significant step forward if Juliet could give up this avoidant behaviour; indeed, it was hoped that once she had talked about the event within this controlled environment, there may no longer be a need for her to inhibit crying. Juliet took some tissues in preparation as she thought she was likely to cry.

How would you go about elaborating the trauma memory to ensure that Juliet remains fully engaged emotionally during the process of reliving?

During imaginal reliving it is important for the therapist to encourage the person to describe the image in the first person, present tense, as if it is happening to them in the 'here and now'. Access to emotion is further facilitated by encouraging activation of as many senses as possible (sight, smell, taste, etc.), so as to fully engage the person in the 'reality' of the memory, including 'anchoring,' or locating, any emotions physically within the body.

It is also important to start and end any imagery at a place where the individual feels safe, so as not to leave them with negative images and feeling unsafe. This may require 'fast-forwarding' in their imagination to either the current moment or some other place of relative safety. It is also important not to interrupt the process of imaginal reliving, no matter how distressing it may become for either the individual or the therapist, as this would have the effect of immediately grounding the person in the present moment rather than keeping them engaged in processing the emotional memory.

Juliet was encouraged to close her eyes, and to recall being in a place of safety just prior to the traumatic event. She was then asked to describe this scene in detail, including sights, sounds and sensory input. She recalled the feeling of the sunshine on her skin and the smell of the cut grass as she ran to see the rabbits which were kept in a stable near to the big country house where her mother worked as a cleaner. Juliet had seen the rabbits before and described the ripping sound as she pulled up some grass on route to poke through the wire for them.

On entering the darkness of the stable it smelt of animals, which she liked. As she knelt down to see the rabbits in their hutch, she was startled by a man with dark hair and wearing blue overalls, who suddenly appeared standing in the doorframe. He pushed the bottom half of the door shut behind him, completely blocking her exit. She clearly felt very uneasy recalling this within the image, and was encouraged to 'stay with it' and locate this feeling in her body, which she noted in both her stomach and throat.

What are emotional hotspots and how would you identify and work with them?

Within the imagery it is important to identify and focus on emotional hotspots. These are parts of the trauma memory that induce intense emotional distress within the image because they are loaded with personal meaning for the individual. These parts of the memory are normally avoided at all costs and are difficult to access emotionally through dialogue alone. Often they are not the most obvious part of the narrative from the therapist's point of view (Grey *et al.* 2002).

In the case of fear memories, exposure to these hotspots helps to reduce fear in the long term, as well as loosening association between **conditioned stimuli**, in this case, men in general, and **unconditioned stimuli,** the specific man in question (Holmes *et al.* 2005; Taylor 2006).

Juliet was encouraged to hold this hotspot of the man in her imagination and was asked to describe him in detail and what she feared was going to happen at this point. She described the man clearly, but could only identify that she thought 'something very bad' was about to happen, as at the age of 4 (her frame of reference within the image) she had no knowledge or experience of what this might include.

While the man pulled down his overalls and exposed his genitalia to her, he talked about how soft the rabbits were, and told her about his 'rabbit'. He asked if she wanted to stroke his 'rabbit' and told her how soft the 'fur' was and how nice it would be for her to kiss his 'rabbit'. Juliet described instinctively knowing that this was wrong and so kept her distance, but she was trapped and unable to get away. The man proceeded to masturbate in front of her, which she did not understand and thought was strange, but despite his best efforts the man was unable to coax her to come closer to him.

Eventually, once he had finished he pulled his overalls back on and crouched down, looking her straight in the eye saying, 'If you ever tell anyone, I will come and get you. I know where you live, and I'll come and get you.' This, for Juliet, was another emotional hotspot. She interpreted it to mean that she was now responsible never to tell anyone or the man would come and kill both her and her mother. The moment filled her with dread, which she located in the pit of her stomach; again, Juliet was encouraged to stay with this emotion for a few minutes before continuing with the image.

After this the man left and she dropped the grass that she had been holding for the rabbits and ran straight back up the hill to the big house to find her mother.

While seeing her mother was immediately reassuring, it produced a second, powerful hotspot within the imagery. Instead of telling her mother everything and having a much desired hug, she was unable to say anything about what had happened and instead locked up emotionally, unable to cry in case she blurted the whole story out and the man would come and kill them both.

Instead of the reaction she had hoped for, her mother was busy cleaning, and although she commented that Juliet had been gone a long while, she just ruffled her hair and suggested she poured some juice for herself from the bag. Juliet felt stunned; again, she was encouraged to stay with this feeling for a few minutes.

As she talked about her mother's reaction within the image and how it felt to have her hair ruffled, she was able to give vent to her emotions and allowed herself to cry. The therapist did not interrupt or even empathise while Juliet was still within the image, but just let the crying happen.

Juliet eventually identified this as the end of the memory, so the therapist encouraged her to 'fast-forward' the image to the relative safety of the present moment and, when she was ready, to open her eyes.

Modifying Juliet's appraisals: Why is congruence (a good fit) between propositional (cognitive) and implicational (emotional) appraisal of the trauma so important?

Juliet's appraisal of the event was that if she ever told anyone about what had happened, the man would come and kill both her and her mother. She believed that she must be very careful around others because something bad could happen at any time (2). There had been two emotional hotspots during reliving involving these appraisals.

Propositionally, that is, logically speaking, for a long time Juliet had not really believed that talking about what had happened would result in the man coming to kill her. Grey *et al*. (2002) term this later appraisal of the trauma a 'secondary appraisal'.

However, because the original threat had been so highly charged emotionally (and therefore processed *implicationally*, that is, on an emotional level), her 'felt' sense had remained that he *would* kill her if she spoke out. Thus there had been a mismatch between her **propositional** (logic-based) and **implicational** (emotion-based) belief systems.

Because her 'felt sense' remained so strong, she had remained scared of dropping her safety behaviours and telling anyone (5), which in turn prevented any new learning from taking place (i.e. learning that nothing bad would happen if she did speak out).

By dropping several of her safety behaviours (5) in one go during therapy:

- 'Never talk about what happened (then or now)'
- 'Never show strong emotions (e.g. cry)'
- 'Try to put thoughts and memories to back of my mind'
- 'Be careful of people, even people you know quite well' (e.g. the therapist),

Juliet was able to experience a new and very different implicational 'felt sense', this time one of safeness; nothing bad had happened and because she was now an adult, bad things were less likely to happen. By sharing her story with the therapist she also learned that, at least sometimes, even relative strangers can be trusted. This enabled a better fit between her intellectual (propositional) and emotional (implicational) appraisals (2), bringing an immediate sense of relief and safeness.

During discussion of the reliving, she expressed her new appraisals as:

'It's helpful to talk about what happened, it was a good thing'
'It's safe to cry'
'Deliberately thinking about the event has given me back control'
'Some people might be safer than I think'.

Why is it important to modify cognitive appraisals within the imagery itself?

In order to restructure and update her emotional memory 'hotspots,' to include these new modified cognitive appraisals, they went over the whole process of imaginal reliving several times over the course of the next few sessions, again recording this for Juliet to play back between sessions for homework.

During this process Juliet verbally inserted the new cognitive appraisals into the hotspots of the trauma memory (i.e. saying out loud at the hotspot within the imagery, 'But now I know the man did not come and kill me or my mum, and wasn't likely to do that anyway'), thereby deliberately 'editing' and updating the appraisal of the emotional trauma memory and allowing the brain to process it in the same way that it does other non-trauma memories (Grey et al. 2002).

How might you work with the remaining features of Juliet's problem: helping her to discriminate between 'then' and 'now' when memories are triggered; reducing current threats; and (continuing to) help her give up her avoidant safety behaviours in order to disconfirm her fears?

Juliet listened to the recordings daily and as she did so they became much easier to listen to than they had been initially. After a few weeks she reported no longer having intrusions or flashbacks and generally felt much better. However, during the week she was asked to drive a male colleague across town alone and she had become quite anxious, although less so than she expected to. She put this down to having pictured the man's face in detail during the imagery, which made it easier for her to discriminate between this man ('now') and the original man in the image who had looked very different ('then'). This had been helpful, and she agreed to continue to consciously make these distinctions between 'now' and 'then'.

While Juliet's appraisals that 'I must be very careful because not everyone who appears good is good' and, 'bad things can happen at any moment' clearly have some truth to them, by avoiding being on her own with men even in relatively benign situations, she had not built up experience or intuition about degrees of safety, appraising all situations as potentially very dangerous. She could stay alone with a man now without feeling overly anxious, and continued to experiment cautiously with

Table 11.1 Posttraumatic Cognitions Inventory (Foa et al. 1999)

Date	Total score	Self	World	Self-blame
06.04.13	176	4.5	7.5	1.0
18.05.13	136	3.5	5.5	1.0
29.06.13	55	2.5	3.0	0

this. [Her scores on the Posttraumatic Cognitions Inventory (see Table 11.1, Foa et al. 1999) had improved significantly since the start of the treatment.]

The therapist therefore encouraged Juliet to continue to drop her safety behaviour of avoiding being alone with men during the course of her normal routine of work, in order build up some experience and to find out more about relative safety. Three fortnightly sessions were spent on this task, which was enough for Juliet to reach her goal of being able to stay on her own with a man for 10 minutes without becoming overly anxious and having to leave. From this she learned that the longer she spent with the man, the less anxious she felt.

Treatment outcomes

Although Juliet had reached all of her goals by completion of treatment, she by no means felt 'home and dry'. Most significantly, she no longer experienced unwanted intrusions or flashbacks about the event. She had been able to cry, not only during therapy, but on another occasion since, when a neighbour's cat had been run over and the neighbour had been upset. Juliet described herself as feeling 'much more human and connected' as a result. She could stay alone with a man now without feeling overly anxious, and continued to experiment cautiously with this.

A continued improvement plan was collaboratively devised in the final session to help keep Juliet moving in the right direction once therapy had ended (Table 11.2).

Table 11.2 Juliet's continued improvement plan

What have you learned from therapy?	Facing my demons in therapy was less scary and more helpful than keeping running away from them.
What strategies have you found most helpful?	Reliving the trauma memory enabled me to reconnect with my emotions at the time and to make more sense of them from an adult perspective.
	Ongoing experiments involving staying with my anxiety until it has subsided, to find out what is safe and not safe.
What do you need to do to maintain/extend change?	Carry on taking small, measured risks around men to help me establish what is 'normal' and safe behaviour.

(Continued)

Table 11.2 (Continued)

What might lead to a setback?	If a man threatens me in any way, or if I feel threatened by a man. I would get away quickly and may not want to experiment again.
How would you recognise this?	I could misconstrue something to be a threat that isn't, or, I could think that something that is really threatening is OK. I would feel more anxious than normal if I felt threatened and would want to get away. *Or* I could stay with it and see . . .
Can you identify skills you have learned, resources, people and agencies that could help manage this set back?	If this happened I could arrange another session with the therapist. Firstly, I could review these notes and decide on a sensible plan of action, going back to working with men I feel really safe with, and gradually working my way back to find if my fears were warranted or not. This is probably what the therapist would get me to do anyway.

Client Name .... Therapist Name .... Date ....

Reflection

What principles of treatment are involved in imaginal reliving of trauma involving fear and anxiety?

The main strength of working with imagery is the access it allows to emotionally laden memories which can then be reappraised and updated in line with current information (Taylor 2006). In the case of fear and anxiety it is helpful to repeatedly replay recordings of the sessions, staying with the anxiety until the person habituates to it over time. This involves the principle of **exposure and response prevention**. Going over the imagery and verbally inserting new appraisals at each hotspot also enables the meaning of the trauma memories to be updated (Grey *et al.* 2002).

In supervision the therapist reflected on and wrote down the advantages and disadvantages of rescripting the remaining imagery that she had finally decided not to undertake with Juliet (Table 11.3). Rescripting takes the form of imaging a different outcome from what happened in the original trauma, imaging an outcome more in line with the person's desired course of action that they were unable to take at the time (Holmes *et al.* 2007: 298). This allows the person to experience the emotions they would have felt had they been able to act in the manner that they would have preferred. The decision not to rescript the image had been based on a number of considerations (see Table 11.3).

Table 11.3 Advantages and disadvantages of using imagery rescripting in Juliet's case

Advantages of rescripting	Disadvantages of rescripting
Juliet felt responsible for other victims of abuse because she did not speak out as an adolescent about what had happened to her. Rescripting could help her to see that speaking out would not have saved others because she did not know the man's name or whereabouts now.	Juliet seemed much improved without rescripting and no longer mentioned feeling responsible or guilty for others towards the end of therapy. It is unethical to give unnecessary treatment. Juliet was paying for treatment privately and may have found the additional sessions too expensive (although this had not been discussed collaboratively).

Conclusion and consolidation of your learning

This chapter has included many new learning points. We suggest Ehlers and Clark (2000) and Taylor (2006) by way of further reading.

Answer the following questions:

Outline at least six of the main features of PTSD.

1

2

3

4

5

6

Name the central feature of Ehlers and Clark's model for PTSD.

List other aspects of Ehlers and Clark's model that it is important to address in treatment.

Briefly relate how the theoretical principles of exposure to fear during reliving in PTSD work.

It would be helpful to re-rate your understanding of PTSD now and to compare this with your original rating. On a scale of 0 to 10, how well do you consider that you understand the condition? (0 = not at all and 10 = completely)

0 —— 1 —— 2 —— 3 —— 4 —— 5 —— 6 —— 7 —— 8 —— 9 —— 10

Again, what gaps in your knowledge are you still aware of that you would like to address?

How do you intend to address these?

Feedback

Think about your experience of reading this chapter and note any feedback for the authors here:

At the end of the book you may wish to collate the feedback together to forward to the following address: nick.wrycraft@anglia.ac.uk

12 Perfectionism

Reader's agenda

Think about what you already know about perfectionism and make a note here of any gaps in your knowledge and understanding about treating perfectionism:

Take a few moments to consider your own agenda or reasons for reading this chapter and make a note of them here:

-
-

The aim of this case study is to help you:

- Define perfectionism
- Recognise the relationship between perfectionism and other problems
- Formulate a case using a CBT model for perfectionism
- Recognise and work with ambivalence to change
- Understand how to employ a range of appropriate CBT strategies to effect change.

Managing your time

The amount of time you decide to spend on this chapter might depend on how much of a perfectionist you are yourself. If you have perfectionist tendencies it is helpful to acknowledge it at this point. It is neither right nor wrong to have these tendencies, although it helps to understand that perfectionists are likely to spend more time trying to understand things very precisely, or, conversely, to procrastinate so as to avoid any possibility of 'getting it wrong'. Take a moment to consider how long you plan to spend reading this chapter, and make a note here:

192 CBT Fundamentals

> There will be a reminder later in the chapter to check whether you have kept track with this.

> ✎ **Exercise**
>
> Take a few moments to consider what perfectionism might involve and how it could affect a person's life, both helpfully and unhelpfully.
>
> (Helpfully)
>
>
>
> (Unhelpfully)
>
>
>
> Now try to come up with a definition for perfectionism that embraces the aspects you have identified above and make a note of your definition here:

Background

Sigurd is a single 27-year-old mature student who has self-referred to the Counselling Service attached to the university he attends. He has been experiencing stress in connection with his work and has been allocated to a cognitive behaviour therapist within the Counselling Service.

Assessment and formulation

What are the main features of perfectionism in Sigurd's case and how might these be linked?

At assessment Sigurd spoke of how he had originally gone straight from school into an apprenticeship; although he had done well in his career and was now a senior technician, he believed that in order to reach his full potential he needed to get a good first degree. He explained how reaching his full potential was something he had never felt able to do, despite having striven to do his best at all times and holding a senior position within a well-respected company. While his parents were pleased for Sigurd, he acknowledged that they had never pressured him to do 'better', realising that any pressure to do better came directly from himself (1) in Figure 12.1).

He identified his main 'rules' in life as 'I must reach my full potential in everything I do, or I will have failed' and 'I mustn't miss opportunities'. He set high standards for himself and hated making mistakes, considering that his parents and employer had given him a lot of undeserved opportunities and that he must not let them down because

1. Self-worth overly dependent on Striving and achievement

2. Inflexible standards
I must reach my full potential or I will have failed
I mustn't miss opportunities
I mustn't make mistakes
I mustn't let others down
I need to work harder than others to get the same grades

3. Cognitive biases
All-or-nothing thinking
Comparing self with others
Overgeneralising
Discounting positives

4. Performance-related behaviour
Checking work ++
Rewriting, correcting
Leaving 'no stone unturned' – reading *everything*
Procrastinating
Refusing invites/breaks

5. Temporarily meet standards

6. Fail to meet standards

7. Avoid trying to meet standards

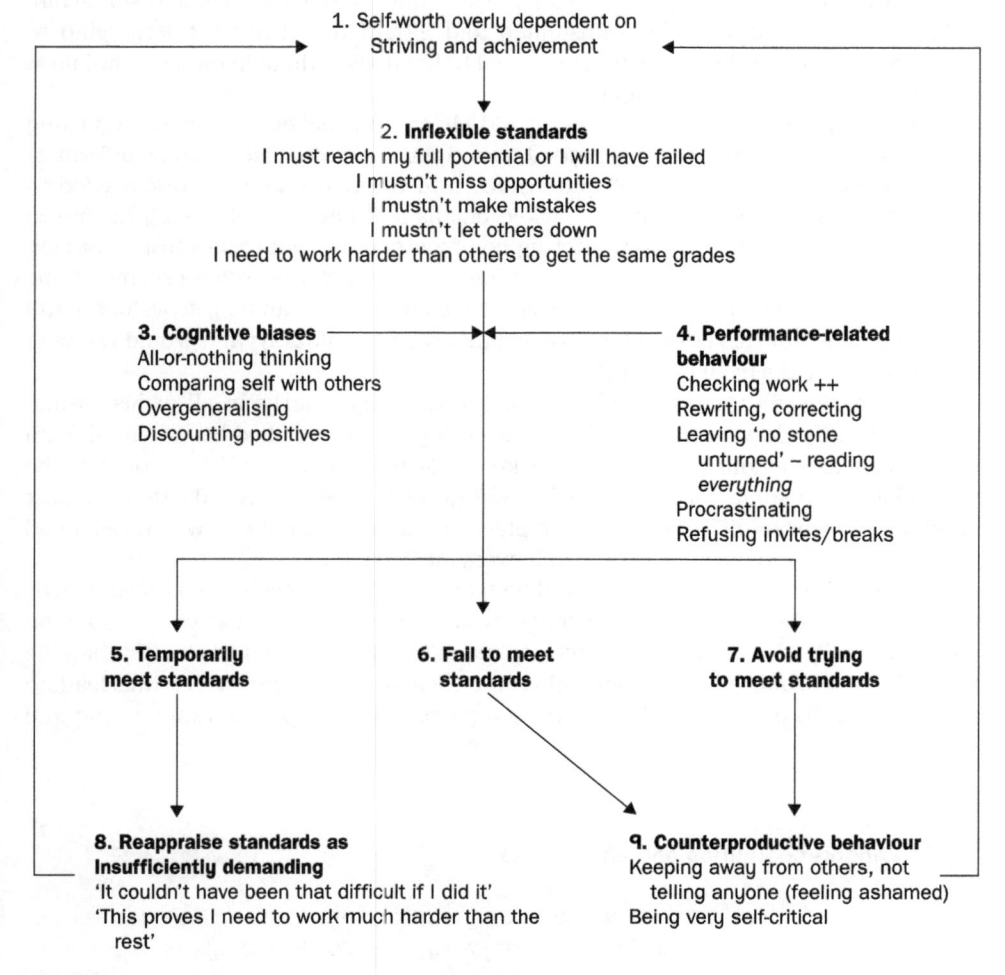

8. Reappraise standards as Insufficiently demanding
'It couldn't have been that difficult if I did it'
'This proves I need to work much harder than the rest'

9. Counterproductive behaviour
Keeping away from others, not telling anyone (feeling ashamed)
Being very self-critical

Figure 12.1 Formulation based on Shafran et al. (2010)

of this. He also assumed that he needed to work harder than others to achieve the same results as them (2).

A number of cognitive biases fed into his perfectionism (3), including **all-or-nothing thinking**, for example, 'I must reach my *full* potential in *everything* I do or I will *fail*' and 'I must read *everything* on the subject or my work will be total rubbish'. His thinking was *overgeneralised* in that he considered slightly negative feedback about one piece of work to mean that all of his work was no good. However, when he received positive feedback he would *discount* this, considering that his lecturer was being 'kind' or wanted to make him feel better about his work because he felt sorry for him. He constantly *compared* himself with the younger students in his cohort, believing that they were much brighter and 'sharper' than he was.

Performance-related behaviour (4) that fed into his perfectionism included reading every piece of literature he could possibly find on the subject, leaving 'no stone unturned' for fear of missing the one vital piece of information that would result in him looking foolish. This was time-consuming and Sigurd found himself struggling to complete the work, although he had managed to hand everything in on time until now, even if it meant staying up all night.

When writing his assignments he would check and recheck his work, adjusting words and sentences until they sounded 'just right'. He recognised this as a form of procrastination, an avoidance of getting down to the real creative work needed to complete the assignment. He also checked emails and Facebook to delay having to work. In class he held back from offering comments to prevent others from 'noticing how little he understood' and would take note of how much time others seemed to be spending on their assignments, making sure he spent longer than they so as 'not to fall too far behind'. For this reason he also declined social invitations and would not take unnecessary breaks from his work.

Despite Sigurd's fears, he had managed to gain high marks in all of his assignments so far (5). However, rather than considering he had reached his potential in an assignment, he thought (8) that the marker must have made a mistake or that the results had been some sort of 'fluke', or that getting good marks indicated the task could not have been difficult in the first place. Thus his sense of self-worth remained dependent on continued striving and achievement (8 back to 1).

On the other hand, if he considered he had (6) failed to reach the high standards set for himself (for example, if he received what he considered 'negative' feedback on his work) or (7) when he avoided trying to reach the standards by procrastinating, he would (9) isolate himself and be severely self-critical for not trying harder, thus leading directly from (9) back to (1), his worth as a person being dependant on striving and achievement.

Another definition and an exercise

The term 'perfectionist' is commonly applied to a person who tries very hard to achieve their best in everything they do. In reality, while many perfectionists may be concerned with doing their best in everything, others are more concerned with perfectionism in one or two areas of life, such as academia, relationships, fitness and/or cleanliness.

Shafran et al. (2010: 9) define perfectionism as: 'The setting of and striving to meet very demanding standards that are self-imposed and relentlessly pursued, despite this causing problems. It involves basing one's self-worth almost exclusively on how well these high standards are pursued and achieved.'

Out of interest, you may wish to consider your own definition of perfectionism in relation to this one. Remember that it is not a matter of one being right and the other wrong.

Consider the strengths and limitations of each definition. Remember, neither is perfect and this exercise may help you to avoid an all-or-nothing approach to defining perfectionism.

My definition

Strengths	Limitations

Shafran et al.'s (2010) definition

Strengths	Limitations

Perfectionism can be associated with a range of different disorders and is therefore referred to as a 'trans-diagnostic' problem. How might the therapist decide whether to treat the disorder or the perfectionism in this case?

Sigurd's presentation clearly involved aspects of social anxiety (his fear of looking stupid in front of others if he did not perform well) as well as elements of low self-esteem (believing others were all brighter and sharper than him). However, as his presenting problem was in relation to perfectionism, the therapist considered it would be most effective to deal with the central issue, namely Sigurd's self-worth being overly dependent on striving and achievement, as treating this was also likely to reduce his social anxiety and improve his self-esteem (Shafran et al. 2010).

What other problems are often linked to perfectionism?

Perfectionism is often connected with a number of other difficulties, most commonly anxiety, mood and eating problems. Some links are demonstrated here:

Anxiety. Standards which are consistently difficult to meet and which are quickly raised when they *are* met can result in a constant state of anxiety. Likewise, if a person breaks one of their rigid rules it can lead to internal conflict and anxiety. Examples of anxiety disorders linked to perfectionism include social anxiety, obsessive compulsive disorder and obsessive compulsive personality disorder – which has as part of its criteria 'signs of perfectionism that interfere with completing a task' and 'excessively devoted to work and productivity' (American Psychiatric Association 2013).

Mood problems. Constantly scanning for mistakes and failures as well as being unable to meet one's personal standards, or experiencing them as ultimately insufficient, tends to result in feelings of inadequacy, frustration, helplessness and ultimately, depression. Harsh self-criticism and **rumination** further add to a depressed mood.

Eating problems. Rigid rules and standards are often applied to eating, body shape, weight and the need for being in control, with the person having a perfect 'ideal' in mind that is both unrealistic and unattainable. Thus perfectionism in these areas can result in anorexia nervosa and/or bulimia nervosa.

Post-traumatic stress disorder. Recent research has also linked perfectionism with PTSD (which is now categorised as a trauma- and stressor-related disorder). PTSD often involves the shattering of ridged rules or assumptions, as well as an all-or-nothing thinking style (Egan *et al.* 2014; Janoff-Bulman 1985; APA 2013).

From these examples it can be seen how perfectionism is a **trans-diagnostic** problem that plays a key role in maintaining a range of different disorders. Therefore perfectionism often needs to be addressed at some point during therapy for these disorders. Determining when to address it will depend on the degree to which it is maintaining the problem (Fairburn 2008).

Because perfectionism is positively reinforced by praise from others and by a sense of personal success when one does do well (despite the difficulties it causes along the way), there is often ambivalence about change (Egan et al. 2013). What might the therapist do from the outset to promote Sigurd's engagement with the process of change?

The central feature of Shafran *et al.*'s (2010) model is that the perfectionist's identity is often overly based on striving and achievement, sometimes to the point where their sense of self-worth may be fused with these.

Another feature of the model is rigid rules and assumptions, which form part of a person's identity. Because of this it is important to go slowly and carefully, allowing the individual time to clarify the problem and become aware of what it is they want to change (or modify) before actively engaging them in the process of change. Even after the difficulty has been resolved, more time is needed to integrate and consolidate any learning from the changes made (James 2001; Stiles *et al.* 1990).

Sigurd had self-referred to the service and was aware that his perfectionism was causing problems. However, he was very fearful of change as there seemed to be so much at stake (Stiles *et al.* 1990). Therefore it was agreed for him initially to find out more about the problem and so it was agreed that his homework would just involve observing and collecting data about the perfectionism. To collect information Sigurd used a data collection tool adapted from Shafran *et al.* (2010) (see Table 12.1).

In the next session the therapist 'unpacked' the data from this. In particular, she asked whether Sigurd considered the behavior he was adopting to reach his high standards was actually helping him to do so. After some consideration, Sigurd began to notice how his behaviour could often be counter-productive. This surprised him, although it looked obvious once it was written down on the paper in front of him. Thus reflecting on the data helped him gain distance and objectivity from the perfectionism, allowing him to clarify the problem and begin to see the need for change (Stiles *et al.* 1990).

Again they mapped these difficulties onto the formulation, adding and making adjustments to it. To find out more about how the formulation applied in real life, the following week's homework involved more data collection, this time including information about thinking biases and any identified 'rules' that might be driving day to day thoughts and behaviour (see Table 12.2).

Sigurd found it interesting to identify the rules driving his thoughts and behaviours and could tie them in clearly with the formulation (2, 3, 4). Having monitored his perfectionistic patterns over two sessions, Sigurd was now beginning to question the helpfulness of perfectionism and his motivation to change was increasing. At the same time he was gradually becoming less anxious about engaging in therapeutic activity.

To promote his willingness to set goals that required making change, the therapist suggested drawing up a 'pros and cons of change' list (Table 12.3). From this Sigurd could see that many of the things in the 'disadvantages of change' box involved fears that looked quite extreme once they were written down. On the other hand, while the advantages of change sounded 'nice' they also seemed a bit 'soft', as if he'd lose the will to do well in favour of feeling comfortable, which he feared.

To mitigate his fears, the therapist initiated a discussion about trying a less all-or-nothing approach to change and whether some of the advantages of perfectionism could be maintained while some of the disadvantages could be minimized. Sigurd expressed relief at this, as until now he had only been able to think in terms of abandoning the perfectionism completely, which he could not contemplate. The therapist explained the concept of behavioural experiments (see Chapter 2) and how Sigurd might try tweaking things gradually to see if this improved matters; if it did not he could always change back.

Table 12.1 Monitoring perfectionism: week 1 (adapted from Shafran et al. 2010)

Date	Area of perfectionism	Perfectionist thoughts	Performance-related behaviour	Emotions (rate their strength from 1–10)
13.03.14	Work: writing my assignment	'I must get the wording right.'	Kept reading it and changing the wording until it sounded 'just right'. Didn't get much new work done.	Frustrated 10
13.03.14 (later)	Work: writing my assignment	'This is taking me forever. I might as well give up.'	Gave up, only to go back and fret over the details again later.	Irritated 9 Despondent 10 Fretful 10
15.03.14	Work: reading	'Everyone else is quicker than me. I need to understand this really properly.'	Tried to read more quickly but kept going back to reread paragraphs.	Frustrated 10 Miserable 8
18.03.14	Work: reading through assignment	'This sounds good, but I don't understand half of it. I bet I've completely missed out the important concepts.'	Reread the research papers to find any bits I've missed.	Angry at myself 10 Frustrated 10 Demoralised 10
22.03.14	Sport – playing five-a-side	'They're all much fitter than me. I must play my best or they won't ask me to play again.'	Tried hard to stay really focused. Got angry with myself for missing a pass.	Frustrated 8 Disappointed 8 Stressed 9
22.03.14	Socialising – after the match	'I totally screwed up and cost us the match.'	Avoided talking to others by helping to tidy up rather than go in with all the others, staying in the shower longer and leaving early.	Embarrassed 8 Guilty 8 Worthless 10

Table 12.2 Monitoring perfectionism: week 2 (adapted from Shafran et al. 2010)

Date	Situation and area of perfectionism	Perfectionist thoughts and thinking biases	Performance-related behaviour	Identified perfectionist rule this is based on	Emotions (intensity rating 1–10)
24.03.14	Work: handing in my assignment	'I've done my best. If it's no good that's all I can do.' All-or-nothing thinking Catastrophic thinking	Asking others about their assignments – checking to see how well they think they did	Unless I work harder than the others I won't do as well. I must reach my full potential (or I'll fail).	Relief 10 Sinking feeling 8 Anxiety 8
24.03.14	Work: given new module guidelines for next term	'I must thoroughly understand this subject before the start of next term or I'll get left behind.' All-or-nothing thinking Comparing myself unfavourably with others Catastrophising Fortune telling	Read the module guide thoroughly. Went to library to get books before the others get them. Download relevant papers to read before term starts.	I must reach my full potential (or I will fail). I mustn't miss opportunities. I need to work harder than others (to be as good).	Anxious 9 Stressed 10 Depressed 8
27.03.14	Potential break from academic work to have some recreation	'This is an opportunity to get ahead. If I don't take it I'll fall behind.' 'I'll be letting others down if I don't do my best.' All-or-nothing thinking Catastrophising Fortune telling	Turned down an offer to go away for a long weekend so I could start planning the next assignment.	I must reach my full potential (or I will fail). I mustn't miss opportunities. I mustn't make mistakes. I mustn't let others down. I need to work harder than others.	Cheated (out of a break) 10 Hard done by 10 Disappointed 10 Tired and bored 10

Table 12.3 Advantages and disadvantages of changing

Advantages of staying the same	Disadvantages of staying the same
No effort needed for inertia	It can be shattering
No risk involved if I stay the same	I'm constantly on edge
My work is a high standard	I rarely feel satisfied with what I do
I enjoy being thorough in my work and knowing that I know everything	Being so thorough is very time-consuming and I don't have much social life
Others think well of me for my achievements	If I do take time out I feel guilty and can't enjoy myself
	If I make a mistake I feel terrible, as if I've let others down really badly
	I often end up procrastinating anyway

Advantages of changing	Disadvantages of changing
It would be nice to enjoy something apart from work without feeling guilty	It will take a lot of effort
I might begin to enjoy my subject better without so much pressure to be the best	I might not succeed, *or* I might end up being a failure
It would be good to feel accepted as part of the team even when I make a mistake	If my work isn't the best, I'd be a 'nobody'
	I might lose respect if I don't do well

> **Stages of change**
>
> Stiles *et al.* (1990) discuss five stages to the process of change:
>
> - Denial
> - Entering awareness
> - Clarification as a problem
> - Active engagement
> - Resolution.
>
> I have borrowed the following story from my CBT training that I think illustrates these stages nicely.
>
> *Denial.* My CBT teacher once had a pair of old, familiar shoes that he loved. They had comfortably moulded to his feet over many years and seemed to

go with everything he wore. One day his wife suggested buying a replacement pair, but he was resistant to this idea, seeing nothing wrong with the old shoes.

Clarification as a problem. One autumn it rained continuously and he started noticing his feet were cold and often damp. He considered having the shoes repaired but, after being quoted an 'extortionate amount', postponed this. His kindly wife (who had had many years of 'being CBT'd' by him) empathised with his dilemma, wondering what he could do about this problem . . .

Active engagement. With encouragement he at last ventured to the shops where he was disappointed not to find an identical replacement pair, but eventually chose a similar style that he quite liked. He wore them home and was pleased that his feet remained dry and warm despite the rain, even though the shoes were not as comfortable as the old ones.

Resolution. For a time he continued wearing the old shoes and kept the new ones for 'best', but could now recognise that they looked shabby, and when his wife suggested that he might bin them, he reluctantly agreed. After a month or two the new shoes began to mould to the shape of his feet and he almost forgot the old shoes, except for using them to illustrate the difficulty of change . . .

Check-in

You have reached mid-point in the case study. It would be useful at this time to reconsider your original agenda items for reading the chapter and whether or not you have reached them. What gaps in your knowledge and understanding have been filled and which remain outstanding?

How is your time management for reading the chapter? If you need to make adjustments make a note here.

Goal setting and measurement

What problem might Sigurd encounter when trying to set realistic goals?

Sigurd was now ready to set some relatively small, flexible goals which would actively engage him in the process of change (Stiles *et al.* 1990). However, he found it difficult to establish specific goals because he no longer knew what a 'normal' amount of time to spend on work would be. He noticed himself wanting a rule to judge this by, but could not see any way of knowing. He was therefore encouraged to remain curious about this and to be flexible about his goals should they need adjusting later. The following are goals he set:

1. To read a research paper in 2 hours without rushing or going back to reread each paragraph.
2. To limit reading to 9–10 papers for his next assignment.
3. To write his next assignment and only check and correct at the end of each paragraph (maximum time for checking and correcting each paragraph, 10 minutes).
4. To recover from mistakes and feedback quickly (within an hour or two).
5. To develop a healthier work–life balance; this would include going with the others for a game of pool once a week.

Each of his goals fitted with the formulation; the therapist was particularly pleased that Sigurd had included the final goal as it would provide an opportunity for him to broaden his basis for self-evaluation to include social opportunities and relationships.

The therapist was used to working with perfectionists and had gained permission to use the 'Clinical Perfectionism Questionnaire' (Fairburn, submitted) as an objective measurement tool for perfectionism. From experience she was aware that a person's mood can sometimes lower as they come to realise the impact that perfectionism is having on their life. She therefore used the PHQ-9 (Kroenke *et al.* 2001) to monitor Sigurd's mood.

Treatment

What do you think the main aims of treatment would be?

From the formulation the main aims of treatment were to help Sigurd broaden his basis for self-evaluation and to develop a more constructive way of responding to perceived failure. It was also important to address his often extreme and unhelpful cognitions and performance-related behaviours.

Working at the least intrusive level, what treatment strategies would you consider for meeting these aims and helping Sigurd reach his goals?

Treatment had already started by asking Sigurd to identify his negative **automatic thoughts** and unhelpful thinking biases (Table 12.1). Using this material, they used thought records (see Chapter 2) to arrive at more balanced thinking, which Sigurd considered made sense (Table 12.4).

Moving from propositional to implicational learning seemed like a big step for Sigurd as he believed there was a lot at stake. How might the therapist encourage him to make necessary real-world changes?

The therapist wondered how Sigurd could find out more about his new thoughts and build a stronger belief in them. Sigurd could see that taking a break would provide him with the information he needed to build on the new thoughts; however, he felt fearful of doing this in case he got left behind with his work. The therapist acknowledged his anxiety, while at the same time encouraging curiosity. Sigurd eventually reasoned that a weekend away would still leave enough time to manage his work, especially if he used the journey to read. He concluded it was worth the risk if it improved his work–life balance, which was one of his treatment goals.

The therapist therefore encouraged him to set up a behavioural experiment (see Chapter 2) to collect data and draw conclusions. He was familiar with experimenting from his work and it made sense to him to apply the same approach here. This involved:

1. Devising a hypothesis to test: 'if I have a break I'll be more relaxed and will work more efficiently afterwards'
2. Devising a means to test this: have a break and see what difference it makes
3. Devising a way of measuring 'being more relaxed' and 'working more efficiently': for example, a subjective 1–10 scale of how relaxed I feel before and afterwards as well as how much work I am able to achieve within a given amount of time, before and afterwards
4. Carrying out the experiment
5. Collecting data
6. Drawing conclusions
7. Repeating the experiment.

This was Sigurd's agreed homework over the next 2 weeks.

A fortnight later he returned having taken a long weekend in Brussels. Although he had felt guilty stopping work, he had really enjoyed exploring the city and wished he had taken an extra day. He had not been able to concentrate reading on the outward journey and had chosen not to read on the return journey home. The agreed data was recorded on his phone (see Table 12.5).

Sigurd concluded his hypothesis had been correct. He felt more relaxed and ready for the new term and his strength of belief in the original thoughts had risen from 65% to 80%, making it more likely that he would act in line with them again. Although he did not plan to repeat the experiment immediately, he could see how regularly playing pool with the others next term might be a good way to take this forward. Thus making one real-world change and learning from experience that it was helpful had started to impact on his **implicational** belief system (see Chapter 2).

Table 12.4 Sigurd's thought record

Date	Situation	Thought % SOB	Feeling %	Evidence for	Evidence against	On balance . . . % SOB	New feeling %
15.04.14	Handing in assignment	'If it's no good there's nothing I can do.' 100%	Sinking feeling 80%	The assignment is now handed in.	I haven't failed before. If I did fail I could always re-submit.	The essay is unlikely to be 'no good'. Even if it was I could re-submit. 75%	Happy to have handed it in 80%
17.04.14	Being given new module guidelines for next term	'I must thoroughly understand this subject before the start of next term or I'll get left behind.' 80%	Anxious 90% Stressed 100% Depressed 80%	How I feel (fearful, panicky and overwhelmed) (Emotional reasoning)	I'm a student. Students learn throughout term. They are not expected to work all through holidays. Other students are having a break. I haven't got left behind before.	'I'm feeling anxious about the new assignment but if I have a break I'll feel more relaxed and ready to start again afresh next term' 65%	Stressed 20% Anxious 70% Depressed 40%
18.04.14	Potential break from academic work and have some recreation	'This is an opportunity to get ahead. If I don't take it I'll be left behind and I'll let others down if I don't do my best.' 100%	Cheated (out of a break) 100% Hard done by 100% Disappointed 100% Tired and dreary 100%	There are only 3 weeks to the break. If I don't use it to get ahead I will have missed the opportunity.	I'm really tired and feeling resentful. If I just keep working I am likely to burn out and not do well. Working long hours isn't necessarily efficient.	If I take a break and go away for the weekend I might feel really refreshed and prepared for the next assignment. I can always do some reading on the train. 65%	A weight lifted 80% Hopeful 70% Relieved 90%

SOB = Strength of belief

Table 12.5 Data from experiment

	Before going away	After going away
Relaxedness	0/10	7/10
Amount of work accomplished in a day	Found and downloaded ten research papers to read, but unable to concentrate on reading.	Able to concentrate and read two research papers in one day.
Amount of work accomplished in a week	Able to tweak assignment but then re-tweaked it again back to how it was before. Gathered the reading material for next term but unable to engage with the topic or concentrate on reading anything about it.	Able to mentally engage with the new topic and read through the module guidelines. Read eight research papers.

Sigurd felt guilty about taking a break from his work, which could undermine his new behaviour. How might the therapist work with Sigurd to mitigate this feeling?

By taking a break Sigurd had infringed his rules: 'I need to work harder than others to get the same grades', 'I mustn't miss opportunities [to work]' and 'I mustn't let others down'. Breaking these rules had led to a barrage of self-critical thinking, resulting in him feeling guilty for having 'deliberately' failed to do his best. Being self-critical reinforces the perfectionism cycle by stressing the idea that one's self-worth is dependent on achieving the standards set by the rules (see Figure 12.1: 9 back to 1 and then 2).

To teach Sigurd how to interrupt the cycle at this point (9), the therapist encouraged him to adopt a more self-compassionate stance, asking him what he would say to a friend who was experiencing burn-out and considering taking a break. At first Sigurd struggled with this, coming up with unhelpful suggestions such as 'Don't worry, you'll probably feel fine in the morning' and 'You usually manage'.

The therapist therefore demonstrated an empathic, supportive alternative: 'This seems very difficult for you. What do you need to make things easier at the moment so you will be able to get on better later? How can I help?' She stressed the need for adopting an empathic, non-judgemental, non-threatening tone towards himself, which would foster feelings of safeness (Gilbert 2005).

Sigurd could see what she meant, but believed it was important to be self-critical because without this threat he'd never get anything done. However, he quickly recognised his all-or-nothing thinking ('never', 'anything') and acknowledged this called for another behavioural experiment.

Over the next week he experimented with identifying and interrupting his self-critical thinking with a kinder tone, giving himself encouragement rather than a telling off to test what impact this had on his attitude to work and on his mood. While this felt odd, he discovered that his mood improved which impacted favourably on his work, so he decided to keep this new behaviour as it was helpful.

Sigurd remained uncertain about how much time it was 'normal' to spend on various aspects of his work. How could he find out what is normal or average?

Sigurd felt anxious about limiting the number of research papers for his next assignment and was concerned he would be disadvantaged by spending only 10 minutes checking and correcting each paragraph. He feared the other students would be doing much more and that he would get left behind.

The therapist therefore suggested carrying out a survey to gather data about the number of research papers other students read and how long they spent writing their assignments. Sigurd agreed and they spent the session devising questions for the survey.

The following week Sigurd returned with information from 20 students suggesting that, on the whole, the amount of time they spent writing their assignments depended on what else was happening in their lives at the time. Something similar held true for the number of research papers they read, although two of the students were more rigorous in their approach. It surprised Sigurd that the majority of the sample did not always prioritise their work and learned from this that maybe he could afford to experiment reducing the number of papers he read for the next assignment, which he decided to do.

How might the therapist help Sigurd start working toward ending therapy and preventing a relapse?

By now therapy sessions were being spaced fortnightly to promote self-reliance, and Sigurd was encouraged to devise experiments independently (Hawton *et al.* 1989). Looking at the formulation, he noticed how his old rules and standards had been somewhat undermined by the work they had undertaken so far and he commented on how 'all-or-nothing' they now looked:

> I must reach my full potential or I will have failed
> I mustn't miss opportunities
> I mustn't make mistakes
> I mustn't let others down
> I need to work harder than others to get the same grades.

The therapist suggested that if he took out some of the extreme language it might make the rules more moderate and less sabotaging. She asked what he would prefer the rules to be and whether he wanted to reword them. After some consideration Sigurd decided on the following:

- I'd like to reach my potential as a well-rounded person.
- It's good to think about my values before deciding what opportunities to take.
- If I make a mistake I can move on and learn from it.
- I'll try to make myself and others proud of me.
- I might chose to work harder than others, but I don't have to do this to prove my worth.

He now felt confident to work independently on experimenting with these new standards and said he would be happy to meet just once more at the start of next term for a follow-up to make sure he was still moving in the right direction.

To consolidate his learning from therapy and plan how to manage any future setbacks they worked together on a continued improvement plan to take things forward (Table 12.6).

Table 12.6 Sigurd's continued improvement plan

What have you learned from these sessions?	1. My perfectionist behaviour (checking, keeping tweaking things, reading absolutely everything and then reading it again, etc.) was making it less likely that my work would get finished or be good. 2. That all-or-nothing thinking makes it seem as if when I'm not succeeding I'm failing. Seeing things on a continuum is much more helpful. 3. Rules are more helpful when they are flexible. 4. Being kinder to myself when I make mistakes helps me not to get depressed, and others seem to be OK when I make mistakes because they make them too. 5. I work better when I take breaks. 6. Having friends is important.
What strategies have you found most helpful?	1. Testing my thoughts for accuracy and helpfulness and taking a more balanced view. 2. Experimenting to find out more about my new balanced thoughts.
What do you need to do to maintain/extend change?	1. Experiment with my new rules to find out if they work better and if I prefer them. Tweak them for a good 'fit'. 2. Continue taking regular breaks from work including social and physical activities. 3. Try to reach my potential across a range of activities that I value. 4. After therapy check in with myself monthly to see how I'm going with this.
What might lead to a setback?	Getting a poor mark/failing at something. Comparing myself with others and thinking I'm not as good. Thinking I constantly need to work harder than others. Being criticised harshly. Getting new assignments. Being given a lot of opportunities.
How would you recognise this?	I'll start to feel panicky and stressed. I'll just keep going without a break. Checking, correcting; saying no to invitations. I'll find it hard to make decisions because of all-or-nothing thinking (seeing one decision as wrong and the other right). I'll be self-critical.

(*Continued*)

Table 12.6 (Continued)

Can you identify skills you have learned, resources, people and agencies that could help manage this set back?	Thought records (opening up my perspective) Behavioural experiments (reality testing) Taking breaks (rest and a change) Socialising (more balanced perspective) Read and follow this continued improvement plan Read through old therapy notes I could return to the Counselling Service for a booster session

Client Name .... Therapist Name .... Date ....

Follow-up session and conclusion of treatment

Why is it helpful to compare both qualitative and quantitative data when evaluating treatment outcomes?

At the follow-up Sigurd looked refreshed and reported looking forward to the new term's assignments. He had been away for a week's walking holiday with a group of students from his cohort and, although they had talked a bit about work, the holiday had been invigorating and refreshing.

On one occasion Sigurd had been leading the walk and had taken the wrong direction, which meant an hour's backtrack. The group members had groaned at first but had later joked good-heartedly about this over dinner. Sigurd realised his mistake had caused problems for the group but they had managed OK and had moved on with a good spirit; in some strange way the mistake made him feel more connected to and accepted by the group. Unpacking this with the therapist, he realised that the 'strange way' involved the groups' acceptance of him as a fallible human being, just like the rest of them, and that mistakes were not the end of the world.

Sigurd was finding his new standards much more workable and was pleased that his marks for the last term had not been compromised as a result of the changes he had made. Together they reviewed the quantitative data outcomes of therapy, mapping treatment against the fortnightly scores, which helped to make sense of them (Table 12.7).

Table 12.7 Treatment outcomes

Date	Clinical Perfectionism Scale*	PHQ-9
Session 1 (Assessment)	39	13
Session 3 (Monitoring)	37	14
Session 5 (Thought records)	33	12
Session 7 (Brussels trip)	25	8
Session 9 (Survey)	25	5
Session 11 (Follow-up)	18	3

* The mean for a control group on the Clinical Perfectionism Scale was 24.17 with a standard deviation of 4.47 (Egan *et al.*, submitted)

Sigurd's mood had initially dropped in session 3 when he realised how much of a problem the perfectionism actually was. However, in session 7 his mood had improved as a result of the weekend in Brussels and in session 11 things had improved considerably after the week away with friends. He found mapping the qualitative outcomes onto the quantitative outcomes in this way interesting and meaningful.

Sigurd thanked the therapist, who reminded him that while it had been a team effort, any changes were ultimately attributable to his own hard work.

Reflections on the case

Looking back on the case, the therapist considered that much of the later treatment success had been as a result of going slowly at the outset and encouraging Sigurd to monitor various aspects of his perfectionism. This prolonged period of monitoring made it clear that his perfectionism was paradoxically sabotaging his performance. The therapist reflected on how helpful it had been to ask him: 'Does this behaviour help you to meet your standards or does it prevent you from reaching them?'

This had focused Sigurd on the effect that his performance-related behaviour was having on his work, and he could see how very often it directly prevented him from reaching his desired standards. This had been a 'penny-drop' moment for him which resulted in a reduction in his anxiety about trying things differently.

Another important thing to address had been Sigurd's self-criticalness whenever he broke one of his rules, especially if he considered he might be letting someone else down. He initially struggled with the idea of self-compassion and found compassionate responses difficult to generate. However, once he applied the same treatment 'rules' to this as to the rest of treatment (i.e. noticing his thinking bias and the opportunity it held for an experiment), it allowed him scope to broaden his outlook.

Perfectionists often strive for a 'perfect' ending to therapy, so towards the end it had been important to encourage independence by spacing sessions out and leaving some unfinished work in progress for Sigurd to continue with alone. This work involved using strategies he was familiar with and felt confident using. He had been positive about ending therapy (unlike some other perfectionists the therapist had worked with) and things had gone to plan in regard to the ending.

Overall, the case had been relatively straightforward. Sigurd had been prepared to try things out once he could see potential benefits and had used his initiative to devise and carry out experiments in line with the formulation.

Significant learning for the therapist had been to go more slowly than normal as Sigurd had been so anxious about making changes. She had found this difficult to do working within a relatively short-term service and had felt pressured to speed things up. However, from experience she knew this would be counter-productive and that time invested at the outset would save time later.

She had been able to build a good therapeutic relationship with Sigurd and had enjoyed working with him toward a satisfactory outcome for them both.

Homework

Can you identify any personal perfectionist rules or standards? These can sometimes be in the form of family sayings that are deliberately passed on, such as 'If a job's worth doing it's worth doing well' or 'Failing to prepare is preparing to fail'.

How have these rules and standards influenced your life so far, both helpfully and unhelpfully?

Is there any way in which you would like to modify these rules?

Over the coming week practice the modified rules and standards and see whether you would like to keep them or adapt them.

Further reading: Fursland *et al.* (2009).

Conclusion and consolidation of your learning

Answer the following questions:

1 Name at least four disorders that are often associated with perfectionism.

2   How might perfectionism be maintaining each of these problems?

3   What is the central feature of Shafran *et al.*'s (2010) model of perfectionism?

4   What thinking biases are common in perfectionism?

5   How might you recognise ambivalence to change?

6   How would you work with ambivalence to change in the case of perfectionism?

7   What treatment strategies would you consider using when treating perfectionism and why?

Feedback

Think about your experience of reading this chapter and note any feedback for the authors here:

At the end of the book you may wish to collate the feedback together to forward to the following address: nick.wrycraft@anglia.ac.uk

13 Assertiveness

> ✏️ **Reader's agenda**
>
> Take a few moments to consider your own agenda or reasons for reading this chapter and make a note of them here:
>
> •
>
> •
>
> The aim of this case study is to:
>
> - Illustrate how to work trans-diagnostically with interpersonal difficulties
> - Demonstrate the use of an idiosyncratic formulation for interpersonal difficulties
> - Highlight some of the difficulties that can crop up in therapy when working with interpersonal difficulties
> - Demonstrate how to work with assumptions driving both assertive and non-assertive behaviour.
>
> **Managing your time**
>
> Take a moment to consider how long you plan to spend reading this chapter, and make a note here:

Introduction

Cognitive behavioural therapy is commonly targeted at specific disorders, and working with assertiveness is sometimes an inherent part of treatment for these disorders, particularly in social anxiety (Padesky 1997). However, at times people can present for treatment experiencing interpersonal problems, such as a lack of assertiveness, apart from a specific disorder.

What impact might a lack of assertiveness have on the therapeutic relationship?

Beliefs and assumptions about relating interpersonally drive these difficulties, and because of this the same problem the person is experiencing outside of therapy can also crop up within the therapeutic relationship itself. The example in this case study involves two assumptions that have potential to play out unhelpfully between the client and therapist, namely, 'I should always obey people in authority' and 'if I say what I think others will not take me seriously and will reject me/my opinion'. While this case study does not focus specifically on difficulties within the therapeutic relationship it does raise awareness of the potential for this.

GP assessment

Aditi is a 23-year-old Asian woman, referred by her GP for CBT for anxiety and depression as a result of bullying and intimidation at work. At the GP appointment she completed the PHQ-9 (Kroenke *et al.* 2001), which indicated moderate depression. While she was waiting for therapy her GP recommended a self-help book on assertiveness, which she read.

CBT assessment and engagement

Aditi was seen by a cognitive behavioural therapist attached to her GP surgery. At the time of assessment she had been signed off work for 2 weeks. It was agreed that weekly evening appointments would suit her needs as she hoped to return to work soon and did not want her employer to know she was having therapy. A contract for six sessions and a follow-up appointment 2 months later was initially agreed, with potential to extend the number of sessions if needed.

At the assessment Aditi's score on the PHQ-9 (Kroenke *et al.* 2001) had improved from 19 to 17 since seeing her GP, which still indicated she was experiencing moderate depression. She put the reduction in her score down to having done something about the problem, which she had found empowering. She thought the depression was likely to resolve once she was coping better at work. For this reason she wanted the focus of therapy to be on thinking and behaving more assertively.

Formulating the difficulty

What models might be appropriate to consider and what would help the therapist decide on which model to use?

When deciding how to formulate the problem a number of things were taken into consideration, including which model would provide the best 'fit'. As people who are bullied often tend to feel inferior to others both the social anxiety model (Wells 1997) and the low self-esteem model (Fennell 1997) were initially considered.

However, neither of these models fitted well with Aditi's experiences as she was neither self-focused nor concerned by physiological symptoms of anxiety. While the bullying *had* impacted on her self-esteem she remained reasonably self-confident outside work. The therapist therefore decided to design an **idiosyncratic** formulation that took into account the background to Aditi's difficulty as well as the short- and long-term maintenance effects of her safety behaviours on the problem.

Data collected during assessment was mapped out collaboratively with Aditi according to this formulation.

Exercise

Few people get through life without experiencing some form of bullying. If you have had particularly difficult experiences with bullying, thinking about this may produce uncomfortable feelings.

If it is not too painful to do so, take a few minutes to consider what you have learned from your experience of bullying, whether this is experience of being bullied, or the experience of being a bully (as both lack assertion skills).

This learning is likely to have formed your personal assumptions and beliefs about bullying. Make a note here of anything you would like to understand better.

CBT formulation

The formulation was collaboratively designed by Aditi and her therapist using the assessment details given below. Using these details, try mapping out the formulation yourself in the space provided below. The formulation needs to demonstrate short- and longer-term maintenance factors (which generally involve the use of safety behaviours).

Aditi explained how she currently lived at home with her extended family, which she described as 'patriarchal and caring'. She was brought up to respect and obey authority figures, especially men and people older than herself (1), which had worked well for her until now. Although she expected to get married soon, she described herself as relatively inexperienced around men compared with other girls in her peer group.

Aditi worked for a pharmaceutical company and described how she was originally assigned a mentor and how keen she had been to please him and make a good impression. The mentor appeared well respected and she initially felt in awe of him (1). From the start there were signs of bullying when her mentor advised her not to comment in meetings as she was very junior and other members of staff would not take her comments seriously (2). She accepted this advice unquestioningly because it fitted with her pre-existing rules and assumptions (1).

Over a period Aditi noticed her confidence being eroded as her mentor became more and more critical of her work, highlighting mistakes in front of others and making derogatory and personal comments in private about her appearance (2). She continued trying to please him but for the first time her rules (1) were no longer working as they had before.

The bullying triggered various negative **automatic thoughts** (2 to 3) which arose out of her rules and assumptions (1). These thoughts led to confusion and anxiety, as well as to dread of having to see her mentor (3 to 4).

To reduce these feelings Aditi began adopting a variety of safety behaviours, including staying within her own work bay, lying low, adopting passive body language and 'playing safe' to avoid comment from the mentor (4 to 5). These avoidance behaviours reduced anxiety, making her feel safer in the short term (5 to 6).

However, in the longer term the reduction of anxiety **negatively reinforced** her safety behaviours (see Chapter 2), keeping her isolated from colleagues, which she found frustrating and depressing (6 to 7). Although she did not have any suicidal thoughts she felt angry with herself for letting him get to her so much. All of this prevented change and maintained the difficulty (7 to 2).

Despite Aditi's efforts, things progressed from verbal bullying to physical intimidation, taking her deeper into the cycle. One afternoon her mentor unexpectedly leaned across, pushing up against her, physically trapping her for some moments. Aditi thought he might become more aggressive if she moved or said anything, but doing nothing allowed him to repeat this behaviour whenever no one was about. Her anxiety rose to a rating of 10/10 at these moments and the mention of his name now caused a surge of dread. Her behavioural response was to try and ignore him and pretend that it was not bothering her, which she hoped would at least not escalate things.

They worked collaboratively on the formulation over the first two sessions until Aditi found a good 'fit' that made sense to her of how the problem was being maintained.

> Now compare the idiosyncratic formulation in Figure 13.1 with your own formulation. Remember, there is no one 'right' formulation, but it does need to demonstrate how the problem is currently being maintained and does have to make sense to the person involved

Assertiveness

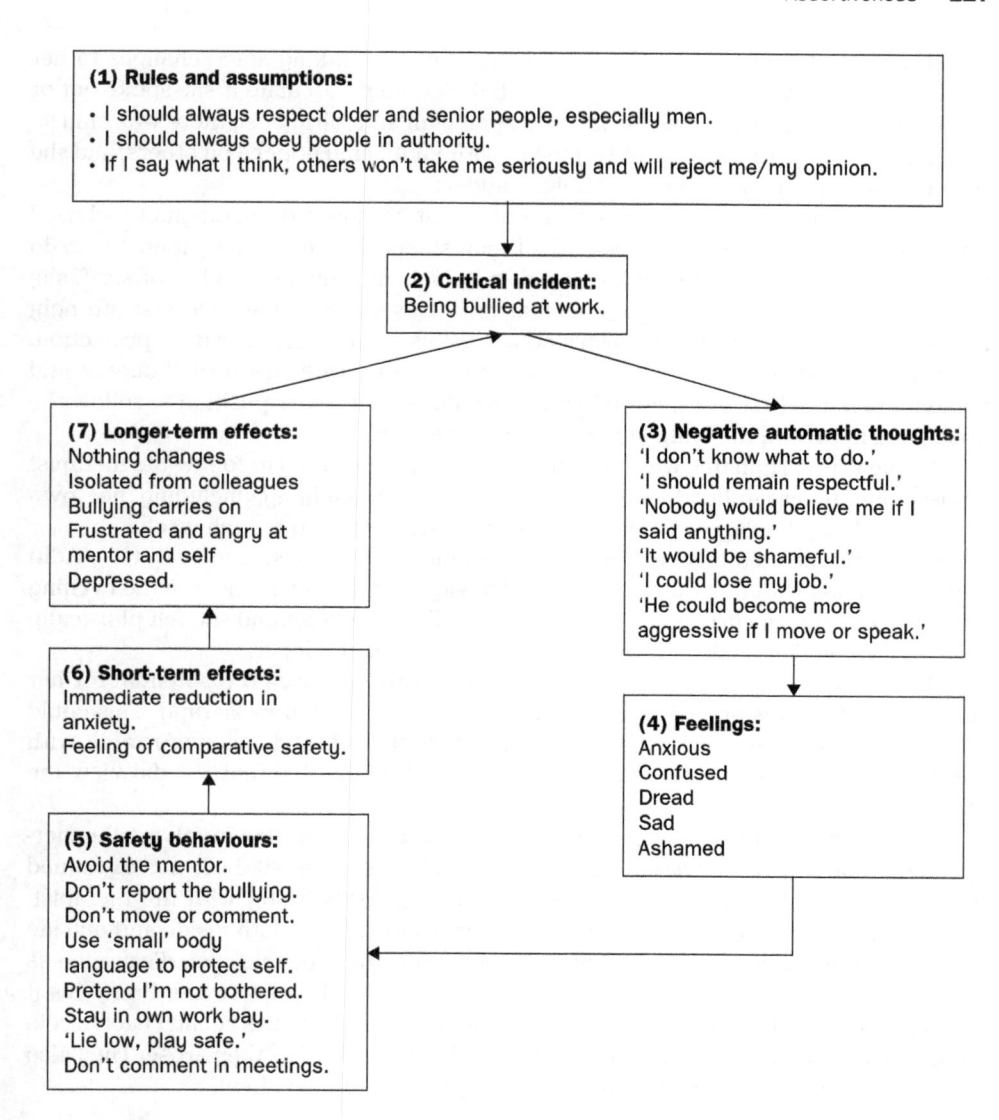

(1) Rules and assumptions:
- I should always respect older and senior people, especially men.
- I should always obey people in authority.
- If I say what I think, others won't take me seriously and will reject me/my opinion.

(2) Critical incident: Being bullied at work.

(3) Negative automatic thoughts:
'I don't know what to do.'
'I should remain respectful.'
'Nobody would believe me if I said anything.'
'It would be shameful.'
'I could lose my job.'
'He could become more aggressive if I move or speak.'

(4) Feelings:
Anxious
Confused
Dread
Sad
Ashamed

(5) Safety behaviours:
Avoid the mentor.
Don't report the bullying.
Don't move or comment.
Use 'small' body language to protect self.
Pretend I'm not bothered.
Stay in own work bay.
'Lie low, play safe.'
Don't comment in meetings.

(6) Short-term effects:
Immediate reduction in anxiety.
Feeling of comparative safety.

(7) Longer-term effects:
Nothing changes
Isolated from colleagues
Bullying carries on
Frustrated and angry at mentor and self
Depressed.

Figure 13.1 Idiosyncratic formulation

Risk

What risks might be involved and how could these be managed?

Bullying inherently involves risk. While Aditi was depressed as a result of the bullying, she otherwise enjoyed her family life and did not currently experience thoughts of harming herself or anyone else.

However, she realised that therapy would involve making some changes to her behaviour in the workplace and feared the bullying might escalate if she spoke out or acted differently. However, as the lab was open-plan and fairly busy there was only so much that her mentor could do or say to her without it being noticed by others, and she recognised that her fears were probably exaggerated.

Aditi explained how the anti-bullying policy at her place of employment advised talking to the individual concerned in the first instance. However, she felt unable to do this for fear that the situation might escalate, which, as a junior member of staff, she considered might put her employment at risk. Despite this, the therapist strongly recommended Aditi to follow the work policy as this would afford her legal protection. Aditi understood this and said she was keen to work with her own thoughts and behaviours in the first instance so that she would be in a better position to follow the policy and approach the bully herself, as recommended.

As she was certain this was the course of action she wanted to follow the therapist advised her to carefully document any instances of bullying, including her own responses. They then agreed to review Aditi's decision about this each week.

Currently the mentor's behaviour was confined to the workplace, and while Aditi had no dealings with him outside work and always left the department in the evening before he did, it was agreed that if things changed at any point and she felt physically unsafe she would immediately raise the matter with her employer.

Another risk factor that the therapist raised with Aditi was the potential for her rule 'I should always obey people in authority' to be activated in therapy. This could result in her agreeing to homework assignments that she felt uncomfortable with and that could prove unsafe. In response to this Aditi admitted that she did view the therapist as an authority figure.

Therefore the importance of genuine therapeutic collaboration involving the therapist and Aditi as equal partners was emphasised (James *et al.* 2001). It was explained how Aditi would be expected to take responsibility for working with the therapist, making sure that things were planned to her own satisfaction both inside and outside the therapeutic environment. Aditi expressed appreciation for this open discussion as it gave her permission to raise any difficulties without feeling awkward. From this it was agreed to routinely include the therapeutic relationship on the agenda each week, making sure that any difficulties were identified and resolved as they arose. They also agreed to keep risk more generally as a weekly therapy agenda item.

Goals of therapy and measurement:

As a contract for six sessions and a follow-up had been agreed, what might be appropriate goals for Aditi within this timeframe?

Aditi established clear goals for treatment:

1   To get back to work within 2 weeks.
2   To be able to move around the lab and speak with colleagues with a maximum subjective anxiety rating of 3/10 within 6 weeks.

3   To restore her self-confidence to a subjective level of 7/10 (currently rated at 2/10 when at work), which would be evident by her contributing in a department meeting despite her mentor's warning (within 6 weeks).

It was agreed that Aditi's mood would be evaluated fortnightly using the PHQ-9 (Kroenke *et al.* 2001). Progress toward her goals required subjective measurement of her anxiety and confidence levels, on a scale of 0 to 10, with 10 representing high and 0 representing no anxiety or confidence. It was agreed to rate these weekly.

> **Check-in**
>
> You have reached the half-way point in the chapter, and it would be helpful to take a few moments to summarise the main points of your learning so far.
>
> Have new questions arisen in your mind that you would like to add to your original agenda?
>
> Are you on time with your original plans? What adjustments, if any, do you need to make? Make a note of these here.

Treatment

How might the therapist clarify what is meant by assertive behaviour and begin to encourage change?

The therapist began treatment with psycho-education, clarifying Aditi's understanding of assertive communication. Aditi identified four types of behaviour she had learned about from the book her GP had recommended:

1   Passive – communicating and behaving in a way that sets aside one's own needs and aspirations in favour of other people's needs and wants.
2   Passive-aggressive – communicating and behaving in a way that is indirect and manipulative.
3   Aggressive – communicating and behaving in a domineering and forceful way in order to get one's own way.
4   Assertive – communicating and behaving in a way that is confident, clear and respectful.

Aditi recognised herself as passive in her interactions with the mentor and older people generally, whereas the mentor was clearly being passive-aggressive and/or aggressive toward her (Hadfield and Hasson 2010).

Using the formulation, the therapist explained how problems typically arise when rules and assumptions about communication styles are held rigidly as either 'right' or 'wrong'. This has the effect of preventing flexible, adaptive responses which allow choice from a range of behaviours according to circumstance. From the formulation Aditi noted her own rules and assumptions that were preventing her from dealing effectively with this new situation (1).

For homework Aditi was encouraged to identify someone assertive (preferably female) whom she would like to use as a role model. In order to raise her awareness she was to watch this person's body language, speech and behaviour and make some notes. At the same time she was asked to monitor her own behaviour, including passive and more assertive responses and the situations that triggered these.

For a role model Aditi chose a strong but kindly female character from a TV detective series she enjoyed watching. She noted the contrast between her role model's confident voice and body language when dealing with her superiors and her own quiet voice and timid body language that was triggered around people in authority. She saw body language as the main thing she would like to work on over the next few sessions. This focus was in line with her goals and meant working behaviourally with her safety behaviours in the first instance (5).

To start with, the therapist asked Aditi to demonstrate in the session how she responds physically when the bully is around and then to demonstrate how her role model would respond in the same circumstance, initially to see how different it would feel. Aditi thought this might be useful but imagined she would feel really uncomfortable acting assertively, which the therapist agreed she might.

To extend any potential learning from this, the therapist suggested they used Aditi's mobile phone to film the role plays so that she could look back on her body language from an observer's viewpoint, that is, beyond her subjective perspective to how the bully might see things. The advantage of using her phone was that she would be in control of the recording and could keep or delete it as she chose (Wells 1997).

Aditi agreed to being filmed on her mobile and started by adopting the 'small' body posture she used when the bully was around, sitting with arms folded across her chest, slightly stooped while keeping her head down to avoid eye contact. When she spoke her voice was quiet and a bit shaky.

The filming was stopped momentarily to allow her to change role into the TV detective. She then acted how she imagined the detective would be in the same circumstance. This time she stood up as she imagined the bully approaching, and although she did not look in his direction, she moved toward him slightly and spoke in a clear, audible voice to (an imagined) colleague standing nearby. These were things she would not contemplate doing in reality.

The filmed role plays took only minutes, but looking back on them was a revelation to Aditi. She commented on how a bully would be much more likely to pick on someone with 'small' body language than someone with bigger (detective's) posture and a firmer voice. Her learning from watching the filmed role plays was that the body language she adopted to make herself feel safer when the bully was around (5) paradoxically enabled the bully to pick on her more easily.

While this seemed obvious in retrospect, Aditi had been following her subjective 'felt sense' up until now rather than thinking logically about the situation. The recording had clarified to her how she wanted to change, and she was keen to take this learning forward by returning to work and trying it out within the workplace. However, the therapist encouraged her to take things slowly and try out anything new in a planned and controlled manner. She was encouraged to view and reflect on the recording again for homework that week.

How can Aditi and her therapist take this learning forward safely, and what is important to consider when role playing the part of a bully?

The following week Aditi and the therapist planned together how to take the learning from this forward in a **graded** way to ensure successful progress and build confidence. Aditi thought the next logical step would be to practise the new body language in a variety of true-to-life role plays with the therapist in the session so that she would be more prepared to make changes in the 'real world' (Hawton et al. 1989).

When role-playing bullying behaviour it is important to reverse roles in the first instance as experiencing the therapist in the role of bully could be upsetting and might damage the therapeutic relationship if not handled sensitively. By reversing the role play at first, with Aditi playing the part of her mentor, it gave the therapist some indication of how to play the part of the mentor and afforded an opportunity for her to model assertive responses. The role play could then be successfully reversed with less risk of causing damage to the therapeutic relationship.

The situation role-played was at Aditi's bench in the lab, with the mentor coming over and leaning up against her. The first role play involved using Aditi's usual safety behaviour of staying within her own work bay, trying to act as if she did not care by not moving or commenting and employing 'small' body language.

Aditi found playing things from the mentor's perspective most enlightening as carrying out the behaviour felt much more deliberate and intentional than she had expected it to. She had been surprised at how easy it had been to get the therapist (acting as her) into the position she wanted, and how empowering it was for the mentor to hold her there for a few moments until he chose to move.

Aditi began to express anger about this and wanted to change roles so that she could inhibit his behaviour with more assertive body language. Before changing roles the therapist discussed things with Aditi, agreeing for the therapist to underplay rather than overplay the role and to come out of role if at any point Aditi choose to.

In the role play the therapist (as mentor) approached Aditi as she was sitting at her bench. This time Aditi stood up as she saw him approaching and moved toward him slightly, making it difficult for him to come up from behind and push against her. At the same time she spoke to (an imaginary) colleague who sits opposite her, asking in a strong voice if she could borrow a book. The therapist (as the mentor) found it difficult to bully Aditi as 'he' had planned in this circumstance, partly because Aditi was positioned differently and partly because a colleague was now involved in the situation; 'he' therefore had no choice but to walk past.

Again, the role play was brief and little was said, but Aditi found it liberating. As they came out of role she laughed at how relatively easily she had influenced the situation by changing her behaviour. In the discussion that followed they referred to the formulation and how safety behaviours had been maintaining the problem (5) and how once they were dropped things improved.

The therapist fed back her experience of being in the role of the mentor and how when Aditi unexpectedly stood up and came towards 'him' it had disabled his intention to come up behind and push against her, and how the only thing left to do had been to walk by and pretend to be going somewhere else.

Aditi said how even though it had only been a role play she had felt anxious about standing up and moving toward the mentor, and that she would not normally dream of doing this. However, talking out loud to the (imaginary) colleague had felt really empowering as she had taken control of her part in the situation, making her presence felt and causing the mentor to lose control of what he had intended to do.

Her learning from this exercise was that employing open and confident body language seemed helpful in sending a clear message that she would not let herself be bullied, although it had felt a scary thing to do.

How can working behaviourally impact on a person's belief system, changing how they think and feel about the situation?

Pondering on the formulation, Aditi commented how behaving differently had changed her original negative thoughts, 'I don't know what to do' and 'He could become more aggressive if I move or speak', at least to some extent. She now had a much clearer idea about what to do and felt less afraid of him becoming aggressive if she moved or spoke. This set her wondering about the validity of other thoughts and assumptions recorded on the formulation.

Behaving differently, even in the role-played situation, had opened Aditi's perspective to new cognitive learning. Role play is a form of behavioural experiment, in this case to test the effect of Aditi's safety behaviours on the outcome of the situation (Bennett-Levy *et al.* 2004).

From working behaviourally Aditi had developed a new thought: 'if I approach rather than avoid him he is less likely to bully me'. She now felt ready to test this in real life.

How might Aditi's learning be taken forward to strengthen these new cognitions?

Aditi was returning to work that week and felt confident enough to try out her newly acquired body language at work. A behavioural experiment incorporating **exposure and response prevention** (which had been explained to her – see Chapter 2) was planned to find out more about her new thought that 'if I approach rather than avoid him he is less likely to bully me'.

Thinking the experiment through more carefully in session she modified the thought, adding a further prediction: 'if I move or speak he might bustle about in an attempt to intimidate me but will be less aggressive in the long run if I approach rather than avoid him. My anxiety will rise but it will go down again if I stay in the situation long enough.'

The experiment that Aditi planned was in line with her second goal and involved moving around the department and speaking to her colleagues rather than remaining in her own work bay as she had done previously. This seemed a relatively 'safe' place to start, and if things went well she planned to go over and speak to a colleague who worked in the bay next to the mentor. She would rate and keep track of her anxiety levels throughout, staying in the situation until her anxiety subsided.

The following week Aditi returned with data collected from the experiment. As predicted, the mentor had tried to intimidate her by bustling around noisily when she approached to talk with the colleague near his area. However, she remained talking with the colleague for a full 3 minutes the first time, until her anxiety reduced from 8/10 to 5/10.

Flushed with success, she had returned twice more on the same day to repeat the experiment, and found that her anxiety only rose to 7 the second time and to 6 the third time, although the mentor had continued to bustle and thump about whenever she approached.

She found it helpful to keep rating her anxiety as each time it went down as predicted, which strengthened her resolve. Her new-found power over the anxiety amused her and the exercise started to feel much less threatening and almost like a game by the third time.

From this Aditi learned that her second prediction had been accurate and that when she moved around and spoke to colleagues the mentor had bustled about in an attempt to intimidate her, but staying in the situation until her anxiety reduced meant she was becoming much less anxious about his behaviour. An added benefit was that she respected herself more when she acted assertively. The experiment was a turning point for her because moving around and talking to her colleagues helped her to see herself as an equal with her colleagues, thus dropping this safety behaviour (5) had undermined her old unhelpful assumptions about always needing to be deferential toward people older than herself (1).

Aditi continued experimenting over the following weeks, routinely venturing out from her workspace and talking to colleagues to build strength of belief in her new thoughts and employing exposure and response prevention when she felt anxious.

On one occasion the mentor caught her off guard and tried to push against her again, but this time, almost without thinking, she had stepped aside and doubled back round behind him. Her anxiety had shot up but she stepped forward again and stood beside him, much to his evident surprise (and her own!). She bravely stayed in the situation until her anxiety had started to settle when the mentor picked up a heavy dish and slammed it down before quickly scuttling back to his own work area. Aditi's anxiety shot up again but she remained where she was, letting her anxiety subside before returning to her area, but this time via a colleague nearer to the mentor, rather than retreating immediately to her bay.

Reflecting on this in the session, Aditi concluded that the mentor was probably angry because he could no longer intimidate her and that she actually viewed him as immature rather than someone in authority to be respected. Again, comparing these conclusions with the formulation, she found herself wanting to adjust her original thoughts and assumptions in light of her new experiences.

How could the therapist encourage Aditi toward achieving her final goal of contributing in a team meeting?

Aditi's confidence at work was growing and she began to consider her third goal, which was to speak up in a department meeting. This would need careful planning and she decided to set it up as a behavioural experiment so that she could learn from it, whatever the outcome (Bennett-Levy et al. 2004).

To help understand the meeting set-up the therapist asked Aditi to map the seating arrangements on paper. The meeting took place around an oblong table facing the screen. The manager sat at the front and the mentor sat opposite and along from the line manager; Aditi sat in front of the mentor and during presentations he would put his feet on her chair, which irritated her.

Reflecting on her diagram, Aditi said she felt 'stuck' in this position, as if she had been directed to sit there and could not sit anywhere else, although this had not actually been the case. She began to consider alternative positions and decided at the next meeting she would sit behind the mentor so he could not put his feet on her chair.

Her experiment was planned as before and involved testing prediction A, that 'if I say something, the others won't take me seriously and will show this by overlooking what I've said' against her alternative prediction B, that 'the others might take my comment seriously and spend time discussing it'.

The following week Aditi reported that things had gone much better than expected. She had been able to contribute to the presentation and the team had discussed her idea for some time.

At one point during the meeting Aditi had played with the idea of putting her foot on the mentor's chair, which made her smile. She realised this would be passive-aggressive behaviour, but even entertaining the idea for a moment presented her with more choices than before, which demonstrated more flexible thinking.

Treatment outcomes

What is the importance of measuring outcomes?

Taking regular measurements affords information about the basic elements of the problem and highlights the effects of any interventions undertaken. Collecting data on an ongoing basis is a more reliable and accurate measure than reflecting retrospectively on this, and Aditi found it interesting and encouraging to consider the progress she was making in such concrete terms.

Her scores on the PHQ-9 (Kroenke et al. 2001) indicated that her depressed mood had improved significantly once she had empowered herself within the working environment, as she predicted it would. Subjective measures showed a correlation between her anxiety and confidence levels, with confidence growing as she learned to tolerate her anxiety and faced her fears (see Table 13.1).

Reaching her therapy goals within six sessions gave Aditi's self-confidence a real boost. However, she still had not spoken to the mentor directly or to anyone else in the department about what had been happening. The therapist was keen for Aditi to address this before finally ending therapy. An extra session was therefore agreed to plan and

Table 13.1 Measurement of treatment outcomes

Date	PHQ-9 Score	Anxiety 0 to 10 (10=high)	Confidence 0 to 10 (10 = high)	Comments
21.12.11	19 (moderately severe)	Not assessed	Not assessed	Score at GP visit.
18.01.12	17 (moderately severe)	10	2	Start of CBT. Improvement put down to having done something about the problem.
25.01.12	Not assessed	10	2	
01.02.12	15 (moderately severe)	8	3	Back to work this week. Discovered that anticipatory anxiety is worse than facing the problem, which improved her mood.
08.02.12	Not assessed	6	4–5	
22.02.12	10 (moderate)	7	6–7	Mentor slammed down equipment but Aditi stood her ground.
07.03.12	8 (mild)	6/5	7	Success at department meeting, anxious but OK.
21.03.12	8 (mild)	5/4	7	Planning the way forward independently.
13.06.12	5 (mild)	3	7–8	Follow-up appointment. Aditi has told her manager and has been assigned a new mentor. The bullying has been dealt with in accord with company policy.

role-play how to explain the situation to her manager and request a different mentor. The session also involved completing a continued improvement plan, on which Aditi clearly outlined the steps she needed to take before the final follow-up session (Table 13.2).

Table 13.2 Aditi's continued improvement plan

What have you learned from these sessions?	That respect needs to be earned.
	Others are likely to take me seriously and value my opinion if I express it.
	That I can take control of my anxiety by approaching things I fear rather than avoiding them.
What strategies have you found most helpful?	Mapping the problem out on paper so I can see it more clearly.
	Role-playing helped me gain the confidence to face things in real life.
What do you need to do to maintain/extend change?	Set new goals.
	Ask mum if she will do role plays with me, reversing roles both ways, to practise what to say and how to say it, so that it comes across confidently.
	Get dad to film us on my mobile phone so I can see what this looks like, and make needed adjustments.
What might lead to a setback?	If the mentor's behaviour gets worse again and I become more afraid and avoidant again.
	If my line manger doesn't take me seriously when I tell him about the problem.
How would you recognise this?	If the mentor would try to push me about again, either emotionally or physically. I would get more anxious and want to avoid him.
	The manager tries to dismiss my problem as 'all in my head' and won't agree to a change of mentor.
Can you identify skills you have learned, resources, people/agencies that could help you manage this setback?	Yes. The formulation and therapy notes would be helpful to refer to, to see what's happening.
	I can involve others at work, either directly or indirectly. Also use family to practise role plays with and use the camera to see how this looks and make changes.
	I could get the union representative involved to ensure my line manager takes me seriously.

Client Name .... Therapist Name .... Date ....

By the time of the two-month follow-up Aditi had spoken to her manager who acknowledged that others had experienced problems with this mentor in the past and readily agreed to a change of mentor. He also commented on the mature manner in which she had handled the difficulty. As a result of challenging her original negative assumption, 'if I say what I think others won't take me seriously,' her self-respect had grown; even her old mentor appeared to be developing some respect for her recently.

Finally, Aditi had thought hard about rewording her old assumptions and had decided on 'respect has to be earned' and 'if I speak up for myself others will usually listen and take my opinions seriously', which seemed to fit with her present reality much better. She planned to build on these two assumptions over the coming months.

Both Aditi and her therapist felt confident to end therapy at this point.

Reflections

Reflecting on the case, the therapist considered that Aditi's determination and preparedness to take calculated risks were major factors in the achievement of her goals. However, it had been important to go at her pace and in the direction she valued going (Veale 2008). By staying with behavioural experiments and exposure and response prevention as the main therapeutic strategies, treatment had remained focused and clear. Working behaviourally had impacted on her **implicational** belief system, undermining her assumptions before focusing directly on them.

The case highlighted the importance of ensuring client safety, while encouraging change and learning through exposure to anxiety-provoking situations. It had also been necessary for the therapist to tolerate a measure of anxiety when Aditi set up experiments that inevitably held an element of risk, however well calculated this had been.

The therapist also considered that openly discussing the potential for Aditi to apply her assumptions within the therapeutic relationship had also been an important factor in mitigating risk.

If Aditi had not been prepared to role-play or to carry out behavioural experiments in the workplace, an alternative would have been to work directly on her cognitions to bring about **propositional learning**, using thought records to question her assumptions about respect. However, without directly engaging with her fears to facilitate emotional learning, therapy would likely have taken longer and been less effective.

Exercise

Over the coming week, monitor and record your own behaviour for any tendencies towards:

1   Passive, apologetic behaviour, including being avoidant of difficult interpersonal situations, or of allowing others to dictate your behaviour by making demands that you feel unable to refuse.

2   Feeling annoyed or angry at situations but being unable to express this for fear of confrontation, so employing manipulative behaviour or sarcasm to get more of what you want from the situation.
3   Behaving in an aggressive manner, either physically or emotionally by openly dominating others, for example.
4   Openly and clearly communicating your thoughts and feelings assertively.

Conclusion and consolidation of your learning

Answer the following questions:

- When working with interpersonal problems, what potential difficulties could crop up within the therapeutic relationship?

- What are the main elements that need to be included in any formulation, especially an idiosyncratic one?

- Can you describe in about 30 words how you might work behaviourally in the first instance to undermine interpersonal assumptions?

Homework

A good place to look out for non-assertive behaviour patterns is in TV soap operas. Assertive behaviour is often harder to find. Try to find a good role model of assertive behaviour and note their respectful attitude and body language. You may want to practise adopting their approach.

Further reading: Hadfield and Hasson (2010).

Feedback

Think about your experience of reading this chapter and note any feedback for the authors here:

At the end of the book you may wish to collate the feedback together to forward to the following address: nick.wrycraft@anglia.ac.uk

14 Clinical supervision in supporting practice

> **Reader's agenda**
>
> Take a few moments to consider your own agenda or reasons for reading this chapter and make a note of them here:
>
> -
>
> -
>
> -
>
> The aim of this case study is to:
>
> - Consider an understanding and definition of clinical supervision and the benefits and advantages
> - Outline models of clinical supervision
> - Discuss the competencies in CBT based clinical supervision.
>
> **Managing your time**
>
> Take a moment to consider how long you plan to spend reading this chapter, and make a note here:
>
> **An understanding and definition of clinical supervision**
>
> What is clinical supervision? Write down your understanding and then compare it to the definition below.

Clinical supervision was first used in the 1920s to identify difficulties in therapeutic relationships that therapists could not detect themselves and to assist in identifying better ways of working with clients (Davy 2002). Clinical supervision is recommended as good practice within all areas of healthcare, encompassing a wide variety of clinical roles. However, due to the differing responsibilities and environments in which healthcare professions work, there are varied understandings and different emphases in how it is implemented across these areas.

In its general use in healthcare professions clinical supervision can be defined as a supportive, formal and structured learning relationship between two or more professionals that enables practitioners to enhance their knowledge and skills and maximise the protection of service users and assume responsibility for their practice in often complex situations (Butterworth and Faugier 1992; Johns 2001; National Health Service Management Executive (NHSME) 1993).

Hawkins and Shohet's (2012: 5, 60) definition, based on counsellors and therapists, is that:

> Supervision is a joint endeavour in which a practitioner together with the help of a supervisor, attends to their clients, themselves as part of their client practitioner relationships and the wider systemic context, and by so doing improves the quality of their work, transforms their client relationships, continuously develops themselves, their practice and the wider profession.

Hawkins and Shohet (2012) emphasise the purpose of supervision as a partnership within a contract between the supervisee and supervisor, for the benefit of the client, yet within an organizational context. Their model of supervision, while emphasising the necessity of focusing on the client–therapist relationship, nevertheless takes into account the influence of other relationships and factors on the therapist and their work.

In clinical supervision the supervisee allocates regular protected time to reflect upon their practice experience, facilitated by an expert and knowledgeable supervisor (Fowler 1996). In most cases the clinical supervisee chooses the clinical supervisor, who is generally an experienced peer and who practises in or has familiarity with the supervisee's area of work and clinical speciality, has undertaken some form of training to prepare for the role and has also received clinical supervision (Fowler 1995; Pover et al. 1998; Sloan 1999).

Clinical supervision is often a one-to-one relationship, although it may also be delivered in a triad or group. Advantages of this approach include that it is an efficient use of time and resources. Also, group clinical supervision has the potential of supporting the development of a team ethos and supporting morale, especially in environments where staff work autonomously, in the case of therapists, or independently in the community.

Clinical supervision is implemented differently among healthcare professions depending on the demands and nature of the role. For example, in nursing, emotional investment, demanding workloads, close involvement with other professions and the presence of significant organisational and political issues necessitate a support-based approach. Furthermore, the differing emphasis and values of the professional codes of conduct of various healthcare professions account for varying approaches to clinical supervision. CBT-based clinical supervision is concerned with the effective application of therapy, and although support is still important, a practice-centred approach is emphasised and the focus is on clinical competence and skill, client work and development (Padesky 1996; Rodolfa et al. 2005; Sloan et al. 2000; Newman 2010; Yegdich 1999a).

It is recommended that the clinical supervisor is a peer as opposed to the supervisee's line manager to avoid role conflict (Edwards et al. 2005; Goorapah 1997; Sloan 1999). For example, a supervisee might be reluctant to discuss an example in which they performed less well in clinical supervision with a manager, who at another time might be considering the same practitioner for promotion, or appraising their performance (Goorapah 1997). However, in some cases, out of practical necessity, a manager may be providing both clinical and management supervision to the same staff. In these circumstances it is advisable that there is clarity and mutual understanding between the supervisor and supervisee as to the differing purposes and boundaries of these relationships.

Training in clinical supervision varies in course length and content, ranging from one-day workshops to modules, and there is a lack of consensus over how to prepare supervisors. Often supervisors learn through practical experience of carrying out supervision, as this is an integral part of CBT training, and therefore therapists become acquainted with the requisite skills to both provide and receive clinical supervision as part of their professional preparation (Sloan et al. 2000).

There is limited guidance and research concerning the length and frequency of clinical supervision sessions in the literature across healthcare professions. Edwards et al. (2005) found clinical supervision sessions were evaluated positively where they were for more than an hour, although Winstanley and White (2003) suggest that sessions ought to be between 46 and 60 minutes. Alternatively, in research with clinical supervision groups among nurses in Scandinavia, both Hyrkäs et al. (2002) and Lindahl and Norberg (2002) stated that sessions lasted for 90 minutes, although this may be due to the additional time required for the needs of a group as opposed to an individual clinical supervision.

Concerning the frequency of clinical supervision, there need to be appropriate intervals between sessions so that the relationship can develop between supervisee and supervisor, and so that the supervisee has adequate time and can actively work on their learning needs and identified actions between sessions. However, it is important that not so much time elapses between sessions such that the action points from the previous session no longer have clinical relevance, or that the supervisee and supervisor struggle with their rapport or remembering the previous session.

In clinical supervision the supervisee chooses what to discuss and brings examples of their clinical work, or cases that they wish to discuss. During the session the supervisor facilitates the supervisee's reflection on their clinical work. This helps the supervisee to identify alternative outcomes and other possible solutions to dilemmas in clinical practice. It also enables the supervisee to better understand their professional learning needs and actions by which these might be addressed (Brunero and Stein-Parbury 2008).

Clinical supervision allows the supervisee to appreciate their capabilities and also supports them in gaining new skills and learning to further develop their competence (Barriball et al. 2004). In order to be effective, it is necessary for there to be a safe and supportive environment. Therefore the relationship between the supervisee and supervisor needs to be open, trusting and mutually respectful, while maintaining discretion and confidentiality (Brunero and Stein-Parbury 2008). As part of the arrangements in establishing clinical supervision it is necessary to discuss the circumstances in which it might be necessary to breach confidentiality.

> **Exercise**
>
> Reflect on what you have read. What are the three main things that you have learned?

The benefits of clinical supervision and characteristics of the supervisor

What do you think can be gained from clinical supervision?

In contrast with the evidence-based focus of CBT, there is limited empirical data to suggest that clinical supervision directly improves clinical outcomes (Bowles and Young 1999; Buus et al. 2013; Sloan et al. 2000). However, from research across healthcare professions there are a wide range of reported benefits. These include:

1. Awareness of own skills and competence
2. Identifying learning needs
3. Setting learning outcomes
4. Considering alternative actions that might have been taken in clinical situations
5. The capacity to identify the extent of individual accountability
6. Better working relationships within the organisation
7. Better working relationships with other healthcare professionals
8. Feeling more in control of work
9. Reduction in work-related stress and improved well-being

(Bégat et al. 2005; Brunero and Stein-Parbury 2008; Hadfield 2000; Hyrkäs et al. 2002; Lu et al. 2005; McVicar 2003; Teasdale et al. 2001; Wallbank and Hatton 2011; Wheeler and King 2000).

Perhaps most importantly, clinical supervision promotes high standards of practice and prioritises the interests of the client. It might be argued that although research cannot provide direct evidence, nevertheless these advantages inevitably contribute to improving the delivery of healthcare and better patient outcomes.

What do you think are the characteristics of a good clinical supervisor?

Often supervisors believe that knowledge is the most important component of clinical supervision. While knowledge and experience are essential qualities of the supervisor, it has also been identified that possessing relevant clinical experience and practice-based credibility are also valued attributes (Fowler 1995). Therefore it is helpful if the supervisor has a good awareness of the clinical landscape that is the supervisee's reality, and either works on a near to peer basis, and/or can ensure that their supervision is focused on facilitating the supervisee's learning. In clinical supervision the relationship that is focused on the supervisee and supervisor understanding problems together and standing shoulder to shoulder empowers the supervisee's learning. This is reminiscent of the collaborative relationship between client and therapist in CBT.

Both Hyrkäs *et al.* (2002) and Sloan (1999) found that effective clinical supervisors demonstrate a high level of commitment, knowledge and empathy. Research by Severinsson and Hallberg (1996) identified that the clinical supervisor was positively regarded where the supervisor seems to be genuine, confirms the feelings of the supervisee and demonstrates understanding. Other characteristics include good listening skills and permitting the supervisee to set the agenda, but also being perceptive to the supervisee's needs and those of clients in the supervisee's care and other professionals with whom they work (Sloan 1999). Finally, Newman (2010) identifies the responsibility of the supervisor to act as a role model.

In summary, effective clinical supervisors combine a range of interpersonal, communication and competency-based skills that serve to facilitate the supervisee in reflecting on their practice. In the next section some different models of clinical supervision are described, to provide some general background before moving on to CBT supervision in particular. What characteristics or attributes do you most value in a clinical supervisor? Consider why you have chosen these and how this has helped your practice?

Check-in

How are you doing with your time-keeping? Have you read as much of the chapter as you need to be able to keep within the allotted time? Are there any changes that you need to make to what you will read?

Models of clinical supervision

Proctor's model

Proctor's (1986) model of clinical supervision is the most widely used and influential within the literature. The model has three stages – normative, formative and restorative – but, in contrast with some other models, these are not used in any prescribed sequence or order.

The *normative* aspect supports practitioners in conforming to high standards of practice and professional conduct and accountability. Normative clinical supervision promotes the safety and wellbeing of clients (NHSME 1993) and considers ethics, values and principles.

The *formative* aspect pertains to development, clinical competence and developing new skills (Milne and James 2002; Spence *et al.* 2001). Formative clinical supervision facilitates the supervisee in analysing, planning and reflecting upon skills, before carrying them out in practice (Hadfield 2000). Formative clinical supervision also involves applying clinical reasoning, and considering alternative actions or approaches, and through reflection learning from experience, and also applying the new knowledge gained from post-registration professional courses (Heaven *et al.* 2006; Spence *et al.* 2001).

The *restorative* aspect of Proctor's (1986) model concerns the supervisee's wellbeing (Bowles and Young 1999; Sloan and Watson 2001). Although a CBT-based approach emphasises the focus of clinical supervision as being upon the skills and clinical competence of the supervisee (Sloan *et al.* 2000; Newman 2010; Yegdich 1999b), reflecting upon how the supervisee feels about their work is an inherent consideration. The results of research in a range of healthcare professions also indicates that the most notable benefit from clinical supervision is in reducing the physical and psychological effects of stress (Bégat *et al.* 2005) and work related strain and improving job satisfaction and sense of reward (Hadfield 2000; Hyrkäs *et al.* 2006; Teasdale *et al.* 2001).

Hawkins and Shohet's seven-eyed supervisor model

Hawkins and Shohet's (2012) model of clinical supervision is a highly popular and widely used framework for clinical supervision in a range of different healthcare professions. The model developed from Hawkins's research into the differing styles adopted by experienced clinical supervisors. The model rests on the premise that even though there is often only the supervisee and supervisor present in clinical supervision, a complex range of other relationships are influential. These include the following:

1. *The client.* In supervision it is identified how the client came into contact with the supervisee, but this is more than simply recounting the facts of the case. It encourages the supervisee to 'stand outside' the relationship with the client in order to appreciate what is occurring.
2. *The supervisee.* The focus is upon the influence of the supervisee on their work but also how they are affected by their work. A common role of clinical supervision is to identify *counter-transference*, or feelings and responses to the client triggered in the supervisee from working with the client and of which they are unaware.
3. *The supervisor.* Often the relationship between the supervisee and client can become replicated in supervision in what is known as a *parallel process*. With regard to this aspect of the relationship the supervisor has to review their own perceptions of the supervisory relationship.

However, other considerations are also important, including the work context (issues within the organisation) and the wider environment (seeing the client in their context, rather than in terms of their mental health issue).

Furthermore, there are two interlinked relationship matrices: client–supervisee and supervisee–supervisor. The model reflects the way in which the relationships interconnect and provides multiple perspectives from which the supervisor can facilitate supervision and assist the supervisor in identifying the subtle influences on their perspective of which they may have been previously aware.

Hawkins and Shohet's (2012) seven-eyed supervisor model involves:

1. Identifying that the supervisee's decisions and interventions match evidence-based practice
2. The context of the client–supervisee relationship
3. The therapist's specific input as an individual and professional
4. The context of the supervisory relationship
5. The context of the supervisor.

There are two further aspects of:

6. The client and supervisee matrix
7. The supervisee and supervisor matrix.

Hawkins and Shohet (2012) conceptualise two styles of supervision:

- Focusing on the supervisee–client relationship through focusing on the session through reports, written notes, case notes or audio or video recordings
- Considering how the client matrix relationship is evident in the clinical supervision.

Within the model these two styles can be further divided into three further categories, depending on the relationship to which attention is directed, and the wider environment within which clinical supervision occurs and the supervisee works with the client.

Let us now outline the stages of the model:

1. *The client and what they present.* This involves the supervisor encouraging the supervisee to consider what the client said and the issues that they chose to focus on and how this links to previous sessions, to encourage the supervisee to focus on the client, their decisions and how this fits into the context of their life. Clarity and accuracy and recall of the details are important in order to avoid fitting the facts to pre-existent assumptions, or convenient theories that may be mistaken.
2. *The supervisee's interventions.* This considers not only the measures that were selected but also the rationale(s) supporting these and their timing, together with other alternatives that might have been used to increase the supervisee's therapeutic range and repertoire of skills and practical competencies.
3. *The relationship between client and supervisee.* In this aspect of the model the supervisor helps the supervisee to realise the conscious and unconscious dynamics that are active in their relationship with the client and to overcome barriers.

4   *The supervisee.* In this stage of the model the emphasis is upon the effects of their work with the client on the supervisee, both conscious and unconscious, in order to optimise their ability to engage with the client.
5   *The supervisory relationship.* Hawkins and Shohet (2012) suggest that there are two perspectives to this stage: the quality of the therapeutic alliance but also the presence of parallel process, or the unconscious dynamics of the supervisee's work with their client.
6   *The supervisor's perspective.* This refers to the supervisor's reflections on their experience in the clinical supervision session.
7   *The wider context.* In this stage of the model a range of factors are involved, differing depending upon the perspective of the client, supervisee and supervisor. These factors include codes of ethics and professional accountability, organisational requirements, other healthcare professions and stakeholders in the client's care and cultural, economic, political and social factors. Furthermore, the specific issues that are regarded as important in the wider context will differ significantly for the client, supervisee and supervisor, depending on their perspectives.

> Can you identify how in your experience of clinical supervision any of these stages of Hawkins and Shohet's (2012) model has altered your perception on a clinical situation or event?

In the next section a model is discussed that offers a structured, CBT competence focused approach to clinical supervision.

A CBT competency based approach

Sloan *et al.* (2000) suggest that although the nature of the discussion that occurs in clinical supervision is very different than therapy, due to the purpose of the meeting and the professional roles of the participants a CBT-oriented approach to clinical supervision ought to be adopted that is focused, structured, educational and collaborative.

They point out that CBT focused clinical supervision ought to involve a range of therapeutically focused activities. These include:

- Presentation of specific cases
- Direct observation
- The CTS-R or other rating scales
- Case presentation
- Behavioural rehearsal

- Joint interviewing
- Direct observation
- Role play
- Audiotapes
- Video recording
- Research and relevant literature.

Milne et al. (2013) claim that these practical elements of CBT-focused clinical supervision are underused and might be better exploited, and that there is a need for the development of clearer standards of competency in CBT-based clinical supervision. Newman (2010) comments that there are practical challenges in assessing therapist competence, as there are a wide range of different condition-specific forms of treatment to master, together with the often difficult reality of engaging and retaining clients in treatment. However, he also identifies that increased competence is a necessary focus of clinical supervision, as it makes it more likely that clients will engage.

Based on the work of Rodolfa et al. (2005), Newman (2010) identifies that the cube model effectively incorporates the range of issues and competencies that might form the basis for CBT-based clinical supervision. The cube model covers foundational competence, functional competence and professional development (Newman 2010). *Foundational competence* refers to professional standards and accountability and practice, while *functional competence* concerns the knowledge and understanding of particular competences together with the technical skills and capabilities to implement these appropriately and effectively with clients. Finally, *professional development* refers to the level of practice of the supervisee, ranging from trainee to advanced therapist and experienced professional. Within the cube model the three areas overlap and are mutually influential (Rodolfa et al. 2005).

Professional development concerns will vary, depending on the level of practice of the supervisee. However, below are listed the range of issues considered within the foundational and functional competencies. Foundational competence includes the following:

- Understanding the empirical basis of treatment – being aware of the research and evidence base supporting CBT-focused explanations of mental health issues, yet at the same time being aware of the limits of knowledge.
- Managing the relationship – technical competence in CBT and a commitment to maintaining positive therapeutic relationships have been identified as producing better client outcomes.
- Cultural competence – understanding the influence of the client's culture allows the therapist to separate views that might be held by a group as opposed to those that are idiosyncratic or due to the client's mental health issue.
- Collaborating with other healthcare disciplines – a commitment to sharing knowledge and clinical skills ensures that the client gains from a cohesive and integrated multi-disciplinary approach.

The functional competence domains pertain to particular knowledge and skills in the following areas:

- Core techniques – depending on the level of experience and development of the supervisee, focus on learning, gaining proficiency in and using a range of techniques, including self-monitoring, asking 'guided discovery' focused questions, new ways of working (such as designing homework and behavioural experiments), activity scheduling, relaxation and controlled breathing, reflecting on existing skills and revisiting old techniques in order that these may be used in the future.
- Acquiring and maintaining functional competence in CBT – through the regular practice-based use of skills with clients but also using the full repertoire of therapeutic interventions and techniques that are available.
- Conceptualising cases in CBT terms – through the use of literature, videos and practising skills through role play in clinical supervision sessions, the supervisee learns a range of technical skills.

In order to support the supervisee in acquiring and maintaining functional competence, it is necessary that at least twice a year the supervisor listen to audio recordings of the supervisee's sessions with clients and give feedback using the CTS-R.

To summarise this section, CBT-based clinical supervision involves practical exercises and activities. The focus is on developing the supervisee's understanding of the foundations of their role and in optimising their skills and proficiency in functional competencies and professional development.

> **Check-in**
>
> What differences and similarities do you see between supervision in general and CBT-based clinical supervision?

Implementing clinical supervision

In this next section we will look at how we might carry out clinical supervision using Hawkins and Shohet's (2012) CLEAR model as a useful template for both formatting individual sessions but also the supervisory relationship as a whole.

Contracting begins by identifying the client's needs and what requires addressing, together with how to use the supervision session(s) and the supervisor's input in the most effective way to achieve the supervisee's goal(s). If meeting for the first time, it might be appropriate to devote the whole session to discussing the contract, mutual expectations and roles and identifying the ground rules. Among the helpful questions that might address the issues in contracting are:

What does the supervisee want to achieve?
What does the supervisee want to use the clinical supervision session for?
What goal(s) or outcome(s) need to be met?
How can the supervisor be of most help?
What is the most difficult challenge for the supervisee at the moment?

Listening refers to the supervisor understanding what the supervisee is imparting and empathising with the content. The supervisor supports the supervisee in gaining new insight into their clinical experiences, through reframing and reflecting back to the supervisee. Often this involves asking questions that identify certain aspects of situations as having more significance than the supervisee previously credited. Here are some of the trigger questions the supervisor might ask:

Tell me some more about that?
Who else was involved?
How do other people feel about that?

Exploration involves questioning and reflecting on the case and identifying new perspectives, ideas and actions to move forward the supervisee's work with their clients. Exploration is also the spirit in which clinical supervision is carried out, in terms of making new discoveries and examining situations with a sense of optimism and enquiry. Exploring is in two phases: the first involves the supervisor working with the supervisee in developing a personal understanding of the importance and meaning of the situation; the second concerns working with the supervisee to develop new options and actions to address the situation. The questions that might be asked in the first phase are as follows:

Are there feelings that you are experiencing and want to express?
How would you describe what you are feeling at the moment?
Does the person you are talking about remind you of anyone else you have known?
Is there a pattern emerging with this relationship that has been evident in others?

In the second part of the exploring phase the questions that might be asked are as follows:

What outcomes do the stakeholders in this situation all want?
What would change to produce the outcome?
What other resources could be used to produce the outcome?
Can you think of alternative ways of producing the outcome?

Action is where, from the range of options generated in clinical supervision, the supervisee identifies their preferred choice and the first actions that need to be taken to move the situation forward. In order to make the action(s) more achievable it might help to enact how this might be carried out in clinical supervision. The following questions might be relevant:

What might be the advantages and disadvantages of each option?
What is it that you wish to achieve with this action?
What will be the first step?
When and at what point in the conversation will you make the step?
Tell me how you might begin to introduce this into the conversation?

Review, finally, is also in two stages. The first involves consolidating and reflecting on the actions that have been taken and what has occurred in clinical supervision. The second examines whether the process was helpful for the supervisee, and if anything was unhelpful how it might be different in future clinical supervision to be more useful. Questions that are relevant for the first phase of the review are as follows:

What will the supervisee do next?
What has been gained from the clinical supervision session?
How has the supervisee been prepared to handle similar situations in future?
What was useful or could have been better helpful about the clinical supervision?

Finally, in the second phase, there is a debriefing and update on progress with regards to the planned change between sessions. The following are among the questions that may be asked in this phase:

How successfully does the supervisee feel the planned action went?
How did the supervisee feel they performed?
What feedback did the supervisee receive from other people?
What does the supervisee feel was successful and what could have been better?
What has the supervisee learned?

Conclusion

Check-in

Were you able to keep to your time schedule? If not, what prevented you?

Think about what you have read in this chapter. What are the three main learning points that have added to your understanding?

1

2

3

> How will what you have read change the way that you use clinical supervision if you are a supervisee, or deliver supervision if you are a supervisor?

In this chapter a definition has been provided and the advantages and benefits of clinical supervision explained. The most frequently used models of clinical supervision, those of Proctor (1986) and Hawkins and Shohet (2012), were described. Proctor's (1986) model provides a flexible and adaptable framework through which to view practice. Hawkins and Shohet's (2012) model offers a clear structure for supervision which incorporates a range of important elements. The model identifies multiple perspectives through which to usefully view the relationships and environments within which client work and clinical supervision occur in order to promote more effective ways of working. The competences that are the focus of clinical supervision in CBT were then discussed.

Throughout the chapter links were made between the practice of CBT and clinical supervision and similarities identified between the way CBT and clinical supervision are carried out. As with CBT practice, central to the supervisor delivering effective clinical supervision are skills of engagement, interpersonal communication and an emphasis on joint working and collaboration. However, the nature of the discussion in clinical supervision is different, with an emphasis on practical competence and proficiency in skills of clinical supervision. The models that have been discussed, especially Hawkins and Shohet's (2012) seven-eyed supervisor model, are useful templates in guiding clinical supervision towards achieving reflective depth and promoting learning.

Very experienced supervisors may well practise in a manner that intuitively applies the model. Correspondingly, the level of experience and proficiency of the supervisee will determine their requirements from clinical supervision. Often very experienced therapists will require clinical supervision that is more focused upon the restorative element of Proctor's (1986) model and the effect of their feelings on their work and vice versa than the formative element of technical competence. However, even very advanced practitioners can still develop their practice, and therefore the formative aspect of clinical supervision ought to continue to feature within clinical supervision.

Feedback

Think about your experience of reading this chapter and note any feedback for the authors here:

Now that you have reached the end of the book you may wish to collate the feedback together to forward to the following address: nick.wrycraft@anglia.ac.uk

Conclusion – developing yourself as a therapist

The intention of this book has not been to provide definitive case studies of specific mental health conditions. Clients with the same problems as those we have discussed might experience them very differently and therefore require a quite different approach. However, this highlights what attracts many of us to working with people in any setting, and not just those focused on mental health. There is the constant potential for people to elude definition, surprise us and disprove our assumptions and expectations. This is a simultaneously humbling but useful reminder that however well trained and informed we become, we can still always learn from the person in front of us.

Within the book we have focused on anxiety-related problems and mild to moderate depression. These represent a narrow band of mental health issues that are often regarded as easily amenable to CBT. However, in reality they represent very different issues which only a highly competent therapist would have the breadth of skills to treat. When beginning to train in CBT there is a bewildering amount to learn and often there is the temptation to try and learn too much too quickly.

Instead it might be more prudent to learn by focusing on just one type of problem at a time. In this way the therapist's range of skills and repertoire of competence can develop on a broad basis in relation to specific conditions that can be developed before moving on to another. So, for example, treating lots of cases where the person is experiencing panic, before moving on to obsessive compulsive disorder, will develop a breadth of skill and confidence, but it should be borne in mind that each new occurrence of mental distress is unique and ought to be viewed as such.

We also suggest sticking to a simple set of criteria to guide your practice as you develop proficiency and skills. Firstly, if you work in a short-term service, for example offering between 6 and 8 sessions, use straightforward therapeutic interventions such as behavioural activation for depression, or exposure and response prevention for anxiety. Also avoid any strategies with which you are not familiar, or do not feel competent to deliver. In order to optimise the use of the time within sessions before assessments, send clients information about CBT so that they know what to expect at assessment and also any questionnaires and assessment tools, so that these can be completed just before attending the session. Furthermore, in sessions try to define problems as closely as possible, and set clear, realistic and achievable goals. It is also important to establish mutual expectations with your client. Good indicators of likely change are whether the person is ready and their completion of homework between sessions.

It is hoped that in this book we have imparted an approach that focuses on using experience to develop professional expertise. If we are to provide the best therapy to clients it is necessary to become the best therapist we can as an ongoing commitment, even after finishing training and education. These activities include attending courses, reading and keeping up to date with current practice and best evidence, and attending regular clinical supervision. Furthermore, having a clear goal as to what areas of practice need to be developed and setting specific goals for learning will lead to continual improvement.

Glossary

Agoraphobia: Fear of open spaces; from the Greek for 'fear of the market place'.

All-or-nothing thinking: As implied, the person sees things as either 'black' or 'white', without any nuance in between.

Ambivalent: Having mixed feelings about someone or something; being unable to choose between two (usually opposing) courses of action.

Analysis: Examination, scrutiny, breaking down and taking apart.

Anticipatory anxiety: Fear of fear.

Assessment: Appraisal of the situation via information gathering. This process is initiated at the first therapy session or 'assessment' meeting and continues throughout therapy as more information comes to light.

Automatic thoughts: Thoughts that come into one's mind unbidden, in contrast to other subjects that have to be consciously considered. Automatic thoughts often go unnoticed at a conscious level as they can become so familiar, a little like wallpaper.

Blueprint: A plan that summarises the client's learning from therapy. This can be used in the event of a lapse and should state clearly what to do.

Cognitions: These include not only thoughts, assumptions and beliefs but also memories and images that the person can recall.

Collude: To act together through a secret understanding. To conspire in a fraud.

Comorbidity: The presence of one or more disorders as well as the primary disorder.

Compulsions: Repetitive behaviours that a person feels driven to perform in response to obsessive thoughts. A compulsion can either be observable by others such as checking (i.e. overt), or a mental act that cannot be observed by others, such as repeating a certain phrase in one's mind (i.e. covert).

Concept: Idea, notion, hypothesis.

Conceptualisation: In this book we have used the words 'conceptualisation' and **formulation** interchangeably to mean a map or framework that is designed collaboratively with the client, using their own **idiosyncratic** details about the problem. The framework usually includes triggers, thoughts, feelings, physiological responses as well as behaviours. These are synthesised into a coherent map that demonstrates how the elements link together and keep the problem going. This conceptualisation or formulation is viewed as a working 'hypothesis' on which treatment planning is based. It is seen as a work in progress and is subject to change as treatment progresses.

Conditioned stimulus: A neutral event in the environment which is repeatedly twinned with an **unconditioned stimulus** becomes a conditioned stimulus, evoking a similar response even when the original unconditioned stimulus is no longer present. However, the power of the conditioned stimulus will diminish and eventually extinguish when the unconditioned stimulus is no longer twinned with the conditioned stimulus at all.

Dichotomous: Divided into two parts.

Differential diagnosis: A diagnostic method used to decide between two or more diagnoses, or to assign two or more comorbid diagnoses.

Ego-dystonic: Related to features of a person's behaviour or attitude that seem contrary to their fundamental beliefs and personality.

Emotional reasoning: Reasoning from how the person feels rather than from logic (e.g. 'I feel stupid, therefore I must look stupid').

Empirical: Derived from or guided by experience or experiment.

Exposure and response prevention: A treatment that involves exposing the person to their fear while preventing their normal response to the fear.

Face validity: The validity of a test at face value. A test can be said to have face validity if it 'looks like' it is going to measure what it is supposed to measure.

Fear hierarchy: This involves listing a wide range of feared situations, gradually increasing in order from the least feared to the most feared.

Feelings: Emotional or moral sensitivity.

Formulation: See **conceptualisation**.

Graded hierarchy: See **fear hierarchy**.

Habituation: Toleration of and acclimatisation to fear, gradually getting used to it till it extinguishes.

Hyperventilation: Over-breathing, resulting in depletion of the amount of carbon dioxide in the blood.

Hypothesis: A provisional idea or proposition which can be used as a basis for testing reality.

Idiosyncratic: Peculiar to the individual, personal, unique.

Imagery rescripting: Deliberately invoking a distressing or traumatic image and then changing the outcome in imagination so that it is in line with the course of action one would prefer to have taken, had one been able to.

Images: Mental pictures or cognitive pictorial reproductions of events. These can be of both past, or of future, happenings. These usually represent strong meaning for the individual.

Imaginal exposure: Exposing oneself to a feared stimulus by imagining this and remaining with the anxiety produced until you have habituated to the discomfort.

Imaginal reliving: This is a form of exposure therapy involving systematic, repeated and prolonged exposure to a traumatic memory which helps to reduce distressing emotions associated with the traumatic memory.

Implicational learning: Learned by direct experience, experiential learning, involving a deep 'felt sense' of knowing.

Invalidate: To quash or negate.

Leading question: A question that subtly prompts a person to answer it in a certain way by giving a hint to the answer within the question. This can result in biased information.

Magical thinking: This involves the belief that one has the power to influence events (either for bad or for good) in magical ways. It includes superstitious thinking that is taken to an extreme.

Metacognitions: Thoughts about one's thoughts (e.g. 'Having a bad thought means I'm a bad person').

Model: This is a term frequently used in the CBT literature. In this book it is used interchangeably with other terms such as 'framework', 'formulation' and 'conceptualisation'. Although different authors often make subtle distinctions between terms, for our purposes this is not necessary. A model is an illustrative structure or plan which represents a hypothesis or theory about how things work in real life.

Mood: State of mind.

Negative reinforcement: A behaviour is negatively reinforced when something adverse goes away as a result of the behaviour (e.g. when a person runs away from a spider their anxiety goes away, thus making it more likely that they will repeat this behaviour another time).

Neutralising: A compulsive act, either physical or mental, whereby an individual with OCD 'undoes' a behaviour or thought that is believed to be 'dangerous' by 'cancelling' it out with another behaviour or thought. This behaviour is also considered a ritual.

Observer perspective: Seeing the situation from the (imagined) perspective of someone else looking on, rather than from one's own frame of reference.

Obsession: An unwanted, recurrent and intrusive thought or image that causes anxiety or distress which the person tries to ignore, suppress, or neutralise with some other thought or action. Obsessions are not just excessive worries about real-life problems.

Paradigm: A typical example or pattern of something that serves as a model.

Paradigm shift: A fundamental change in approach, or of basic assumptions.

Paradoxical: A statement or proposition that seems self-contradictory or impossible, but in reality expresses a possible truth.

Positive data log: A journal or log-book in which positive information is collected.

Positive reinforcement: A behaviour is positively reinforced when something pleasant is added as a result of the behaviour (e.g. when a person does their work and feels a sense of achievement as a result of this, making it more likely that they will repeat this behaviour another time).

Process issue: An issue that arises out of the process of therapy, as opposed to the content of it. An example of this might be if the therapist asks the client to engage in something that has not been agreed to collaboratively and the client does not complete the assignment because they have not agreed to it (rather than because the content of the homework is too difficult).

Propositional learning: Learning other than from direct experience, intellectual learning.

Reinforcers: Environmental events that can strengthen behavioural responses if the behaviour is contingent on the event.

Reliability: The extent to which a measure gives a similar result if it is administered more than once to the same person.

Rumination: Dwelling compulsively on the causes and consequences of one's distress rather than working out a solution.

Safety behaviour: A self-protective measure that is adopted to help a person feel safer and less anxious in the short term, but which contributes to the difficulty they are trying to alleviate in the longer term.

Schema: A framework or network of interrelated knowledge, ideas, opinions, biases and prejudices which are built up over the course of a lifetime. Schemas help people make sense of experiences, guiding perception and memory, and have a profound impact on personality. While schemas do not cause chronic emotional disorders, by dominating what people notice, attend to, and remember, they have a powerful maintaining influence on them (Zimbardo *et al.* 1995). Although there are subtle differences between the terms 'schema' and 'beliefs', for clarity, within this text the terms are used interchangeably.

Social learning theory: Learning gained by modelling and imitation.

Synthesis/synthesising: Combining, constructing and integrating into a whole. Making a new sense of the parts by combining them into a whole.

Therapeutic impasse: A point in therapy which both therapist and client can find no way round, leading to a sense of being 'stuck'.

Trans-diagnostic: Occurring across a range of different disorders, not classified as a disorder in its own right.

Unconditioned stimulus: A fundamentally powerful event in the environment that evokes a reflex in a person or organism.

Validated measure: A measure which is authorised as a trustworthy and accurate measure of whatever it is supposed to be measuring.

Validity: Validity indicates that a measure is identifying the phenomenon it is claiming to be measuring.

Variable: The variable is the 'thing' that can be altered to bring about a different result or consequence.

References

Alden, L.E. (2005) Interpersonal perspective on social phobia. In W.R. Crozier and L.E. Alden (eds) *The Essential Handbook of Social Anxiety for Clinicians*. Chichester: Wiley.

American Psychiatric Association (2000) *Diagnostic and Statistical Manual of Mental Disorders*, 4th edition, text revision. Washington, DC: APA.

American Psychiatric Association (2013) *Diagnostic and Statistical Manual of Mental Disorders*, 5th edition. Washington, DC: APA.

Arntz, A. and Weertman, A. (1999) Treatment of childhood memories: Theory and practice. *Behaviour Research and Therapy*, 37, 715–740.

Barkham, M., Margison, F., Leach, C., et al. (2001) Service profiling and outcomes benchmarking using CORE-OM: Towards practice based evidence in the psychological therapies. *Journal of Consulting and Clinical Psychology*, 69, 184–196.

Barriball, L., White, A. and Munch, L. (2004) An audit of clinical supervision in primary care. *British Journal of Community Nursing*, 9(9), 389–397.

Beck, A.T., Rush, A.J., Shaw, B.F. and Emery, G. (1979) *Cognitive Therapy of Depression*. New York: Guilford Press.

Beck, J.S. (1995) *Cognitive Therapy: Basics and Beyond*. New York: Guilford Press.

Beck, J.S. (2001) *Cognitive Behavior Therapy: Basics and Beyond*. New York: Guilford Press.

Bégat, I., Ellefsen, B. and Severinsson, E. (2005) Nurses' satisfaction with their work environment and the outcomes of clinical supervision on nurses' experiences of well-being – a Norwegian study. *Journal of Nursing Management*, 13, 221–230.

Bennett-Levy, J. (2003) Mechanisms of change in cognitive therapy: The case of automatic thought records and behavioural experiments. *Behavioural and Cognitive Psychotherapy*, 31, 261–277.

Bennett-Levy, J., Butler, G., Fennell, M., Hackmann, A., Mueller, M. and Westbrook, D. (2004) *Oxford Guide to Behavioural Experiments in Cognitive Therapy*. Oxford: Oxford University Press.

Billett, E.A., Richter, M.A. and Kennedy, J.L. (1998) Genetics of *Obsessive-Compulsive Disorder*. In R.P. Swinson, M.M. Antony, S. Rachman and M.A. Richter (eds) *Obsessive Compulsive Disorder: Theory, Research and Treatment*, pp. 181–206. New York: Guilford Press.

Borkovec, T.D., Alcaine, O.M. and Behar, E. (2004) Avoidance theory of worry and generalised anxiety disorder. In R.G. Heimberg, C.I. Turk, and D.S. Mennin (eds) *Generalised Anxiety Disorder: Advances in Research and Practice*, pp. 77–108. New York: Guilford Press.

Borkovec, T.D. and Sharpless, B. (2006) Generalised anxiety disorder: Bringing cognitive behavioural therapy into the valued present. In S.C. Hayes, V.M. Follette and M.M. Linehan (eds) *Mindfulness and Acceptance: Expanding the Cognitive-Behavioral Tradition*. New York: Guilford Press.

Bowles, N. and Young, C. (1999) An evaluative study of clinical supervision based on Proctor's three function evaluative model. *Journal of Advanced Nursing* 30(4), 958–964.

British Association for Behavioural and Cognitive Psychotherapies (2010) *Standards of Conduct, Performance and Ethics in the Practice of Behavioural and Cognitive Psychotherapies*. Available from http://www.babcp.com/files/About/BABCP-Standards-of-Conduct-Performance-and-Ethics.pdf (accessed 16 May 2014).

Brunero, S. and Stein-Parbury, J. (2008) The effectiveness of clinical supervision in nursing: An evidence based literature review. *Australian Journal of Advanced Nursing*, 25(3), 86–94.

Butler, G. (2008) *Overcoming Social Anxiety and Shyness: A Self-Help Guide Using Cognitive Behavioral Techniques*. New York: Basic Books.

Butterworth, T. and Faugier, J. (1992) *Clinical Supervision and Mentorship in Nursing*. London: Chapman & Hall.

Buus, N., Cassedy, P. and Gonge, H. (2013) Developing a manual for strengthening mental health nurses' clinical supervision. *Issues in Mental Health Nursing*, 34, 344–349.

Chambless, D.L., Caputo, G.C., Bright, P. and Gallagher, R. (1984) The assessment of fear in agoraphobics: The body sensations questionnaire and the agoraphobic cognitions questionnaire. *Journal of Consulting and Clinical Psychology*, 52, 1090–1097.

Clark, D.M. (1989) Anxiety states: Panic and generalized anxiety. In K. Hawton, P.M. Salkovskis, J. Kirk and D.M. Clark (eds) *Cognitive Behaviour Therapy for Psychiatric Problems*. Oxford: Oxford University Press.

Clark, D.M. and Wells, A. (1995) A cognitive model of social phobia. In R. Heimberg, M.R. Liebowitz, D.A. Hope and F.R. Schneier, *Social Phobia: Diagnosis, Assessment and Treatment*, pp. 69–93. New York: Guilford Press.

Cuijpers, P., van Straten, A. and Warmerdam, L. (2007) Behavioral activation treatments of depression: A meta-analysis. *Clinical Psychology Review*, 27, 318–326.

Cully, J.A. and Teten, A.L. (2008) *A Therapist's Guide to Brief Cognitive Behavioral Therapy*. Houston: Department of Veterans Affairs South Central MIRECC.

Dalgleish, T. and Power, M.J. (2004) Emotion specific and emotion non-specific components of posttraumatic stress disorder (PTSD): Implications for a taxonomy of related psychopathology. *Behaviour Research and Therapy*, 42, 1059–1088.

Davy, J. (2002) Discursive reflections on a research agenda for clinical supervision. *Psychology and Psychotherapy: Theory, Research and Practice*, 75, 221–238.

Dugas, M.J., Gagnon, F., Ladouceur. F. and Freeston, M. (1998) Generalised anxiety disorder: A preliminary test of a conceptual model. *Behaviour Research and Therapy*, 36, 215–226.

Edwards, D., Cooper, L., Burnard, P., Hannigan, B., Adams, J., Fothergill, A. and Coyle, D. (2005) Factors influencing the effectiveness of clinical supervision. *Journal of Psychiatric and Mental Health Nursing*, 12, 405–414.

Egan, S., Piek, J., Dyck, M., Rees, C. and Hagger, M. (2013) A clinical investigation of motivation to change standards and cognitions about failure in perfectionism. *Behavioural and Cognitive Psychotherapy*, 41(5), 565–578.

Egan, S., Hattaway, M. and Kane, R.T. (March 2014) The relationship between perfectionism and rumination in post-traumatic stress disorder. *Behavioural and Cognitive Psychotherapy*, 42(2), 211–223.

Egan, S. J., Goodier, G. H. G., Shafran, R., Lee, M., Fairburn, C., Cooper, Z., Doll, H. and Palmer, R. (submitted). The reliability and validity of the clinical perfectionism questionnaire in eating disorder and community samples. Manuscript under review.

Ehlers, A. and Clark, D. (2000) A cognitive model of posttraumatic stress disorder. *Behaviour and Research Therapy*, 38, 319–345.

Fairburn, C.G. (2008) *Cognitive Behavior Therapy for Eating Disorders*. New York: Guilford Press.

Fairburn, C.G. (submitted). *The Clinical Perfectionism Questionnaire*.

Fennell, M. (1997) Low self-esteem: A cognitive perspective. *Behavioural and Cognitive Psychotherapy*, 25(1), 1–26.

Fennell, M. (2006) *Overcoming Low Self-Esteem Self-Help Course: A 3-part Programme Based on Cognitive Behavioural Techniques*. London: Robinson.

Fennell, M. (2009) *Overcoming Low Self Esteem: A Self-help Guide Using Cognitive Behavioural Techniques*. London: Constable and Robinson.

Fennell, M. and Brosan, L. (2011) *An Introduction to Improving Your Self-esteem*. London: Robinson.

Foa, E., Ehlers, A., Clark, D. et al. (1999) The Posttraumatic Cognitions Inventory (PTCI): Development and validation. *Psychological Assessment*, 11, 303–314.

Foa, E.B., Huppert, J.D., Leiberg, S., Langner, R., Kichic, R., Hajcak, G. and Salkovskis, P.M. (2002) The Obsessive-Compulsive Inventory: Development and validation of a short version. *Psychological Assessment*, 14(4), 485–496.

Formica, M.J. (2009) The me in you: Parallell process in psychotherapy. *Psychology Today*. http://www.psychologytoday.com/blog/enlightened-living/200901/the-me-in-you-parallel-process-in-psychotherapy (accessed 25 October 2013).

Fowler, J. (1995) Nurses' perceptions of the elements of good supervision. *Nursing Times*, 91(22), 33–37.

Fowler, J. (1996) The organization of clinical supervision within the nursing profession: A review of the literature. *Journal of Advanced Nursing*, 23, 471–478.

Fresco, D.M., Mennin, D.S., Heimberg, R.G. and Turk, C.L. (2003) Using the Penn State Worry Questionnaire to identify individuals with generalized anxiety disorder: a receiver operating characteristic analysis. *Journal of Behaviour Therapy and Experimental Psychiatry*, 34, 283–291.

Fuller, R. (ed.) (1995) *Seven Pioneers of Psychology*. London: Routledge.

Fursland, A., Raykos, B. and Steele, A. (2009) What keeps perfectionism going? In *Perfectionism in Perspective*. Perth: Centre for Clinical Interventions. Available at http://www.cci.health.wa.gov.au/docs/3%20What%20keep%20perfectionism%20going.pdf (accessed 2 May 2014).

Gilbert, P. (ed.) (2005) *Compassion: Conceptualisations, Research and Use in Psychotherapy*. Hove: Routledge.

Gilbert, P. (2007) *Psychotherapy and Counselling for Depression* (3rd edition). London: Sage.

Gilbert, P. (2009) *Overcoming Depression*. London: Robinson.

Goorapah, D. (1997) Review article: Clinical Supervision. *Journal of Clinical Nursing*, 6, 173–178.

Green, S.M., Anthony, M.M., McCabe, R.E. and Watling, M.A. (2007) Frequency of fainting, vomiting and incontinence in panic disorder: A descriptive study. *Clinical Psychology and Psychotherapy*, 14, 189–197.

Greenberger, D. and Padesky, C. (1995) *Mind over Mood, Change How You Feel by Changing the Way You Think*. New York: Guilford Press.

Grey, N., Holmes, E. and Brewin, C. (2001) It's not only fear: Peri-traumatic emotional 'hotspots' in post-traumatic stress disorder. *Behavioural and Cognitive Psychotherapy*, 29, 367–372.

Grey, N., Young, K. and Holmes, E. (2002) Cognitive restructuring within reliving: A treatment for peritraumatic emotional 'hotspots' in posttraumatic stress disorder. *Behavioural and Cognitive Psychotherapy*, 30, 37–56.

Hackmann, A. (2004) Panic disorder and agoraphobia. In J. Bennett-Levy, G. Butler, M. Fennell, A. Hackmann, M. Mueller and D. Westbrook (eds) *Oxford Guide to Behavioural Experiments in Cognitive Therapy*, pp. 59–78. Oxford: Oxford University Press.

Hadfield, D. (2000) Clinical supervision: Users' perspectives. *Journal of Child Health Care*, 4(1): 30–34.

Hadfield, S. and Hasson, G. (2010) *How to Be Assertive in Any Situation*. Harlow: Pearson Education.

Hawkins, P. and Shohet, R. (2012) *Supervision in the Helping Professions* (4th edition). Maidenhead: Open University Press.

Hawton, K., Salkovskis, P., Kirk, J. and Clark, D.M. (eds) (1989) *Cognitive Behaviour Therapy for Psychiatric Problems: A Practical Guide*. Oxford: Oxford University Press.

Heaven, C., Clegg, J. and Maguire, P. (2006) Transfer of communication skills training from workshop to workplace: The impact of clinical supervision. *Patient Education and Counselling*, 60, 313–325.

Heimberg, R.G., Horner, K.J., Juster, H.R., Safren, S.A., Brown, E.J., Schneier, F.R. and Liebowitz, M.R. (1990) Psychometric properties of the Liebowitz Social Anxiety Scale. *Psychological Medicine*, 29, 199–212.

Hirsch, C.R. and Mathews, A. (2012) A cognitive model of pathological worry. *Behaviour Research and Therapy*, 50, 636–646.

Hirsh, C.R. and Holmes, E. (2007) Mental imagery in anxiety disorders. *Psychiatry*, 6(4), 161–165.

Holmes, E.A. and Mathews, A. (2005) Mental imagery and emotion: A special relationship? *Emotion*, 5(4), 489–497.

Holmes, E.A. and Mathews, A. (2010) Mental imagery in emotion and emotional disorders. *Clinical Psychology Review*, 30(3), 349–362.

Holmes, E.A., Grey, N. and Young, K.A.D. (2005) Intrusive images and 'hotspots' of trauma memories in posttraumatic stress disorder: An exploratory investigation of emotions and cognitive themes. *Journal of Behaviour Therapy and Experimental Psychiatry*, 26, 3–17.

Holmes, E., Arntz, A. and Smucker, M. (2007) Imagery rescripting in cognitive behaviour therapy: Images, treatment techniques and outcomes. *Journal of Behaviour Therapy and Experimental Psychiatry*, 38, 297–305.

Hyman, B.M. and Pedrick, C. (1999) *The OCD Workbook: Your Guide to Breaking Free from Obsessive Compulsive Disorder*. Oakland, CA: New Harbinger Publications.

Hyrkäs, K., Appelqvist-Schmidlechner, K. and Paunonen-Ilmonen, M. (2002) Expert supervisors' views of clinical supervision: A study of factors promoting and inhibiting the achievements of multiprofessional team supervision. *Journal of Advanced Nursing*, 38(4), 387–397.

Hyrkäs, K., Appelqvist-Schmidlechner, K. and Haataja, R. (2006) Efficacy of clinical supervision: Influence on job satisfaction, burnout and quality of care. *Journal of Advanced Nursing*, 55(4), 521–535.

Jacobson, N.S., Dobson, K.S., Truax, P.A., *et al.* (1996) A component analysis of cognitive-behavioral treatment for depression. *Journal of Consulting and Clinical Psychology*, 64, 295–304.

James, I.A. (2001) Schema therapy. *Behavioural and Cognitive Psychotherapy*, 29, 401–404.

James, I.A. and Barton, S. (2004) Changing core beliefs with the continuum technique. *Behaviour and Cognitive Psychotherapy*, 32, 431–442.

James, I.A., Blackburn, I.M. and Reichelt, F.K. (2001) *Manual of the Revised Cognitive Therapy Scale (CTS-R)*. Northumberland, Tyne and Wear NHS Trust.

Janoff-Bulman (1985) in Resick, P.A. (2001) *Stress and Trauma*. Hove: Psychology Press.

Janoff-Bulman, R. (1985) The aftermath of victimization: Rebuilding shattered assumptions. In C.R. Figely (ed.), *Trauma and Its Wake*. New York: Brunner/Mazel.

Johns, C. (2001) Depending on the intent and emphasis of the supervisor, clinical supervision can be a different experience. *Journal of Nursing Management*, 9, 139–145.

Kolb, D.A. (1984) *Experiential Learning: Experience as the Source of Learning and Development*. Englewood Cliffs, NJ: Prentice Hall.

Kolb, D.A. and Fry, R. (1975) Towards an applied theory of experiential learning. In C. Cooper (ed.) *Theories of Group Process*. London: John Wiley.

Kroenke, K., Spitzer, R.L. and Williams, J.B. (2001) The PHQ-9: Validity of a brief depression severity measure. *Journal of General Internal Medicine*, 16(9), 606–613.

Lewinsohn, P.M., Biglan, A. and Zeiss, A.S. (1976) Behavioural treatment of depression. In P. O. Davidson (ed.) *The Behavioral Management of Anxiety, Depression and Pain*, pp. 91–146. New York: Brunner/Mazel.

Lindahl, B. and Norberg, A. (2002) Clinical group supervision in an intensive care unit: A space for relief, and for sharing emotions and experiences of care. *Journal of Clinical Nursing*, 11: 809–818.

Lu, H., While, A.E. and Barriball, L.K. (2005) Job satisfaction among nurses: A literature review. *International Journal of Nursing Studies*, 42(2): 211–227.

Marchand, A., Todorov, C., Borgeat, F. and Pelland, M. (2007) Effectiveness of a brief cognitive behavioural therapy for panic disorder with agoraphobia and the impact of partner involvement. *Behavioural and Cognitive Psychotherapy*, 35, 613–629.

Marks, I.M. (1987) *Fears, Phobias, and Rituals*. Oxford: Oxford University Press.

McVicar, A. (2003) Workplace stress in nursing: A literature review. *Journal of Advanced Nursing*, 44(6), 633–642.

Meyer, T.J., Miller, M.L., Metger, R.L. and Borkovec, T.D. (1990) Development and validation of the PennState Worry Questionnaire. *Behviour Research and Therapy*, 28(6), 487–495.

Milne, D. and James, I. (2002) The observed impact of training on competence in clinical supervision. *British Journal of Clinical Psychology*, 41(1), 55–72.

Milne, D.L., Reiser, R.P. and Cliffe, T. (2013) An $N=1$ enhanced evaluation of clinical supervision. *Behavioural and Cognitive Psychotherapy*, 41, 210–220.

National Health Service Management Executive (NHSME) (1993) *A Vision for the Future: The Nursing, Midwifery and Health Contribution to Health and Health Care*. London: The Stationery Office.

National Institute for Health and Clinical Excellence (NICE) *Obsessive-Compulsive Disorder: Core Interventions in the Treatment of Obsessive Compulsive Disorder and Body Dysmorphic Disorder.* Clinical Guidance 31. London: NICE. http://guidance.nice.org.uk/CG31/NICEGuidance/pdf/English (accessed 19 May 2014).

National Institute for Health and Clinical Excellence (2010) *Depression: The Treatment and Management of Depression in Adults* (updated version), National Clinical Practice Guideline 90. Leicester: British Psychological Society and Royal College of Psychiatrists.

National Institute of Mental Health (2013) *Anxiety Disorders.* http://www.nimh.nih.gov/health/topics/anxiety-disorders/index.shtml (accessed 19 May 2014).

Newman, C.F. (2010) Competency in conducting cognitive–behavioural therapy: Foundational, functional, and supervisory aspects. *Psychotherapy*, 47(1), 12–19.

Northumberland, Tyne and Wear NHS Trust (2013) *Obsessions and Compulsions: A self-help guide.* www.ntw.nhs.uk/pic (accessed on 25 October 2013).

Nursing and Midwifery Council (2008) *The code: Standards of conduct, performance and ethics for nurses and midwives.*

Padesky, C.A. (1994) Schema change processes in cognitive therapy. *Clinical Psychology and Psychotherapy*, 1(5), 267–278.

Padesky, C.A. (1996) Developing cognitive therapist competency: Teaching and supervision models. In P.M. Salkovskis (ed.) *Frontiers of Cognitive Therapy*, pp. 266–292. New York: Guilford Press.

Padesky, C.A. (1997) Clinical Tip: A more effective treatment for social phobia? *International Cognitive Therapy Newsletter*, 11(1), 1–3.

Padesky, C.A. and Greenberger, D. (1995) *Clinicians Guide to Mind over Mood.* New York: Guilford Press.

Padesky, C.A. and Mooney, K.A. (1990) Clinical Tip: Presenting the cognitive model to clients. *International Cognitive Therapy Newsletter*, 6, 13–14.

Pover, J., Cooper, J., Turner, A. and Jones, M. (1998) Putting supervision into practice in a medical unit. *Nursing Times Learning Curve*, 1(11), 2–4.

Power, M.J. and Fyvie, C. (2013) The role of emotion in PTSD: Two preliminary studies. *Behavioural and Cognitive Psychotherapy*, 41, 162–172.

Proctor, B. (1986) Supervision: A co-operative exercise in accountability. In M. Marken and M. Payne (eds) *Enabling and Ensuring: Supervision in Practice* (2nd edn). Leicester: National Youth Bureau for Education and Training in Youth and Community Work.

Rachman, S. and Hodgson, R. (1974) Synchrony and desynchrony in fear and avoidance. *Behaviour Research and Therapy*, 12(4), 311–318.

Rachman, S. and Shafran, R. (1999) Cognitive distortions: Thought-action-fusion. *Clinical Psychology and Psychotherapy*, 6, 80–85.

Robson, P. (1989) Development of a new self-report questionnaire to measure self-esteem. *Psychological Medicine*, 19(2), 513–518.

Rodolfa, E., Bent, R., Eisman, E., Nelson, P., Rehm, L. and Ritchie, P. (2005) A cube model for competency development: Implications for psychology educators and regulators. *Professional Psychology: Research and Practice*, 36(4), 347–354.

Rogers, C. (1980) *A Way of Being.* Boston: Houghton Mifflin.

Salkovskis, P.M. and Westbrook, D. (1989) Behaviour therapy and obsessive ruminations: Can failure be turned into success? *Behaviour Research and Therapy*, 27, 149–160.

Sanders, D. and Wills, F. (2005) *Cognitive Therapy, An Introduction* (2nd edn). London: Sage.

Saver, B.G., Van-Nguyen, V., Keppel, G. et al. (2007) A qualitative study of depression in primary care: Missed opportunities for diagnosis and education. *Journal of the American Board of Family Medicine*, 20, 28–35.

Sawyer, N. (2007) Ten top tips for behavioral experiments. Unpublished leaflet.

Schwartz, J.M. (1996) *Brain Lock: Free Yourself from Obsessive Compulsive Disorder*. New York: Regan Books.

Severinsson, E. and Hallberg, I. (1996) Clinical supervisors' views of their leadership role in the clinical supervision process within nursing care. *Journal of Advanced Nursing*, 24, 151–161.

Shafran, R., Egan, S. and Wade, T. (2010) *Overcoming Perfectionism: A Self-Help Guide Using Cognitive Behavioural Techniques*. London: Constable and Robinson.

Sloan, G. (1999) Good characteristics of a clinical supervisor: A community mental health nurse perspective. *Journal of Advanced Nursing*, 30(3), 713–722.

Sloan, G. and Watson, H. (2001) Illuminative evaluation: Evaluating clinical supervision on its performance rather than the applause. *Journal of Advanced Nursing Practice*, 35(5), 664–673.

Sloan, G., White, C. and Coit, F. (2000) Cognitive therapy supervision as a framework for clinical supervision: Using structure to guide discovery. *Journal of Advanced Nursing*, 32(3), 515–524.

Spence, S.H., Wilson, J., Kavanagh, D., Strong, J. and Worrall, L. (2001) Clinical supervision in four mental health professions: A review of the evidence. *Behaviour Change*, 18(3), 135–155.

Spitzer, R.L., Kroenke, K. and Williams, J.B.W., for the Patient Health Questionnaire Primary Care Study Group (1999) Validation and utility of a self-report version of PRIME-MD: The PHQ Primary Care Study. *Journal of the American Medical Association*, 282, 1737–1744.

Spitzer, R.L., Kroenke, K., Williams, J.B.W. and Lowe, B. (2006) A brief measure for assessing generalized anxiety disorder. *Archives of Internal Medicine*, 166(10), 1092–1097.

Stiles, W.B., Elliott, R., Llewelyn, S.P., Firth-Cozens, J.A., Margison, F.R., Shapiro, D.A. and Hardy, G. (1990) Assimilation of problematic experiences by clients in psychotherapy. *Psychotherapy*, 27(3), 411–420.

Stokes, C. and Hirsch, C.R. (2010) Engaging in imagery versus verbal processing of worry: Impact on negative intrusions in high worriers. *Behaviour Research and Therapy*, 48, 418–423.

Swinson, R.P., Anthony, M.M., Rachman, S. and Richter, M.A. (1998) *Obsessive Compulsive Disorder: theory, Research and Treatment*. New York: Guilford Press.

Taylor, S. (2006) *Clinician's Guide to PTSD: A Cognitive-Behavioral Approach*. New York: Guilford Press.

Teasdale, J.D. (1996) Clinically relevant theory: Integrating clinical insight with cognitive science. In P.M. Salkovskis (ed.) *Frontiers of Cognitive Therapy*, pp. 26–47. New York: Guilford Press.

Teasdale, J.D. and Barnard, P.J. (1993) *Affect, Cognition and Change: Remodelling Depressive Thought*. Hove: Lawrence Erlbaum.

Teasdale, K., Brocklehurst, N. and Thom, N. (2001) Clinical supervision and support for nurses: An evaluative study. *Journal of Advanced Nursing*, 33(2), 216–224.

Veale, D. (2003) Treatment of social phobia. *Advances in Psychiatric Treatment*, 9, 258–264.
Veale, D. (2008) Behavioural activation for depression. *Advances in Psychiatric Treatment*, 14, 29–36.
Veale, D. and Willson, R. (2005) *Overcoming Obsessive Compulsive Disorder: A Self-Help Guide Using Cognitive Behaviour Therapy*. London: Robinson.
Veale, D. and Willson, R. (2007) *Manage Your Mood: Using Behavioural Activation Techniques to Overcome Depression*. London: Robinson.
Wallbank, S. and Hatton, S. (2011) Reducing burnout and stress: The effectiveness of clinical supervision. *Community Practitioner*, 84(7), 31–35.
Watson, J.B. (1970) *Behaviorism*. New York: Norton.
Wells, A. (1997) *Cognitive Therapy of Anxiety Disorders: A Practical Manual and Conceptual Guide*. Chichester: Wiley.
Wells, A. (2006) The metacognitive model of worry and generalised anxiety disorder. In G.C.L. Davey and A. Wells (eds) *Worry and its Psychological Disorders: Theory, Assessment and Treatment*, pp. 179–200. Chichester: Wiley.
Wells, A. and Clark, D.M. (1997) Social phobia: A cognitive approach. In G.C.L. Davey (ed.) *Phobias: A Handbook of Description, Treatment and Theory*. Chichester: Wiley.
Westbrook, D., Kennerley, H. and Kirk, J. (2007) *An Introduction to Cognitive Behaviour Therapy: Skills and Applications*. London: Sage.
Wheeler, S. and King, D. (2000) Do counselling supervisors want or need to have their supervision supervised? An exploratory study. *British Journal of Guidance and Counselling*, 28(2), 279–290.
Wills, F. and Sanders, D. (1997) *Cognitive Therapy: Transforming the Image*. London: Sage.
Winstanley, J. and White, E. (2003) Clinical supervision: Models, measures and best practice. *Nurse Researcher*, 10(4), 7–32.
Yegdich, T. (1999a) Clinical supervision and managerial supervision: Some historical and conceptual considerations. Journal of Advanced Nursing, 30(5): 1195–1204.
Yegdich, T. (1999b) Lost in the crucible of supportive supervision: Supervision is not therapy. *Journal of Advanced Nursing*, 29(5), 1265–1275.
Young, C. (2007) *An Introduction to Coping with Panic*. London: Robinson.
Zimbardo, P. McDermott, M., Jansz, J. and Metaal, N. (1995) *Psychology: A European Text*. London: HarperCollins.

Index

Activity record (example) 61–2
Activity Schedule (example) 60 (*also see* behavioural activation)
Advantages and disadvantages of changing (example) 200 (*also see* Perfectionism)
Agenda setting (*see* components of CBT and CTS-R and Dreyfus's model of competence)
All-or-nothing thinking (example) 194
Anxious predictions record (example) 76
Application of change methods (*see* components of CBT and CTS-R and Dreyfus's model of competence)
Assertiveness 213–29

Bandura 7 (*see* Social learning theory)
Beck (Aaron) 7
Beck (Judith) 37
Behavioural activation (*also see* activity schedule and activity scheduling)
  understanding of 26–7
  definition 27
  practical example 59–60
  valued directions (role of) 59
Behavioural experiments (BE)
  case specific examples
    low self-esteem, anxiety and depression 78
    panic disorder with agoraphobia 98–100
    social anxiety disorder 114–16
    generalised anxiety disorder (GAD) 164–5
  assertiveness 224
  difference with ERP 31
  planning of 203
  principles of 31–3
  role play as a behavioural experiment 222–3

Behaviour therapy (understanding) 7, 8, 9
  behaviourism 7
  classical conditioning 7
  operant conditioning 7

CBT
  definition 36
  principles of 7, 37
CBT assessment
  contrast with generic mental health assessment 17
  definition 17
Clinical supervision 230–43
  benefits of clinical supervision 233
  characteristics of a good clinical supervisor 233–4
  CBT based clinical supervision 231–2
  CBT competency based approach to clinical supervision 237–9
  clinical supervision/ managerial supervision 232
  definition 231
  frequency of clinical supervision 232
  Hawkins and Shohet's seven eyed supervisor model 235–7
  implementing clinical supervision 239–41
  length of clinical supervision sessions 232
Cognition (definition) 16
Cognitive levels (understanding) 11–14
  assumptions (definition and understanding) 12–13
  automatic thoughts (definition and understanding) 11–12
  core beliefs (definition and understanding) 13
  negative automatic thoughts (definition) 12, (examples of) 91, 146
Cognitive therapy (understanding) 7 (*see* Beck)
Cognitive therapy scale rating (CTS-R) 37–50

CTS-R Cognitive therapy specific items 39–40
CTS-R general items 39–40
Cognitive cycle 39–40
Dreyfus's model of competence 40–2
revised Cognitive therapy scale rating (CTS-R) 39–40
Collaboration (*see* components of CBT and CTS-R and Dreyfus's model of competence)
Collaborative approach
 in working with a person with panic disorder with agoraphobia 89–90
 in working with a person with assertiveness issues 218
 methods of promoting collaboration 55
 principles of collaboration 56
Compassionate self-talk (example) 165 (*also see* Self-compassionate stance examples)
Components of CBT 37–8
 agenda setting 38
 checking- in 38
 orientation 37
 periodic summaries 38
 setting homework 38
 summarising session and client feedback 38
Conceptual integration (*see* components of CBT and CTS-R and Dreyfus's model of competence)
Continued improvement plan (case specific examples)
 mild-to-moderate depression 64
 low self-esteem, anxiety and depression 83–4
 panic 100–1
 social anxiety disorder 117
 obsessive compulsive disorder (OCD) 136
 obsessive compulsive disorder (OCD)- mental compulsions 153
 generalised anxiety disorder (GAD) 168–9
 post-traumatic stress disorder (PTSD)- single episode trauma 187–8
 perfectionism 207–8
 assertiveness 226
Core beliefs
 definition 13
 examples of 13
 role within CBT 13, 14
Cost-benefit analysis (example) 126
CTS-R
 definition 39
 items 42–50
  agenda setting and adherence 42
  application of change methods 49
  collaboration 44
  conceptual integration 47–8
  eliciting appropriate emotional expression 45–6
  eliciting behaviours 46
  eliciting key cognitions 46
  feedback 43–4
  guided discovery 47
  homework setting 49–50
  interpersonal effectiveness 45
  pacing and efficient use of time 44–5
Cultural issues 141–2, 144, 150, 152, 155

Darwin "*Origin of species*" 7
Depression (symptoms) 53
Dreyfus's model of competence 40–50
 classification 41
 explanation 40–2
 scoring system 41
 stages of competence 40–1
 agenda setting 43
 application of change methods 49
 collaboration 44
 conceptual integration 47–8
 eliciting appropriate emotional expression 45–46
 eliciting behaviours 46
 eliciting key cognitions 46
 feedback 43–4
 guided discovery 47
 homework setting 49–50
 Interpersonal effectiveness 45
 pacing and efficient use of time 44–5

Ego dystonic (definition) 142
Eliciting behaviours (also components of CBT and CTS-R and Dreyfus's model of competence)
 Eliciting appropriate emotional expression (*see* components of CBT and CTS-R and Dreyfus's model of competence)

260 Index

Eliciting key cognitions (*see* components of CBT and CTS-R and Dreyfus's model of competence)
Emotional hotspots (definition) 184, (example) 184, 186(*see also* Imaginal exposure)
Exposure and response prevention (ERP)
  principles of 24 (*also see* behavioural experiments examples 98–100 and graded hierarchy, hierarchy of feared situations)
  example 222–4 (*also see* Behavioural experiments)

Feedback (*see* components of CBT and CTS-R and Dreyfus's model of competence)
Formulation
  definition and understanding 20
    case specific examples
      mild to moderate depression 56–8
      low self-esteem, anxiety and depression 72–5
      panic disorder with agoraphobia 91–4
      social anxiety disorder 108–9
      obsessive compulsive disorder 128–9
      obsessive compulsive disorder– mental compulsions 147–8
      Generalised anxiety disorder (GAD) 162–3
      post-traumatic stress disorder- single episode trauma 179–82
      perfectionism 192–4
      assertiveness 216–17
    role within CBT 17

Generalised anxiety disorder (GAD) 158–73
  avoidance theory 161
  co-morbidity 160
  definition 158
  features/ characteristics of GAD 158, 159, 161
  Generalised Anxiety Disorder Assessment (GAD-7) 159, 170
  Penn State Worry Questionnaire (PSWQ) 160, 164, 169, 170

Graded hierarchy (purpose of) 24–6 (*see also* ERP)
  hierarchy of feared situations (example) 130–2
Guided discovery (*see* components of CBT and CTS-R and Dreyfus's model of competence)

Homework setting (*see* components of CBT and CTS-R and Dreyfus's model of competence)
Homework tasks (purpose of) 60
Hot thoughts (definition and examples of) 11–12 (*also see* Automatic thoughts)
Hypothesis testing (examples) 133–5, 137, 146, 150, 151

Imagery
  example in the case of OCD- mental compulsions 151,
  relating to GAD 161, 167–8(*also see* Worry history outcome chart)
Imagery re-scripting (*also see* Imaginal exposure)
  regarding non-anxiety based PTSD 176
  contrast of Imaginal exposure and Imagery rescripting 188–9
Imaginal exposure (in PTSD)
  appropriate use of 175, 177
  contrast of imaginal exposure and rescripting 188–9
  explanation 183
  example 183–7
  considerations 178
Interpersonal effectiveness (*see* components of CBT and CTS-R and Dreyfus's model of competence)

James et al 39–40 (*see* CTS-R)

Kolb and Fry 3 (*also see* learning cycle and reflection)

Leading questions (examples) 145
Learning cycle 3–5 (*see also* Kolb and Fry and Reflection)
  explanation 4
  stages of 4–5

Low self-esteem, anxiety and depression
    68–86
  self-esteem (definition) 70
  safety behaviours in low self-esteem 71
  Robson's self-concept questionnaire 75,
    78, 85

Magical thinking (definition) 143 (*also see*
    TAF)
Mild to moderate depression 52–67
Models
  definition and purposes 4
Models of CBT
  ABC model 19–20
    examples 56–8, 63, 142–3
  Clark and Wells' model of social anxiety
    108–9
  Ehler's and Clark's PTSD Model 179–82
  Fear and avoidance model 9
  Fennell's model of low self-esteem 72
  Four systems model 18–19
  Hirsch and Matthews's cognitive model
    of worry 162–3
  Interacting cognitive subsystems model
    15–17
  implicational learning
    case specific examples
      mild to moderate depression 65
      low self-esteem, anxiety and
        depression 77
      panic disorder with agoraphobia 99
      social anxiety disorder 112, 118
      obsessive compulsive disorder
        (OCD) mental compulsions 148,
        155
      post-traumatic stress disorder- single
        episode trauma 185–6
      perfectionism 203
      assertiveness 227
    professional skills, development and
      learning 17
    understanding of 16
  propositional learning
    case specific examples
      mild to moderate depression 65
      low self-esteem, anxiety and
        depression 77
      panic disorder with agoraphobia
        99
      social anxiety disorder 118

obsessive compulsive disorder-
    mental compulsions148
  post-traumatic stress disorder
    (PSD)- single trauma episode
    185–6
  assertiveness 227
  professional skills, development and
    learning 17
  understanding of 16
  Wells' metacognitive model of worry 161

Obsessive compulsive disorder (OCD)
    121–39 (*also see* OCD and mental
    compulsions)
  features of 122, 124
  co-morbidity 122
  diagnostic criteria 123
  neuroscience of OCD 130
  types of 122
  understanding of 122, 124, 125
OCD mental compulsions 140–57
  neuroscience of mental compulsions
    149
  Revised Obsessive Compulsory
    Inventory 126–7, 137, 146, 154

Pacing (*see* components of CBT and CTS-R
    and Dreyfus's model of
    competence)
Panic diary 96–7
Panic disorder with agoraphobia 87–103
  understanding of panic disorder and
    agoraphobia 88–9, 95,
  Agoraphobic Cognitions Questionnaire
    94, 101
  Body Sensations Questionnaire 94, 101
  diagnostic criteria 89
  physiology of panic attacks 96
Patient Healthcare Questionnaire (PHQ-9)
  use as a measurement tool 32
Perfectionism 191–212
  Clinical Perfectionism Questionnaire
    202
  definition 194–5
  monitoring (examples of) 198, 199
  comorbidity with:
    anxiety 196
    eating problems 196
    mood problems 196
    PTSD 196

Post-traumatic stress disorder (PTSD) –
    single episode trauma 174–90
  diagnostic criteria 175
  neuroscience 177
  post-traumatic cognitions inventory
    (PTCI) 178, 187
Pros and cons of change list (example)
    197–200

Reflection (*also see* Learning cycle and
    Kolb and Fry)
  case specific examples
  mild to moderate depression 65–6
  low self-esteem, anxiety and depression
    85
  panic disorder with agoraphobia 101–2
  social anxiety disorder 118–19
  obsessive compulsive disorder (OCD)
    138
  obsessive compulsive disorder – mental
    compulsions 154–5
  generalised anxiety disorder 170–1
  post-traumatic stress disorder (PTSD)
    single episode trauma 188–9
  perfectionism 209
  assertiveness 227
  skills involved in 4
  stages of 3
Risk
  case specific aspects of
  mild-moderate depression 54–5
  OCD 125–6
  assertiveness 217–18
Role-play (examples) 134, 220–2

Safety behaviours
  definition and understanding of 21, 23
  disorder specific safety behaviours 22

  example of 107
  safety behaviour in a case of social
    anxiety 107
Self-compassionate stance (examples) 82,
    205 (*also see* Compassionate
    self-talk examples)
Self-critical thinking (example) 205
Self-critical thoughts records and
    alternative (example) (80–1)
Self-monitoring (example) 111–13
Skinner 7, 8, 9 (*also see* behaviourism and
    behaviour therapy)
Social anxiety disorder 104–20
  social anxiety (features) 105
  social phobia (definition) 106
  social anxiety scale 111
Social learning theory 7 (*also see*
    Bandura)
Stages of change 200–1
Superstitions 21
Supervision
  use of 97–8, 99, 124–6, 188–9

Thought-Action-Fusion (TAF) 143–4
  morality TAF 143
  probability TAF 143
Thought records
  purpose of 27–8
  explanation of 28–9, 30–1
  examples 28, 30, 203–4
  five column thought record 28
  seven column thought record 30

Worry free time (example) 166
Worry history outcome chart 167
4W Finds
  example 91
  the role of 17

COGNITIVE BEHAVIOURAL THERAPY FOR MILD TO MODERATE DEPRESSION AND ANXIETY
A Guide to Low-intensity Interventions

Colin Hughes and Stephen Herron

9780335242085 (Paperback)
2014

eBook also available

Cognitive Behavioural Therapy for Mild to Moderate Depression and Anxiety provides information and support using evidence-based, low-intensity psychological treatments involving cognitive behavioural therapy (CBT) for mild to moderate mental illness. The book closely mirrors the key components of assessment, therapeutic relationship, treatment of low mood, anxiety and panic, sign posting and basic psychopharmacology

Key features:

- Supports the low-intensity worker (Psychological Well-Being Practitioner) with patient self-management
- Designed as a core text for Modules I and 2 of the Postgraduate Certificate for Low-intensity Therapies Workers (IAPT)
- It is a useful practical companion to all who have an interest in or work directly with clients who experience common mental health problems

www.openup.co.uk

OPEN UNIVERSITY PRESS
McGraw - Hill Education

MENTAL HEALTH NURSING CASE BOOK

Nick Wrycraft

9780335242955 (Paperback)
September 2012

eBook also available

This case book is aimed at mental health nursing students and those going into mental health settings, such as social workers. The cases include a wide range of mental health diagnoses from common problems such as anxiety or depression through to severe and enduring conditions such as schizophrenia. The cases will be organised into sections by life stage from childhood through to old age.

Key features:

- Uses a case study approach which provides a realistic context that students will find familiar
- Each case study will commence with a practice focused scenario
- Provides a commentary offering insights, perspectives and references to theories, research and further explanations and discussion

www.openup.co.uk

OPEN UNIVERSITY PRESS
McGraw - Hill Education